THE LOMÉ CONVENTION AND A NEW INTERNATIONAL
ECONOMIC ORDER

Publications of the John F. Kennedy Institute,
Center for International Studies, Tilburg, The Netherlands
Nr. 11

THE LOMÉ CONVENTION AND A NEW INTERNATIONAL ECONOMIC ORDER

edited by
Frans A.M. Alting von Geusau

with contributions from

J.C. Anyiwo	K.B. Lall
L.J. Brinkhorst	E. Lof
H. Coppens	T. Palánkai
C. Dodoo	B. Persaud
Th. Dams	H. Stordel
G. Faber	J.J.C. Voorhoeve
R. Kuster	I.W. Zartman

A.W. Sijthoff — Leyden — 1977

ISBN 90 286 0217 8

Printed in The Netherlands.

PREFACE

The Conclusion on February 28, 1975 of the Lomé Convention between forty six African, Caribbean and Pacific States, and the European Community and its member states has no doubt been an important event in world development cooperation. The Convention cannot merely be seen as the continuation of an historical — formerly colonial — relationship. It also reflects efforts to devise a new type of relationship between countries of most unequal economic development. The negotiation and conclusion of this Convention moreover took place amidst intensive and world-wide discussions on the establishment of a new international economic order, which could bring more justice and equality in international relations.

Against this background, the John F. Kennedy Institute organized, from December 10-13, 1975, an International Colloquium on "The Lomé Convention and World Development Cooperation: Old Links or a New Departure?"; its eighth major Colloquium on current and crucial international problems.

The present volume brings together most of the working papers prepared for the Colloquium, as revised by the authors between March and August 1976.

Chapter 1 is a revised version of the Opening Address to the Colloquium by the Netherlands' State Secretary for Foreign Affairs.

Chapters 3, 5, 6, 7, 8 and 9 are revised versions of the papers presented to the Colloquium.

Chapter 2 integrates the analyses of two papers, which had been presented separately.

Chapter 4 has been written later at our specific request.

Chapter 10 partly reflects the discussions during the Colloquium. It was completed in June 1976.

The Institute is grateful to the authors for their contributions to this volume.

I am particularly grateful to Dr. J.W. Schneider s.j. and to

Messrs. R. Kuster, J.A. van Lith and A.J. Vingerhoets, who constituted the research team preparing the Colloquium. I am most thankful to Dr. J. Westhoff, delegate of the Commission of the European Communities in Jamaica for his invaluable assistance especially in preparing chapter 2 of this volume.

The Institute is indebted to the Netherlands' Ministry of Science and Education, the European Communities and the American Embassy for their financial support towards the Colloquium and to A.W. Sijthoff International Publishing Company for publishing this volume.

I am especially grateful to Miss M.C. Hinkenkemper, executive secretary, Miss Annelies Vugs, secretary and Mr. R. Kuster, research-fellow to the Institute, who have done most of the work in connection with this volume.

August 1976   F.A.M. Alting von Geusau

TABLE OF CONTENTS

XI

ABOUT THE AUTHORS

Frans A.M. Alting von Geusau is Professor of the Law of International Organizations at Tilburg University and Director of the John F. Kennedy Institute.

J.C. Anyiwo is Senior Consultant Systems Engineer, Nigerian Institute of Social and Economic Research, Consultancy Services Unit, Lagos.

L.J. Brinkhorst is State Secretary for Foreign Affairs of the Netherlands.

H. Coppens is Lecturer at the Free University of Amsterdam.

C. Dodoo is Legal Expert at A.C.P. Secretariat, Brussels.

Th. Dams is Professor and Director of the Institut für Entwicklungspolitik, University of Freiburg (i.Br.).

G. Faber is Research Fellow at the Free University of Amsterdam.

R. Kuster was at the time of the Colloquium Research Fellow at the John F. Kennedy Institute.

K.B. Lall is Ambassador of India to Belgium and to the EEC, Brussels.

E. Lof is Research Fellow at the Free University of Amsterdam.

T. Palánkai is Associate Professor of the Karl Marx University of Economics, Budapest.

B. Persaud is Assistant Director Commodities Division, Commonwealth Secretariat, London.

H. Stordel is Deputy Director of the Manufacturers Division of UNCTAD, Geneva.

J.J.C. Voorhoeve is staff-member of the Policy Planning and Program Review Department, Worldbank, Washington.

I.W. Zartman is Professor at the Department of Politics, New York University.

LIST OF TABLES

GLOSSARY

AASM	Associated African States and Madagascar
ACP	African, Caribbean, Pacific
ASEAN	Association of South East Asian Nations
BTN	Brussels Tariff Nomenclature
CAP	Common Agricultural Policy
CAR	Central African Republic
CCA	Commercial Cooperation Agreement
CET	Common External Tariff
CFA	Communauté Financière Africaine
CMEA	Council for Mutal Economic Assistance
DAC	Development Assistance Committee
EC	European Communities
EDF	European Development Fund
EEC	European Economic Community
EFTA	European Free Trade Association
EIB	European Investment Bank
FAO	Food and Agricultural Organization
GATT	General Agreement on Tariffs and Trade
GNP	Gross National Product
GSP	Generalized System of Preferences
IBRD	International Bank of Reconstruction and Development
IDA	International Development Association
IFC	International Finance Corporation
IUGS	International Union of Geological Societies
IMF	International Monetary Fund
LTA	Long Term Arrangement regarding International Trade in Cotton Textiles
Machreq	Egypt, Lebanon, Syria and Jordan
Maghreb	Algeria, Morocco, Tunesia
MIFERMA	Société Anonyme des Mines de Fer de Mauritanie
NATO	North Atlantic Treaty Organization
OAU	Organization of African Unity

OCT	Overseas Countries and Territories
ODA	Official Development Assistance
OECD	Organization for Economic Cooperation and Development
OPEC	Oil Producing and Exporting Countries
STABEX	Stabilization of Export Earnings
UA	Unit of Account
UNCTAD	United Nations Conference on Trade and Development
UN(O)	United Nations Organization
US(A)	United States of America
USSR	Union of Soviet Socialist Republics

Part One

THE CONVENTION IN PERSPECTIVE

Chapter 1

LOMÉ AND FURTHER

by *Laurens Jan Brinkhorst*

The Lomé Convention, which entered into force on April 1st 1976, has turned a new leaf in cooperation between the EEC and a large number of developing countries. An early effort to find out what sort of prospects the convention will open up appears to be useful and called for. The Lomé Convention is not merely the continuation of the previous association agreements between the EEC and some African countries. It is a new relationship bound to involve the EEC increasingly in the developing North-South relationship. The effort at this stage to identify strong and weak points in the convention is not a purely academic exercise. It is oriented towards its optimal implementation.

Interdependence and Development Cooperation

Before giving some comments on the Lomé Convention itself I want to make just a few remarks to place the agreement in its general political perspective. Inevitably this perspective will be coloured by the way in which I interpret and evaluate relations between the Netherlands, the EEC and the Third World.

I do not want to say much about the relationship between the Netherlands and Europe. Geographically small and relatively vulnerable on account of its internationally oriented economy, the Netherlands is forced to rely on European cooperation in many spheres of government activity. The events of the past decades have led to such interdependence among the EEC countries that it has become difficult and in some areas almost impossible for individual member states to conduct autonomous policies. The fact that many national measures, actions and developments transcend national boundaries has continually increased the necessity for coordination and joint planning and for appropriate decision-making and intervention, some of it supranational. A very recent and striking example of this necessity for community action is to be found in the field of energy. As the outcome of the EC-summit meeting in December 1975 showed that the Community framework has become so inevitable and indispensable that even strong centrifugal forces have had to give way to a community approach.

The EEC framework has also become increasingly important and indeed compelling for the policies of the individual member states as regards their international relations outside Europe. This applies above all, of course, to international economic relations, including economic relations with developing countries, to which the Lomé convention is directly relevant.

In other words, the objective reality of greater and ever increasing interdependence, especially in the economic field, is forcing the individual member states to view their relations with the outside world more and more in European terms. The outside world already views them as such. Indeed, paradoxical as it may seem, third countries see European unification as a more logical, accepted and advanced process than it sometimes is in the eyes of the member states themselves.

There are some who consider this integration process, this Western European group formation, to be dubious or even harmful. Insofar as these are the views of hardened nationalists I need not dwell on them further. But there are those who are justifiably apprehensive of inward-looking attitudes and preoccupations with internal problems and possibilities which one often finds when any group is formed, and their views should be taken seriously. They believe that the attitudes of the EC will hamper the necessary global cooperation.

I have two comments to make on this. Firstly it is not only inevitable but also a good thing for relatively equal countries having a natural affinity to form a group, especially where geographical proximity has caused the countries to establish innumerable mutual ties. It is a good thing not only for the individual countries with a view to settling their regional problems, but also for the world at large. The thin dividing line between national and international events, the interrelationship of national, regional and global processes, increasingly demands worldwide deliberation, coordination and management. If this management is to be effective, it is desirable, indeed necessary, for countries to get together at sub-global level for joint decision-making and action in an intergovernmental or supranational context, whichever is more appropriate and acceptable. This has recently been brought out only too clearly in practice. I need only mention the 1975 discussions concerning the New International Economic Order, culminating for the time being in the 7th Special Session of the UN General As-

4

sembly in New York, and the talks on energy and economic development in Paris. In my opinion group action will prove more and more indispensable if effective, i.e. concrete and binding decisions are the desired objective rather than exercise in rhetoric.

Secondly, and as regards the EEC in particular, the feared tendency towards self-centredness, has indeed not been absent in the past and has justifiably given rise to concern. However, this tendency should not be viewed in isolation but seen in its historical context. One cannot altogether avoid a certain degree of self-preoccupation when one is trying to sort things out in a formative stage of group activity. But one should not confuse this with autarchy, or what could be called "structural introversion". As new internal structures become more clearly defined and more stable, there will be more outward orientation. In fact, the outward-looking trend is already manifesting itself within the EEC and will continue to do so in the future. Recent outside influences and pressures, both political and economic, have done much to foster this process.

I am of course referring in particular to the economic challenges resulting from the recession and the energy crisis, which have underlined the external vulnerability of the EEC, and to the strongly worded and emphatic demands made on it by the outside world. As the 7th Special Session of the UN General Assembly showed, the outside world, and in particular the Third World, does not attach very much importance to sympathies expressed or intentions stated by the individual member states. What the outside world is interested in are effective reforms, which can only be undertaken jointly at EEC level. So it is at the EEC level, where the effective power lies, that the member states will be addressed. At that level they will have to show their good will and will be judged.

Actual developments, then, seem to be giving steadily less support to the historically justifiable fear concerning attitudes of self-centredness within the EEC. And it is certain that the international situation will not have it otherwise in the future.

In support of this, I should like to examine the international setting in which the EEC is placed.

I am certainly not so ethnocentric as to describe Western Europe as a sort of Greater Netherlands. And yet we can draw a certain parallel between the international position of the Netherlands and that of the EEC. Like the Netherlands, the EEC is highly dependent on relations with outside countries and is in that respect relatively vulnerable, if anything but small.

The EEC too is linked to many countries through a fine network of multifarious relations. Its dependence on others in the matter of security is obvious. By far the most important trade bloc in the world, it is highly dependent on imports and exports. Moreover, the EEC cannot but have innumerable political and cultural ties with the rest of the world whose fortunes and misfortunes have been so largely determined by the actions of its member states in the past.

Given this whole complex of relations in a wide variety of fields, some of which imply a high degree of dependence, the position of the EEC can best be described by the key-word *interdependence*. Given these closely interwoven international relationships, to follow a course of self-centredness, self-sufficiency and autarchy is hardly a realistic option for the future. It would meet unsurmountable practical obstacles and imply intolerable financial burdens. Moreover, this path would have disastrous effects on international relations; it would entail great security risks and it would generally antagonise other countries because it would be interpreted as a way of shirking one's responsibilities towards an international society which has been largely shaped—and not always in a positive sense—by the behaviour of the EEC member states.

Seen in this light it is most unrealistic to view the EEC as a "Super-power in the making", as has been suggested. The only real option the EEC has, is what I would call a conscious strategy of interdependence—optional interdependence, that is a strategy in which a deliberate choice is made for mutually dependent relations, cooperation and partnership.

I hasten to add that this may not be as nice as it sounds. Interdependence is not, as some people think, a magic way of obtaining a just and safe world. On the contrary, interdependence can itself constitute a controversial international problem and give rise to tensions and conflicts.

This is the case when interdependence is particularly unbalanced or asymmetrical, that is when the dependence of one party is much greater than that of the other party involved. There is no equality then, no even distribution of costs and benefits and hence no harmony of interests. That is why I have in mind an optimal balance of dependencies when I argue the case for a strategy of interdependence. Only in this way will it be possible to arrive at joint management of the inter-relationship which is mutually acceptable and beneficial.

What consequences will this have for the EEC's relations with the Third World? To be brief it means that a lot of changes, adjustments and restructuring will have to take place to put right the historically evolved imbalance in the relations between the EEC and the developing countries, particularly the former colonies of the EEC member states. During the colonial period this imbalance was in many cases nothing short of a relationship of exploitation. The dominant negotiating position of the former colonial powers caused the unequal relations to survive after decolonisation, even when these relations were incorporated into the framework of the EEC. The initial EEC association arrangement was hardly one that provided for basic restructuring, tailored as it was to the wishes of some to continue the old relations on the old basis. Although the two subsequent Yaoundé conventions did bring adjustments and improvements they in turn did not fundamentally alter the position of imbalance.

The question of balance or symmetry is one of the principal criteria according to which the Lomé Convention should be judged. Will it retain, not to say reinforce, one-sided dependence and vulnerability? Or will it correct the asymmetry either by increasing the EEC's dependence or by reducing that of the ACP countries, or both? Will it allow the ACP countries to try and reach a certain degree of "decoupling", should they so desire, in order to achieve more self-reliance or, more important perhaps, a greater measure of collective self-reliance of all the developing countries including non-ACP countries? Or will it impede this necessary intensification of the cooperation among developing countries?

I do not claim to have the ultimate answer to these crucial questions. However, I do have an opinion on the matter. Before I offer it I should like to mention one general point which should be kept in mind when evaluating the Lomé convention. Lomé cannot be viewed in isolation; it is not independent of earlier developments. The very relationship between the EEC countries and the ACP countries has a long history and is necessarily conditioned by it—for better or for worse. One cannot deny the historical context. Instead, one should recognize it and use it as a starting point from which to look for new directions and new vistas. The Lomé convention is not the be-all and end-all of the EEC's relation with the Third World. What we are concerned with is whether Lomé is a step in the right direction, a step which offers possibilities for a restructuring of the cooperation system, which contains assurances for the future and which promotes further progress towards a more just, New International Economic Order.

The Main Provisions of the Lomé Convention

Turning to the main provisions of the Lomé Convention it is my strong conviction that a careful weighing of all the elements involved cannot but lead to a positive conclusion, albeit with reservations. In a few words I would put it like this: the Lomé convention contains a number of provisions that, taken together, make for a fresh impetus to international development cooperation in general, on a global scale; these provisions relate to the core of international development cooperation and have long been urged without much success, on numerous occasions in numerous international fora. I refer particularly to the *integrated approach* which the agreement reflects, its *binding character,* the elements of *automaticity* and *long term commitments,* its concentration on the *poorest countries* and the *poorest population* strata, the participatory structure of *decision making,* and some of the *policy instruments* that are likely to constitute useful precedents.

By presenting an *integral framework* for a complex set of relations between the two groups of countries involved, the convention covers and interlinks virtually all areas of development cooperation and the various forms of activity they require—areas such as: trade, industrialisation, social development assistance and balance of payments support. The disadvantages of a fragmentary approach, which has proved so inadequate in the past, can thus be avoided.

A number of provisions impose *explicit obligations* on the parties to the Convention, with a strong emphasis on the obligations of the European Community. These provisions are self-executing, which means that both governments and private parties can base claims directly on the articles of the Convention itself.

The *5 year duration* of the Convention enables the ACP countries to plan their trade and development programmes for an extended period of time. The fixed life span of the Convention allows for adjustment of the relationship after 5 years or for opting out altogether. Freedom of action is further guaranteed by the fact that any ACP country or the Community can denounce the Convention, according to art. 92.

Concentration on the poorer countries and population groups is explicitly provided for in the Convention. This emphasis on the needs of the least developed countries and most needy sections of the population is fully in line with, not to say anticipates, the relatively recent re-orientation of official international development policies in the same direction.

As far as the *decision structure* is concerned, it is significant that the implementation of the convention—and thus the management of the relationship—is entrusted to joint bodies, in which EC and ACP countries have an equal voice. Furthermore, the arrangement for arbitration in case of dispute, which by the way is of a binding character, also reflects this bipartite, egalitarian approach.

As for the *policy instruments*, I would like to mention some of the more salient ones. Striking, of course, is the *absence of reverse preferences,* which in the past have given rise to many and, in my view, justified misgivings. Indeed, their abolition is a major step in the direction of a better equilibrium between two partners of unequal strength. As such this step could serve as a valuable precedent for the restructuring of global trade relations between rich and poor countries, which are still largely governed by rules written for trading partners of comparable strength.

With respect to imports into the Community, the EEC gives *full rebates on tariffs and other import restrictions* on 96% of all ACP trade. For agricultural products special arrangements have been made because of the restrictive import regulations under the Common Agricultural Policy. However in the past the EC has shown itself willing to remedy certain injustices resulting from these import regulations. I refer to the special arrangement for beef from the ACP countries. Such special allowance for the export interests of the parties to the convention should also be insisted upon in the future, and not just in rare cases only.

For sugar, a crucial export product, the EEC has yielded to ACP demands for a considerable import quota at a *guaranteed price* which at present is much higher than the world market price. A novelty of the scheme, and possibly a useful precedent for price setting for vital export products in the future, is the automatic yearly adjustment of the sugar price in relation to the internal sugar price in the Community, which in turn is linked to inflation. Quite new and again, I think, exemplary to global trade relations between industrialised and developing countries, is the relaxation of the origin rules to be applied in the framework of the Lomé Convention. The ACP countries are treated as one customs area. Other developing countries forming a tariff union with ACP countries are also entitled to favourable treatment in this respect.

The most striking feature, certainly the one that has drawn most attention, is *the system to stabilise export earnings (STABEX)* of certain products of the ACP countries. Which are the possible effects of this new tool in the range of development cooperation instruments?

9

It is true that the arrangement is not revolutionary in that it does not interfere with the functioning of the international market mechanism governing trade in the products in question. The STABEX arrangement is also quite modest in terms of both funds available (375 million units of account) and products covered. It will certainly not provide benefit to all ACP countries. Nevertheless the mechanism has considerable significance. After so many years of fruitless deliberation, it is a new and concrete step on the way to a broadly based arrangement for the commodity question, one which the developing countries have long regarded as particularly important. The admittedly modest scale of STABEX has the advantage, incidentally, that it does not hamper the creation of more ambitious global commodity regulations, as is sometimes erroneously suggested. The attitude of the Group of 77 (comprising almost all developing countries) shows that they are not afraid of that, either. The 77 are more inclined to see the geographically limited STABEX system as a favourable precedent for a regulation on a wider scale. Considering the results of the 7th Special Session of the UN General Assembly on this point as well, it can at least be said that the STABEX arrangement has helped to take this part of commodity policy out of the realm of theoretical observations and place it in the realm of reality. This is a considerable gain, and also a demonstration of the fact that we sometimes have to make a start with arrangements on a limited scale, regional ones for instance, before we can proceed to realising the same idea throughout the world.

The amount of financial aid in the Lomé Convention is less than half the figure of eight thousand million units of account which the ACP had originally asked for on the basis of calculations concerning inflation, population growth and degree of development. The countries formerly associated are therefore no better off in real terms. We should also remember that this group includes many of the least developed countries. However, where the allocation of aid is concerned, a positive point is that internationally accepted norms in the matter have already been translated into the terms of the Convention. The emphasis is clearly on the least developed, a number of ACP countries having been added to the official UN list. Attention is also being directed to the poorest groups in the ACP and to projects of interest to two or more ACP countries, for which part of the EDF funds have been earmarked.

Finally, a word on the provisions for industrial cooperation, largely introduced by the ACP itself. This element of the relations between ACP and EEC is of exceptional importance, considering that this is where the greatest imbalances in the relation between rich and poor are to be found. Polarisation is the most acute in the matter of capital investment and the associated problems of openness and control.

In the framework of the Convention an attempt has been made to avoid the two extremes, neither of which are in the interest of the host countries. These are domination by foreign investors and a complete rejection of all international investment, including full nationalization. The arrangement ultimately decided upon strikes a balance between the two. It may well constitute a conceptual breakthrough by setting new guidelines in the field of industrial relations between developed and developing countries which, if they prove effective, may be capable of a wider application.

All the broad provisions that I have only touched upon just now are as many positive elements of the Lomé convention. I must add, however, that the proof of the pudding is in the eating. Much depends on the will and effort with which the agreement is implemented. I have no doubt that it will need continuous pressure both from inside the EC and from the ACP countries jointly to achieve optimum implementation. The forces of reluctance and evasion are not to be underrated. In this sense we all have to be alert about our own readiness to meet responsibilities and see to it that others will not shirk them either.

The political significance of the Lomé Convention

This brings me to the political dimension of the Lomé Convention. It is clear that the Convention does not have the same significance to all the countries involved, and that their motives for participating have been different. It has been a simpler matter for some of the ACP countries and, for that matter, of the EEC member states, than for others. The ACP countries, and specially some of them, such as Tanzania and Nigeria, have been especially careful from the outset to obtain symmetry in their relations with the EEC.

This watchful and independent attitude has had a favourable effect on the negotiations themselves and the final result. The parties at the negotiating table were of equal status and it can even be said that the ACP regularly surpassed the EEC as far as initiatives and negotiating tactics were concerned. This gave the ACP self-confidence and convinced them that strong action, and above all common action, could eventually bring balanced results.

I should like to go a little more deeply into this aspect of the now famous ACP Unity during the negotiations. After attempts to reach agreement in 1972 had been in vain, an effort by the English-speaking African countries to establish formal links with the French-speaking group was finally successful in the spring of 1973. Their unity was formally confirmed at the meeting of heads of state of the OAU in May 1973, when a number of guidelines for negotiations were adopted. Their unity has in fact never been seriously threatened since, although there have been differences of opinion between the groups of countries within the ACP. The very protracted negotiations have created a sense of solidarity between the English-speaking and the French-speaking countries, and for that matter between the Caribbean region and Africa as well, which is a factor of political significance. We have gone full circle. The very countries which in the past had alienated their former colonies from each other culturally and administratively, have now, after uniting themselves in the Community, contributed to the cohesion of their former colonies through these negotiations with the ACP.

Another significant factor here is that responsibility for the Community's part in the negotiations has rested with the European Commission. The Yaoundé Conventions were predominantly negotiated by the Council! Through the new approach, the bilateral relations of the various EEC member states with individual ACP countries have merged into one collective EEC approach to the ACP-group as a whole. The relations of the Nine with the ACP have thus changed from bilateral to multilateral, managed by bipartite bodies. This is not to say that all member countries of the EEC have tried with equal conviction to reduce the one-sided dependence of former colonies. Some have clearly had more difficulty with this than others—and still have—but it must be remembered that it is not so easy to re-think and re-structure economic and historic ties.

I also accord political significance to the attitude of the ACP with regard to the other developing countries and the Group of 77. From the outset, the fact that ACP countries are members of the Group of 77 has affected their attitude with regard to their link with the EEC. For a long time the EEC was firmly entrenched in the limited framework of the old relations with the ACP according to the formulas laid down both in the former association agreements and in the treaty of accession of the United Kingdom, Denmark and Ireland. The majority of the ACP countries, however, kept insisting on a connection between their ties with the EEC and the wider problems of North-South relations. They did this mainly in two ways. On the one hand they took political and material elements from international discussions and tried to get these incorporated into the Convention. On the other hand, they paid very great attention to openings in the Lomé Convention for the benefit of non-ACP developing countries. The great persistence of the ACP countries in urging liberalisation of the rules of origin of the Convention, so as to enable all developing countries to benefit, was a symptom of this endeavour. Thus, attempts by the EEC to arrive at a common standpoint with the ACP countries in international discussions on the North-South problems have not been successful. The majority of ACP countries wanted to avoid giving the appearance of wishing to shut themselves off, with the EEC, from the rest of the world, and especially from their fellow developing countries. On the whole the EEC countries have respected this attitude, if not always with the same enthusiasm.

The suggestion that the Lomé Convention is detrimental to non-ACP developing countries would then seem to be unfounded. There are figures to prove this. The level of EEC trade with associated countries has remained more or less constant, which means that it has deteriorated relatively. In comparison, trade with non-associated developing countries has increased much. The association arrangement has not apparently hampered this. Rather, it should be argued that the preferential treatment has saved the associated countries from losing still more ground. Nor should it be forgotten that the ACP countries include by far the majority of the least developed countries, which according to UN standards are in need of special attention and treatment.

These conclusions as to the global implications and significance are confirmed by sources which are above suspicion. The comments on the Lomé Convention made by non-ACP developing countries are generally positive. They have accorded catalytic value to the elements of renewal mentioned earlier, such as the STA-BEX mechanism. I need only mention the positive comments put forward so far by third countries. And even such strange bedfellows as the US, China and Sweden are on record with favourable statements.

Lomé and further

Does all this mean that we can pat ourselves on the back and embark on the next five years with self-satisfaction? In spite of my positive evaluation, I shall be the first to deny this. The Convention is no more than a step, be it an important one, in the right

13

direction. It is, however, anything but the last step. The process of restructuring of the international economic system, particularly as regards the relations between the highly industrialised countries and the Third World, requires much more if it is really to lead to a New International Economic Order worthy of the name, i.e. a relationship of interdependence characterised by reciprocity and symmetry rather than one-sided dominance and asymmetry. It will require much more of the same policies and instruments, and much more in the sense of new policies and instruments. More specifically, not only have some aspects of the Lomé Convention to be globalised so as to extend its positive features to countries other than those of the EC and the ACP, the convention has also to be supplemented by new, more far-reaching schemes. This is not to be taken as a belittling of the Lomé convention. As I hope to have made clear it is a distinctly positive development at the present juncture. Future events will prove its relevance and significance, provided the implementation is as good as the intentions on paper. That, of course, is dependent on the sincerity and firmness with which especially the European partners to the convention, play the role assigned to them. It is up to all of us, politicians, opinion makers, officials, to see to it that this is done—in both the letter and the spirit of the convention. Only then will it be—to cite the preamble—establishing a new model for relations between developed and developing states, compatible with the aspirations of the international community towards a more just and more balanced economic order!

Chapter 2

THE ROAD TO LOMÉ

by *C. Dodoo* and *R. Kuster**

By concluding the Lomé Convention, Contracting Parties are:

> "*Resolved* to establish a new model for relations between developed and developing States, compatible with the aspirations of the international community towards a more just and more balanced economic order".

According to several official comments, the agreement should be seen as unique in history, both by its contents and the way it was brought about. The extent to which the Convention is considered to have created a new system of relationships, was indicated already in chapter 1. The more important policy instruments will be dealt with more fully in chapters 3-7 below.

The Lomé Convention has replaced the earlier Yaoundé Conventions of Association between the EEC (of the six) and the African and Malagasy associated states, the Arusha Convention between the EEC and Kenya, Tanzania and Uganda, as well as special relationships between Britain and a number of Commonwealth countries. It also includes countries which did not have any special relationships with member-states of the enlarged community (compare annex I).

How did this "unique" relationship emerge? In this chapter, we shall review the road to Lomé, beginning with the French request in 1956 to associate its overseas countries and territories with the new economic community, resulting in the addition of part Four and the "Implementing Convention relating to the Association with the community of the Overseas Countries and Territories" to the Treaties of Rome. The next step on the road to Lomé was set when the majority of French colonies acquired independence, re-

* This chapter could not have been written without the many insights and most invaluable assistance offered to the authors by Dr. J. Westhoff, delegate of the Commission of the European Communities in Jamaica. The authors wish to express their sincere gratitude to him.

15

sulting in the first Yaoudé Convention of 1963. Some African commonwealth countries availed themselves of the opportunity—opened in the abortive negotiations on Britain's accession to the EEC in 1961-63—to conclude separate agreements with the community. The enlargement of the EEC on January 1st, 1973 finally enabled a new and broader relationship, not in the least because of the growing political strength of the developing countries and the growing awareness among EC members of their responsibilities towards the developing countries. It set the stage for negotiation and agreement on the policy instruments of the new Convention.

The Treaty of Rome and the Association of Overseas Countries and Territories[1]

In Part Four of the Rome Treaty and the Implementing Convention, the conditions of Association of the Overseas Countries and Territories of France, Italy, the Netherlands and Belgium were laid down for a five year period.

The association policy of the EEC can only be understood within the framework of the French colonial policy after the Second World War. For the association of the overseas countries and territories with the EEC was particularly the consequence of the special constitutional, economic and monetary relations of France with its colonies.

At the time of the negotiations on the establishment of the EEC, France still had many colonies in Africa which were directly governed from Paris and were subject to a kind of direct economic colonialism. This meant that the colonies' economies were developed corresponding to the French national economy and that they were, in fact, a part of it. France formed together with its colonies a centralised and closed area, which was determined by special relations between France and its colonies, such as the trade system, the monetary system of the "zone franc" and also budgetary aid. The commercial relations were also very important. In 1956, for example, 23% of imports to France came from and 32% of its exports went to its overseas territories. Furthermore, the economic and trade policy which France applied within the monetary sys-

1. Jhr. Drs. G. van Benthem van den Bergh, "De Associatie van Afrikaanse Staten met de Europese Economische Gemeenschap", A.W. Sijthoff, Leiden, 1962, pp. 45-61. Gordon L. Weil, "A Foreign Policy For Europe?", College of Europe, Bruges, 1970, pp. 139-145.

tem of the "zone franc" implied that its colonies were strongly dependent on the French market for the sale of their products. For the products from its overseas territories had been exempted from tariff and/or quantitative import restrictions on the French market and certain tropical products could even be sold against guaranteed prices on the French market which were higher than the world market prices (the "surprix" system). These special relations implied that France claimed a special treatment of its African colonies as a condition to become a member of the EEC. For France it was not possible to accept the establishment of a customs union, implying a free trade area with a common external tariff vis-à-vis non-EEC members, including its African colonies. France wanted to create to some extent a link between its overseas territories and the EEC because of the economic and monetary unity it formed with its colonies.

France therefore claimed that the overseas countries and territories should be associated with the EEC, implying the establishment of a free trade area between the overseas countries and territories and the EEC.

However, in the report of the Spaak Committee that formed the basis of the negotiations that resulted in the Rome Treaty, the problem of the relations with the overseas countries and territories has not been treated at all. Only during the meeting of the Six Ministers of Foreign Affairs in May 1956 in Venice did France raise the question of its overseas territories for the first time. For tactical reasons, however, France waited till the Brussels negotiations of February 1957 on the definitive text of the EEC Treaty, to put forward its demand for association of the overseas countries and territories as a condition sine qua non to the establishment of the EEC.

Furthermore, France claimed from the other EEC members that they should participate in the financial aid which it was giving to its colonies. France contributed yearly a considerable amount to the development of its overseas territories. This financial burden might have hampered its competitive position on the common market. By asking their future partners to participate in this financial assistance simultaneously some sort of compensation would be given for the opening of the French overseas markets to their products. However, the French claims cannot be explained by economic motives alone. There was also a political motive. France also tried to promote a broader cooperation between two continents with complementing economies, which perhaps might be able to play a very important role in the world power relations in the future. In this the French government tried to strengthen its political position in Africa and in the world.

However, the French claims, mentioned above, were strongly opposed by the other EEC countries. Especially Germany and the Netherlands were against the French plans. They did not like a regional approach of development aid and they considered the financial contributions which were necessary too high in relation to the development aid that could be given to non-associated countries. Germany and the Netherlands were also afraid that the preferential treatment of the associated territories would harm the exports from other developing countries to the Common Market. This could have indirect effect on the German and Dutch exports to these countries, because their trade relations were traditionally more directed on Commonwealth Africa and Latin America than on the French colonies. Furthermore the Eurafrica conception was not so popular in Germany and the Netherlands. They did not want to be involved with the French colonial policy.

In the end, however, Germany and the Netherlands had to accept the association of overseas countries and territories because France claimed acceptance from the other EEC members as a condition for signing the Rome Treaty. Furthermore, they attached great importance to the success of the "Relance Européenne" and they wanted to avoid a failure like the European Defence Community in 1954.

After France had agreed to a Community procedure for the distribution of financial aid, and the granting of tariff-free quota's for bananas to Germany and for coffee to Benelux and Italy from third countries,[2] the association of the overseas countries and territories was a "fait accompli".

The six EEC members agreed that the non-European countries and territories "maintaining special relationships with Belgium, France, Italy and the Netherlands", should become associated with the EEC (Part IV of the Rome Treaty (arts. 131-136) and the Implementing Convention).

The purpose of association is dealt with in article 131 of the EEC treaty: "The purpose of association shall be to promote the economic and social development of the countries and territories and to establish close economic relations between them and the Community as a whole".

2. EEC Treaty, "Implementing Convention on the Association of the Overseas Countries and Territories with the Community", art. 15.

18

The association agreement was characterized by two main elements, namely:
— the progressive establishment of a free trade area between the EEC and the associated countries and territories, by the reciprocal reduction of tariffs and quantitative restrictions;[3]
— the establishment of a European Development Fund (EDF) for the purpose of granting Community financial aid to the associated countries and territories to promote their social and economic development. The resources of the first EDF amounted to 581.25 million u.a. for the five year period.[4]

The Independence of overseas countries and territories and the Association Conventions

The association found its basis in an agreement between the six member states of the Community without participation by the overseas countries and territories concerned. It was established by the EEC on their behalf. Shortly after the coming into force of the Rome Treaty most former territories achieved independence. At their request the association regime has been continued until the end of the said period of five years with some adaptations on the institutional level that gave a right of say to the newly independent states. At the same time these states requested that negotiations for a possible new association treaty would take place on the basis of complete equality of all states concerned.

However, the proposal for a new convention was strongly opposed by Germany and the Netherlands. According to them the association agreement should have been considered as a transitional arrangement which should disappear when the associated countries would attain full political and economic independence and that a possible new association agreement should legally be based on article 238 of the EEC treaty, which provides for association between the EEC and non-member states.

France, however, held the view that, the association should be a permanent framework for Euro-African cooperation and it should be based on article 131 of Part IV of the Rome Treaty, the original basis of the association. This would imply that the associated countries were entitled to ask for continuation of the association and, which was more important, to receive development aid.

3. EEC Treaty, Part Four, "Association of the Overseas Countries and Territories", arts. 133-134. Implementing Convention, arts. 9-15.
4. Implementing Convention, arts. 1-7.

However, the problem of the legal basis of a new association agreement was not explicitly solved. It would be concluded without indicating its legal basis.[5]

The Yaoundé I Convention

After Germany and the Netherlands had given up their objections to the continuation of the association, and in return France agreed in principle to a reduction of the common external tariff on a number of tropical products it was possible to agree on a new convention.

The negotiations between the European Community and 17 African States and Madagascar (AASM) resulted in a Convention which was signed on July 20, 1963 in Yaoundé, the capital of Cameroon. However, it did not enter into force until June 1, 1964 because of a delay in the ratification procedure. This was a consequence of the cooling of relations between the Dutch and the French after the breakdown of the negotiations of accession between Britain and the EEC. This new convention, which was officially called "The Convention between the European Community and the African and Malagasy States associated with the Community" was concluded again for a period of five years implying that it had to expire on May 31, 1969.

There were a few differences between the Yaoundé Convention and the Implementing Convention as a result of changes in the political situation and necessary economic adjustments. These economic adjustments were the consequence of internal developments within the EEC, especially brought about by the establishment of the common agricultural policy. The free trade principle of the first association agreement was maintained, namely, the reciprocal granting of tariff preferences for industrial products and for some tropical products. However, on a certain number of tropical products, such as coffee, tea, cocao and tropical fur, the EEC preferences were unilaterally reduced or even abolished by reducing the common external tariff in order to meet the wishes of the non-associated developing countries which was strongly supported by Germany and the Netherlands. Furthermore, the agricultural products exported by the associated countries to the EEC, which were comparable to or competitive with agricultural products produced within the EEC, were controlled by special trade arrangements. However, to give some compensation to the associated countries

5. Weil, *op. cit.* p. 92.

for the abolition of a number of preferences and the establishment of new trade arrangements for certain agricultural products, the financial aid by the EDF was increased from 581.25 million u.a. to 730 million u.a. The changed political situation was expressed by the fact that for the first time joined association institutions were set up to administer the Yaoundé Convention, namely, the Association Council, the Parliamentary Conference of Association and the Court of Arbitration.[6]

The Yaoundé II Convention

In December 1968 the negotiations on the renewal of the Yaoundé I Convention started between the EEC and AASM, which was in line with the Yaoundé I provisions according to which the negotiations on a possible renewal of the Convention should start in the course of 1968. During the negotiations, however, some problems arose because the AASM wanted far more than the EEC was willing to give and furthermore the EEC countries could not agree again on a guiding philosophy for the new Convention. Nevertheless a new Convention was signed in July 1969, in Yaoundé. It entered into force on January 1, 1971. Despite the complaints of the associated countries, the new Yaoundé Convention did not fundamentally change the pattern established earlier. There were only a few small differences.

In general it improved certain technical rules and the resources of the EDF were increased from 730 million u.a. to 918 million u.a. This was done to compensate the reduction of preferential arrangements which was a continuation of the trend of Yaoundé I.

Trade and financial and technical cooperation under the Yaoundé Conventions

Repeating the foregoing both Yaoundé Conventions included trade, technical and financial cooperation as well as institutions composed on a basis of parity.

In order to promote the mutual trade relations, the association treaty provided for a free trade area between the Community on the one hand and each of the associated countries on the other hand by the gradual elimination of tariffs and quantitative restric-

6. R. Cohen, "Europe and the developing countries", in Ph. P. Everts, "The European Community in the world", Rotterdam University Press, 1972, p. 112.

tions that had been completed in principle on July 1st, 1968.[7] As a consequence the AASM benefited from the inter-communal regime with the exception of temperate agricultural products and processed foodstuffs for which a special regime has been established.

From their side the AASM could maintain or institute tariffs or quantitative restrictions for products originating from the European Community in order to meet their development needs, to obtain means for their budget or in the event of difficulties in their balance of payments.[8] They should however, apply the most-favoured-nation principle vis-à-vis the EEC and they were not allowed to discriminate between the member states of the EEC.[9]

Although the provisions of the Yaoundé Conventions aimed at improving trade relations between the EEC and the AASM, especially in favour of the AASM, the results of the Yaoundé Conventions, did not entirely meet expectations. Exports by the AASM to the EEC have increased more slowly than their exports to all developed countries and the exports of all developing countries to the EEC. Yet two factors have to be taken into consideration. The AASM got preferences for only one third of their export products, the remaining products came in freely from all countries. Moreover, in order to allow for the interest of third developing countries, the common customs tariff and consequently the preference has been reduced for some important export products (e.g. for cocoa from 9% to 4% and for coffee from 16% to 7%). Even though the results could have been better the fact remains that without preferences the AASM would not have been able to maintain their position on the common market with respect to the other developing countries. Besides the trade regime has contributed to a considerable extent to a greater economic independence of the AASM because their import as well as their export has increased more with respect to the EEC states with which they had no special ties in the past as with respect to those EEC states with which these ties existed. Because of the not too satisfactory results in the trade area other means in favour of the export products from the AASM have been looked for like export promotion.

7. Convention of Association between the EEC and the AASM, Yaoundé I, arts. 2-3, art. 6 (1,2).

8. Yaoundé I Convention, arts. 3 (2), 6 (3). Convention of Association between the EEC and the AASM, Yaoundé II, arts. 3 (2), 7 (2).

9. Yaoundé I Convention, arts. 3 (2)-4 (1), 6 (4)-7. Yaoundé II Convention, arts. 3 (3)-4 (1), 7 (3), 11.

This seemed to become necessary after the Community had started to grant preferences to the non-associated states with its system of general tariff preferences which came into effect on July 1, 1971.

However, the effect of the GSP scheme on the preferential treatment of the associated countries was very limited because it was constructed in such a way that it affected the tariff advantages enjoyed by these countries only to a very limited extent (see also chapter 3).

The financial and technical assistance granted by the Communities within the framework of the association from January 1st, 1958–January 31st, 1975 amounted to a total of 2381.25 million u.a., 170 million through the European Investment Bank and the rest through the EDF. Although this assistance constitutes only 7% of the total development aid given by the original six member states, it has been of great importance to the associated countries where it represented on an average 20% of the total public aid received.

A characteristic of the Community aid was that it was given mainly in the form of grants. Moreover, close cooperation existed between donors and recipients. The initiative for the submission of a request for aid lays with the associated countries; appraisal of a project took place by the Commission in cooperation with the state concerned. The decision to finance a project rested with the institutions of the Community, but the competent authorities of the associated states were responsible for the execution of projects financed by the Community.

As far as the use of the assistance given by the Community is concerned a development can be seen during the years. During the first period of association the emphasis was mostly on the strengthening of the economic and social infrastructure; exclusively grants have been given. Under the first Yaoundé Convention accent has been laid down on interventions in direct productive sectors such as agriculture. The second Yaoundé Convention stressed furthermore industrialization, export promotion and the development of tourism.

Both Yaoundé Conventions had provisions for the granting of technical assistance for exceptional aid in the event of serious difficulties, for loans on special terms, for interest rate subsidies, for normal loans granted by the European Investment Bank and for contributions to the formation of risk capital.

In general the technical and financial assistance has been considered as satisfactory and adapted to the needs of the associated states which together with the Community within the framework of the Common institutions established the policies and guidelines of the financial and technical cooperation.

The Overseas Countries and Territories

Those overseas countries and territories which did not become independent and for whose foreign policy the EEC countries are still responsible continued to be associated with the EEC on the basis of Part IV of the Rome Treaty.

Up to now the structure of this association has been settled by decisions of the EEC Council of Ministers for five year periods, corresponding with the periods of the Yaoundé Conventions.

The characteristics of these associations of the OCT are nearly the same as the conventions mentioned above. The most important difference is that the association of the OCT does not have joint institutions. Furthermore, the association arrangements of the OCT are normally negotiated between the responsible EEC countries with the other EEC members.

The Commonwealth countries of comparable economic structure and production

The negotiations that resulted in the first Yaoundé Convention, coincided in part with the negotiations on the accession of the United Kingdom to the Community following the declaration by Prime Minister Macmillan, in July 1961. One of the most important problems treated during those negotiations concerned the relations with the Commonwealth countries. In his introduction on the possible solutions of the problems brought forward by the negotiations, Mr. Heath has proposed the association of the Commonwealth developing countries without making a distinction between South East Asiatic states on the one hand and dependent and independent states in Africa, the Caribbean and the Pacific on the other hand. The latter group of states has been treated as a separate group for the first time in the so-called classification "Deniau", classification according to the essential characteristics of the export trade of the Commonwealth countries and of the kind of problem posed with regard to the provisions of the Rome Treaty. On the basis of this classification it has been decided that for the dependent Commonwealth States, association would be the best solution whereas the independent states in Africa and the Caribbean could accede to the new Yaoundé Convention; if so desired other arrangements could be looked for.

In January 1963, the negotiations with the United Kingdom have been broken off after the initialling of the Yaoundé Convention but before the signing of this Convention. However, this did not have any effect on the possibility of admitting developing Commonwealth countries to the group of associated countries. For under these circumstances some of the member states of the EEC, especially Germany and the Netherlands, only wished to proceed to the signing of the Convention after safeguarding that the developing Commonwealth countries could also benefit by this Convention.

This guarantee has been given by a Declaration of Intent issued by the Six on April 1/2, 1963, which came simultaneously into force with the signing of the first Yaoundé Convention and which has been repeated at the signing of the second Yaoundé Convention. This declaration, which was meant to stress the open character of the association, says that the EEC is willing to extend the Yaoundé Convention or other similar instruments to other countries having an "economic structure and production comparable with those of the AASM".

These non-associated developing countries (notably the Commonwealth countries) could choose out of the following possibilities:

— Participation in the Yaoundé Convention, which governed the relations between the Community and the AASM.
— Conclusion of one or more special association agreements on the basis of article 238 of the Rome Treaty, which could cover reciprocal rights and obligations, especially in the field of trade.
— Conclusion of simple trade agreements with a view to facilitate and to develop their trade with the EEC.

According to the EEC point of view the developing countries from the Commonwealth area could not be allowed to suffer from the failure of the negotiations between the EEC and the United Kingdom. Thus, it would not be reasonable to refuse them the privileged links with the Community, which they had been allowed to expect. Furthermore some EEC countries, such as Germany and the Netherlands, saw in this declaration of intent a possibility to reduce the post-colonial aspects of the Yaoundé Convention. [10]

10. Charles Schiffmann, "A negotiation and a convention", The Courier, No. 31, Special Issue, March 1975, p. 4.

The association agreements with Nigeria and the East African Community

Nigeria and the three East African States, Uganda, Tanzania and Kenya have appealed to this declaration and all four have opted for the second solution, a special association based on article 238 of the Rome Treaty. The first association agreement was signed with Nigeria in Lagos on July 1, 1966 and it should expire on the same day as the Yaoundé I Convention. However, this association agreement was never brought into force for it could not be ratified before its expiry date because of internal political problems in Nigeria (Biafra). Since then, a new request for negotiations has never been submitted by the Nigerian government until the start of the negotiations of the Lomé Convention. The association agreement with Tanzania, Uganda and Kenya, which had established on June 6, 1967 the East African Community, was concluded in Arusha on July 28, 1968. This association agreement also never came into effect because it was impossible to ratify it before its expiry date (May 31, 1969). However, with the three East African countries a second Arusha treaty has been concluded which existed during the same period as the second Yaoundé Convention.

The difference with the Yaoundé Convention was that the Lagos and Arusha agreements did not include any technical and financial clauses, they had not been requested either. As for trade and the institutions, the provisions are comparable with those of the Yaoundé Convention with a few exceptions. In order to take into account the interests of the associated states of the Yaoundé Convention, the preferential treatment for some important export products of Nigeria and the East African States had been subjected to some quantitative limitations. Moreover, the three East African States were obliged to see to it that the overall volume of tariff concessions and the balance of concessions among the member states are maintained during the lifetime of the treaty.

Furthermore, the institutional provisions were less far-reaching than those of both the Yaoundé Conventions, because the Arusha and Lagos agreement were more limited in scope. There was only provided for an Association Council and a Court of Arbitration. One Commonwealth state, Mauritius, has appealed to the first option of the declaration of intent and has acceded to the second Yaoundé Convention. The agreement making Mauritius the 19th member of the Yaoundé Convention was signed at Port Louis, the capital of the island, on May 12, 1972.

The enlargement of the EEC, and the Negotiations of the Lomé Convention

On January 1, 1973 Great Britain, Denmark and Ireland became full members of the European Community with the same rights and obligations as the original six members. This implied that the question of association of developing countries with the EEC got new importance because Great Britain's accession to the EEC entailed several problems concerning the Commonwealth developing countries:
— The Commonwealth African countries were strongly dependent on the British market as the most important outlet for their export products.
— Britain was very anxious to keep the markets in its former colonies and that is why it was necessary, in its own interest, to work out a reciprocal satisfying arrangement for them.
— It would be inconsistent with the provisions of the Rome Treaty to maintain separate preferences (Commonwealth preferences) of EEC members towards third countries outside the EEC areas. [11]
On the ground of these problems the EEC development policy, which was almost completely limited to French Africa, was not acceptable for Great Britain. According to the British point of view it was necessary to establish machinery to ensure that to those Commonwealth countries for which it was needed, possibilities should be given to safeguard their trade and economic interests within the enlarged Community.

Great Britain's strong trade relations with the developing Commonwealth countries implied that it was considered necessary to guarantee the privileges enjoyed by each party concerned. Therefore, two possibilities for the future policy of the EEC vis-à-vis developing countries were put forward during the negotiations on the accession of Great Britain to the EEC:
— The first possibility would be to replace the association policy vis-à-vis French Africa by a global development policy.
— The second possibility, which was chosen at the end, was to extend the association policy to the Commonwealth countries in Africa, the Caribbean and the Pacific, and to improve its contents.

However, at the summit meeting of the EEC in Paris, in October 1972, it was decided that besides the regional association policy a

11. B.W.T. Mutharika, "The trade and economic implications of Africa's association with the enlarged European Economic Community", Economic Bulletin for Africa, Vol. X, No. 2, May 1974, p. 42.

global development policy ought to be developed step by step. [12] This was expressed by the communiqué of the Summit Conference: "The Community must, without detracting from the advantages enjoyed by countries with which it has special relations, respond even more than in the past to the expectations of all the developing countries". This implied a dilemma between "conserving the privileges of the associates" (strongly supported by the French government) and "measures such as most-favoured-nation tariff reductions or the generalized scheme of preferences, which are important for non-associated developing countries" (mainly supported by the Dutch and the German governments).

This dilemma was the consequence of the fact that these measures, in so far as they benefited the non-associated developing countries, could have a diminishing effect on the advantages of the associated developing countries.

In accordance with the second possibility, the EEC made a detailed and precise offer of association to twenty independent Commonwealth developing countries situated in Africa, the Indian and Pacific Oceans and the Caribbean under Protocol 22 of the accession treaty with Great Britain, Denmark and Ireland. In this protocol the declaration of intent of 1/2 April 1963 was inserted and the proposal has been made to these independent Commonwealth countries that the negotiations envisaged for the conclusion of an agreement based on one of the formulae contained in the declaration should begin as from August 1st, 1973. Accordingly those independent Commonwealth countries which chose to negotiate within the framework of the first formula have been invited to participate side by side with the AASM in negotiating the new convention to follow the second Yaoundé Convention. The offer of association was, however, not made to the developing countries in Asia and Latin America which implied several problems for these countries. The extension of the number of associated countries will cause more competition from preferential imports into the EEC. This will be encouraged by the agreements between the EEC and the Mediterranean countries. Furthermore, the size of the preferential EEC market is considerably increased by the accession of Great Britain, Denmark and Ireland. For the Asian Commonwealth developing countries and Pakistan there is not only the establishment of these new preferences against them in the British

12. Hans-Broder Krohn, "Das Abkommen von Lomé zwischen der Europäischen Gemeinschaft und den AKP-Staten", Europa-Archiv, Folge 6/1975, pp. 177-178.

market, but also the loss of their Commonwealth preferential treatment there as well. [13]

Reactions of the AASM and the Commonwealth developing countries [14]

The negotiations on the new convention should safeguard what has been achieved in the Yaoundé Convention and its fundamental principles in the field of trade relations, financial and technical cooperation and joint institutions. It has been particularly stressed that the extension of the policy of association should not be the source of any weakening in the Community's relations with the AASM, the associated states of the first hour.

This declaration is of the utmost importance in the light of the difficulties that had to be overcome before the negotiations could start.

The AASM were not too happy with the idea to have to share their benefits, especially in the field of trade, with the Commonwealth countries. They also thought that the increase in the number of associated states would reduce the financial and technical assistance which they received from the EEC under the Yaoundé Convention. Furthermore they were afraid to lose their identity by the arrival of the new partners as Nigeria alone has already a population almost equal to the joint populations of the eighteen AASM.

However, during a meeting at Nouakchott, in April 1972, three months after the successful completion of the negotiations with Britain, Denmark and Ireland, the AASM decided to join the Commonwealth countries in the forthcoming negotiations for the enlargement of the association.

The Commonwealth countries could not decide so quickly because their reactions were much more hesitant and much more mixed. Some countries considered that association with the EEC would imply greater possibilities to develop their exports and to stimulate economic development. Others, however thought that association with the EEC would introduce inflexibilities in their economic policies and would be therefore harmful to economic development. There were also some Commonwealth countries

13. John Pinder, "The Community and the developing countries: Associates and outsiders", Journal of Common Market Studies, 1973, no. 1, p. 53.
14. Mutharika, *loc. cit.* Pinder, *loc. cit.*

which were afraid to have to submit to a regime established without their participation, a regime according to their point of view that aims at the continuation of the old colonial ties in a new shape.

Bloc-to-bloc negotiations

Various factors have contributed to overcome the mutual distrust. Negotiations at the Third Unctad Conference in Santiago de Chile showed that for the time being not much could be expected from a world wide arrangement.

Contacts between the Commonwealth countries and the AASM and a better acquaintance with the Yaoundé Convention showed that fear for neo-colonialism was without foundation. The Commonwealth countries have noted, moreover, with satisfaction that the African countries which never had colonial ties with the member states have been invited by the Community and have accepted to participate in the negotiations (Soudan, Ethiopia, Liberia and Guinea Bissau).

Although from the side of the Community it has been envisaged to admit to the negotiations only those Commonwealth countries that had opted specifically for the first formula, this idea has been dropped and instead the Community declared its intention to negotiate a global arrangement on the basis of the first formula. Yet the deciding factor in accepting the invitation to the negotiations could have been the possibility to establish in this way the unity of Africa and to remove the artificial borders from the colonial past.

It was very fortunate that at the moment of choice the presidency of the Organization of African Unity rested with Nigeria. By its presidency Nigeria had more responsibility and consequently less liberty of movement than an ordinary member and once Nigeria had declared itself for negotiations, it was certain that the other members of the OAU would have to follow.

By putting its full economic and political weight into the negotiations with the EEC in favour of the poorest developing countries, Nigeria saw in doing this a possibility to improve its prestige in Africa and at the same time it would be considered as the inspirer of the African unity.

In May 1973, the African trade ministers agreed, during a meeting at Abidjan, to the principle of having a bloc-to-bloc negotiation with the EEC and to compose a charter of eight principles to guide them. This was confirmed by the OAU summit meeting at

Addis Ababa a fortnight later. The Caribbean and the Pacific countries followed very soon and at the time when the negotiations were formally opened in July 1973, there were three separate groups of countries on the one side as opposed to the Community. Therefore there were three separate spokesmen for the one side, one for each group:

1) Under the auspices of the OAU those of the member states of the OAU which were to take part in the negotiations had formed themselves into the African group and acted through one spokesman. Before the emergence of this African group there were the French-speaking African countries, hitherto organised in an exclusive association entailing the enjoyment of preferential treatment by the EEC under the Yaoundé Convention. There were also the three East African countries of the East African Community enjoying preferential trade arrangements with the EEC under the Arusha Convention. Bearing in mind their acquired status and special privileges it was a great achievement for the Commonwealth countries, to have been readily accepted into the fold of the AASM and Arusha groups, and together, to form the African group for negotiations with the EEC.

Their guiding principles for the negotiations consisted of: [15]

(a) The principle of non-reciprocity in trade and tariff concessions given by the EEC;

(b) the extension, on a non-discriminatory basis, toward third countries, of the provisions on the right of establishment;

(c) the revision of the rules of origin must be formulated so as to facilitate the industrial integration of African countries and, in particular, they must grant the status of original products to all goods which have been produced in one or several of the African countries (whether or not they are members of African groupings) or which have been processed in accordance with mutually accepted criteria, irrespective of whether or not they enjoy preferential relations with the EEC;

(d) a revision of the provisions on the movements of payments and capital to take account of the objective of monetary independence in African countries and the need for monetary co-operation among African countries;

(e) the dissociation of EEC financial and technical aid from any particular form of relationship with the EEC;

(f) free and assured access to EEC markets for all African prod-

15. Eric Christopher Djamson, "The Dynamics of Euro-African Co-operation", Martinus Nijhoff, The Hague, 1975, pp. 35-36.

31

ucts including processed and semi-processed agricultural products, whether or not they are subject to the common agricultural policy of the EEC;

(g) the guaranteeing to African countries of stable, equitable and remunerative prices in EEC markets for their main products in order to allow them to increase their export earnings;

(h) any form of agreement concluded with the EEC should not in any manner adversely affect intra-African co-operation.

2) The Caribbean countries organised under the Caribbean Economic Community, also had their own spokesman. They had accepted the following guiding principles which hardly differed from the principles of the African group: [16]

(a) Rejection of reciprocity;

(b) free entry into the Community for all their products, with special arrangements for sugar, bananas and citrus in particular;

(c) relaxation of the rules of origin;

(d) a guaranteed volume of sugar exports to the Community;

(e) development aid, dissociated from particular forms of relationship with the EEC, on terms which do not compromise their dignity and self-respect;

(f) any institutions to be limited strictly to the economic and technical aspects of the relationship;

(g) no constraints on economic cooperation with other developing countries;

(h) no impairment of cooperation between the Caribbean countries themselves.

3) Likewise the Pacific countries, organised under the South Pacific Economic Community, had their own spokesman.

Process and nature of the negotiations

Because the second Yaoundé Convention would expire on January 31, 1975, article 62 of the convention provided that the negotiations for a new convention should start at least 18 months before the expiry date. That is why the special provisions in articles 109-114 of the Treaty of Accession were only applied till January 31, 1975. These provisions determined the status quo for the special relations between the six old member states of the EEC and the 19 AASM as well as between Great Britain and those Commonwealth countries which would fall under the declaration of intent.

16. Pinder, *loc. cit.* p. 62.

On the initiative of the European Community a first ministerial conference—between the Community and 41 invited states—took place in Brussels on July 25/26, 1973. At this Conference, the invited states decided to enter into negotiations with the Community. It was agreed that such negotiations would be conducted on ministerial level.

Actual negotiations on the conclusion of a new Convention began shortly after a second ministerial conference on October 17/18, 1973 in Brussels, in which both sides presented their basic negotiating positions.

Although negotiations took place between the Community and its nine member states, and 46 developing states, they have formally and in fact been conducted as bilateral negotiations. As a consequence, they required both sides—the nine and the forty-six—to adopt a common negotiation position prior towards facing each other.

The establishment of the Community's negotiation position was relatively easy because of the obligations under protocol 22, the experience with the Yaoundé and Arusha Conventions and the proposals of the EEC Commission, especially the Memorandum of April 1973. [17]

While negotiations took place on ministerial level or—as the case may be—in meetings of the Committee of ambassadors and plenipotentiaries, the Community agreed on October 15/16, 1973, that the Commission would conduct negotiations—between those sessions—on behalf of the Community and its member states.

The procedure thus agreed upon broadly followed the precedents set by the previous Yaoundé Conventions; the clearer division of tasks between the Commission and the Council apparently prevented the re-emergence of the dispute of competence, which had complicated the negotiations of the two Yaoundé Conventions. On the ACP side however, it was much more difficult to establish common negotiation positions because of the large number of countries, the diversity of each country's problems and the complexity of the long and laborious negotiations themselves.

At the opening conference in July 1973, which was a formal one, the statements made by the three separate spokesmen setting out the respective guidelines of their group for the negotiations

17. "Memorandum of the Commission to the Council on the Future Relations between the Community, the Present AASM States and the Countries in Africa, the Caribbean, the Indian and Pacific Oceans referred to in Protocol 22 to the Act of Accession", COM (73) 500/fin. April 4, 1973.

revealed that the African group, the Caribbean group and the Pacific group all had common objectives and aspirations. In their statements they agreed to principles which deal with the main objections against the Yaoundé model.

It came as a natural and logical consequence for these three separate blocs of countries to form themselves into the homogenous group called the ACP for the purposes of the negotiations. Thus, in October 1973, at the second session of the joint Council of Ministers for the negotiations, the African, Caribbean and Pacific countries spoke through one spokesman. It was a moment of great historical significance. For the first time in the history of economic relations, 44 developing countries had bound themselves to negotiate collectively with the EEC.

Inspired by their common objectives and unanimity of action, the ACP countries were enabled the more effectively to negotiate with the EEC. It is a source of great pride that despite the large number of countries, the diversity of each country's problems and the complexity of the long and laborious negotiations themselves, the ACP countries stood united at all times and presented a common front. This ACP unity might be explained by several factors:
— it was considered the only successful negotiating technique, towards the EEC;
— the ACP's perceived common economic interests during the negotiations;
— a growing consciousness of their combined political power at the negotiating stage;
— the catalyzing force of Nigeria;
— the consequences of the better relations between Britain and France (e.g. accession of Britain to the EEC);
— the awareness of potential economic power (OPEC). [18]

After the opening conferences on ministerial level in July and October 1973, negotiations started between the Commission on behalf of the Community and the Ambassadors of the ACP states

18. This ACP unity was strengthened during the first meeting of the Council of Ministers of these countries, held in Guyana on June 5/6, 1975, where it was decided to institutionalise the cooperation between the members of the ACP. The ministers signed an agreement known as the Georgetown Agreement. Until the permanent secretariat foreseen in the agreement was set up, the action of the group was coordinated by an ad hoc administrative secretariat, which was also responsible for coordination during the negotiations on the Lomé Convention.

in plenary sessions and by January 1974 many technical meetings were in progress.

The meetings between January 1974 and July 1974 were characterized by a good deal of hard bargaining. However, not much progress has been made in this stage even though a better understanding of each of the problems could be achieved. The differences of view between the EEC and the ACP continued to be many.

The ACP states had to maintain their own unity on issues which would have very different effects among their economically diverse members. The EEC was often taken up with difficult domestic economic and political problems. This implied that the Brussels technical negotiators were not able to put forward solutions. That is why the ACP countries took the initiative, inviting the Community to a ministerial conference to be held at the end of July, 1974 at Kingston, Jamaica. This conference gave a strong impulse to the Brussels negotiations by arriving at a number of conclusions, such as the dropping of any reciprocity requirements on the trade side and a definite agreement on the system for export earnings stabilization as proposed by the Commission of the EEC. Furthermore it was agreed that priority should be given to industrialization in the new Convention. The ACP memorandum on industrialization served as a draft for the provisions on industrial cooperation in the new Convention. The size of financial aid and the question of sugar exports to the EEC, continued to be areas of disagreement. [19]

The conclusions, mentioned above, served as a basis for the continuation of the negotiations that took place after the summer holidays 1974 in four working groups in which the Community was represented by the Commission and the ACP states by a limited number of their Ambassadors. Progress in negotiations after the Kingston Conference was in the beginning very slow. During this time the experts and ambassadors were putting finishing touches to drafts but they did not succeed in getting down to the things which mattered.

An important role has been played in this phase by the meetings of the two bureaux composed on the ACP side of their chairman accompanied by a representative of each regional grouping and on the Community side by the Commission assisted by a representative of the presidency of the Council. This phase of the negotiations has been concluded in December 1974, in Brussels by the

19. Isebill V. Gruhn, "The Lomé Convention: inching towards interdependence", International Organization, Vol. 30, No. 2, Spring 1976, p. 253.

adoption of a text with many alternative versions. The ministers tried to solve these differences during a plenary meeting in the Egmont Palace on 13-15 January 1975.

Because of insufficient preparation they did not succeed and therefore they decided to resume the negotiations at the end of January again on Ministerial level between the Community and the enlarged bureau of the ACP states. These negotiations have been successfully concluded, in the morning of February 1, 1975 after a final marathon conference which started on January 30, 1975.

The decisive negotiations on Ministerial level have been conducted by the Council—though with active participation of Commissioner Cheysson.

As had been the case with the two Yaoundé Conventions, the Lomé Convention refers to neither Part IV nor article 238 of the EEC Treaty as its legal basis. Due to their scope and the differing interpretations—as between the Commission and the European Parliament on the one hand and the Council of Ministers on the other—the Yaoundé Conventions had been made into so-called mixed agreements, to which both the Community and its member states are parties. In legal terms, the Lomé Convention has been given the same character.

Negotiating the Lomé Convention: The major issues

Trade cooperation

Trade cooperation between the EEC and the ACP countries is provided for in title I of the Lomé Convention which contains only 15 articles. However, this section raised the most difficult problems during the negotiations and some of them had to be resolved at the very end of the negotiations. It was quite a difficult task to establish the trade relationships between the nine industrial member states of the EEC and 46 developing ACP countries because of the great diversity of situations, traditions and attitudes among the EEC and ACP countries. The most important issues in the trade field were:
— Access for ACP goods to the Community market
— The principle of non-reciprocity in trade commitments
— Access for Community products to the ACP markets
— Rules of origin
— Non-tariff barriers. [20]

20. The Courier, No. 31, Special Issue, March 1975, p. 23.

Access for ACP products to the Community market

The principal demand of the ACP countries was that goods originating in ACP countries, encompassing agricultural and semi-agricultural products, manufactured and semi-manufactured products whether or not they are covered by the Common Agricultural Policy, should be imported into the EEC free from customs duties, levies and other charges having equivalent effect and also free from any quantitative restrictions.

The community showed a remarkable development in its attitude and approach. It granted such access with exceptions for agricultural products which fall directly or indirectly under the Community's Common Agricultural Policy. The ACP countries were annoyed by the experience of the AASM in 1972 when the Community was not willing to grant tariff concessions for early fruit and vegetables. Thus from the start of the negotiations the ACP countries requested total and unrestricted access to the EEC market for all their agricultural products.

However, the Community took the attitude that no negotiations could take place regarding these products and consequently on the offer made by the Community on this point in July 1974. The Community did not make clear, however, on which ground this distinction between agricultural and industrial products could be justified, a distinction which has not always been made during other negotiations.

Bearing in mind that the economies of the ACP countries are fundamentally agricultural and as 80% of the ACP export products are agricultural, the CAP which aims to ensure sufficient income for farmers inside the EEC and to maintain a balance within the EEC between supply and demand of these agricultural products for Community consumers, is harmful to the interests of the ACP countries. The fixed domestic agricultural prices which are protected by levies on imports hinders the access of some of the ACP agricultural products to the EEC market. Furthermore, the granting of subsidies for production and export implies unfair competition for similar commodities in foreign markets. [21]

At Kingston, however, the Community took note of the request of the ACP states to improve the Community offer and accepted to examine this request with the ACP states during the negotiations.

21. E. Olu Sanu, "The current negotiations between Africa and the EEC", paper read at the Europa Institute of the University of Amsterdam, on Friday, 22nd March 1974, pp. 11-12.

On the strength of this acceptance the ACP states insisted on the forming of a special working group for agricultural products but this group could not make any progress as the Community declared itself not to be able to add anything to its offer because of its above mentioned position.

Under pressure of the ACP states the Community has amended its offer but the request of the ACP states to include the results in the Convention or at least in a protocol has been refused by the Community with the same argument. Eventually it has been decided that in the minutes of the signing of the Convention a declaration would be inserted in which the offer of the Community would be included, which minutes exceptionally could be published.

> "For the purposes of applying Article 11 (4) of the Convention, the Community is prepared, for the purposes of achieving the aims set in Article 1 to begin an examination of requests by the ACP States that other agricultural products referred to in Article 2 (2) (a) of the Convention should benefit from special treatment.
>
> This examination will cover either new agricultural productions for which there would be real possibilities of export to the EEC, or current products not covered by the provisions for implementing the treatment referred to above, insofar as these exports might assume an important position in the exports of one or more ACP States." [22]

This offer contains an improved and enlarged version of the special regime provided for under the Yaoundé Convention. Under the Yaoundé and Arusha conventions the agricultural products falling under the CAP and imported from the associated states, were treated in the same way as those from third countries. However, when the substantial economic interest of one or several associated states concerned in such products was established, the possibility of a more favourable system was provided for within the framework of the Yaoundé and Arusha arrangements. In the Yaoundé and Arusha conventions the concept of economic interest was however not clearly defined. The EEC alone had the right to define this concept taking into account the economic, political and social interest of the agricultural sector within the Community. This implied an important obstacle to the development and

22. ACP-EEC Convention of Lomé, annex II to the Final Act, joint declaration on Article 11 (4) of the Convention.

diversification of the products of the associated states. The ACP countries therefore categorically rejected this concept during the negotiations on the Lomé Convention. [23]

The new regime under the Lomé Convention for agricultural products falling under the CAP which amount to 5.8% of the ACP agricultural exports to the EEC, does not remove the protection offered for products originating in the Community itself by the CAP, but it is more favourable than the general regime with regard to products from third countries. This percentage of 5.8, mentioned above, seems to be very small at first sight. However, this is an average, which means that it can be very important for certain ACP countries individually. Thus, levy reductions were given for some CAP-products originating in ACP countries which are of actual export economic interest to those ACP countries such as maize, rice, millet and sorghum and processed rice and cereal products. Some fruit and vegetables may even be imported duty-free or at very reduced duty without the need to observe a marketing timetable. Furthermore, special measures have been made to allow the ACP countries to export a certain amount of beef and veal to the EEC. Tobacco and meat originating in ACP countries are also exempted to some extent from measures that may be adopted by the Community to safeguard its own domestic production [24] (see further chapter 7).

The principle of non-reciprocity in trade commitments

Under the Yaoundé Conventions the obligations in the field of trade resulted from the acceptance of a free-trade area as a basis for the mutual trade relations between the contracting parties. In the beginning of the negotiations on the new Convention the French and Belgian delegations and the Commission still held the view that the new association should continue to be based on the principle of a free-trade area.

On the basis of this principle the AASM from their side too had to remove their trade barriers for products originating in the European Community and to grant so-called reverse preferences under the Yaoundé Convention. The AASM, Togo and Zaire excepted, were used to grant the EEC reverse preferences and some of them supported the concept of reciprocity on political grounds. [25]

The importance of these reverse preferences has been exag-

23. Sanu, *loc. cit.*, p. 12.
24. The Courier, *loc. cit.* pp. 23. 38.
25. Pinder, *loc. cit.* p. 64.

gerated considerably, however. First of all, not all AASM did grant these preferences and secondly so many exceptions had been accorded that in fact all AASM were free to do as they liked. Still, the ACP countries and more in particular the Commonwealth countries considered these obligations as too far reaching and outdated. Thus, the ACP countries demanded that there should be no reciprocity in the trade and tariff concessions given by the Community having regard to the yawning gap of disparity between the levels of economic development of the EEC and the ACP countries. Reverse preferences would prevent the ACP countries from buying in the cheapest markets. The Community has accepted that in view of their present development needs the ACP countries shall not be required for the duration of the Convention to grant reciprocal treatment to imports of products originating in the Community. [26]

Another reason for the EEC to abolish the reverse preferences was because of the opposition by the USA which considered it to be discriminating. The USA went as far as to decide under the 1973 Trade Reform Act, section 604 b (adopted with a view to the Tokyo Round of Trade negotiations in the GATT) "that generalized tariff preferences will not be granted to any developing country which accords preferential treatment to the products of a developed country other than the USA, unless the President has received assurance satisfactory to him that such preferential treatment will be eliminated before January 1, 1976".

The USA is not so much concerned about the loss to their own exports caused by these preferences, which is not great, but much more about the shape of the world trading system. The world might be divided into North-South blocs, which would be an economic and political disadvantage. [27]

Thus, the importance of the abolition of the reverse preferences for the ACP countries lies mainly in the fact that they will not be excluded from the United States' GSP, which is very important for the Caribbean (see further chapter 3).

Access for Community products to the ACP markets

Notwithstanding the principle of non-reciprocity dealt with above, the ACP countries "shall not discriminate among the Member States and shall grant to the Community a treatment no less

26. ACP-EEC Convention of Lomé, art. 7 (1).
27. Pinder, *loc. cit.*, p. 66.

favourable than the most favoured nation treatment". [28] This last formula has been used on purpose to permit those ACP countries which wish to give preferential treatment to the Community to do so; but this preferential treatment has to be given to all the EEC member states because discrimination between the nine is not allowed. The ACP countries insisted, however, that the EEC most favoured treatment "shall not apply in respect of trade or economic relations between ACP states or between one or more ACP states and other developing countries". [29] The EEC has refused, however, that exceptions could be made in favour of certain developed countries and it requested that the non-discrimination and most-favoured nation clause would not only apply to imports but to exports as well. [30] Here the Community went further than in the Yaoundé Convention where only non-discrimination has been asked as regards to export duties. [31] Because of the comparatively unimportant obligations of the ACP countries and the growing importance of the commodities, the Community could not accept that one of the member states is treated less favourably than its partner states from the Community or than a third industrial country. This point has created great difficulties until the very last but at the end the ACP countries have accepted a formula that met the wishes of the Community: "In their trade with the Community, the ACP countries shall not discriminate...". [32]

This implies that the ACP countries are free to choose the instruments of their own trading policies with the EEC and with other countries, on condition only that these policies are not discriminatory.

Rules of origin

Laborious negotiations also took place on the rules of origin which enable the customs administrations in the Community to identify exactly which products they can regard as having originated in the ACP states and eligible as such for free access. According to the Convention, the concessions granted by the Community relate to products originating in ACP countries. The definition of the rules of origin assumed great importance during negotiations since a restrictive definition would weaken the effectiveness of the trade concessions.

28. Lomé Convention, art. 7 (2) (a).
29. Lomé Convention, art. 7 (2) (b).
30. Lomé Convention, art. 7 (2) (a).
31. Yaoundé, II Convention, art. 4 (1).
32. Lomé Convention, art. 7 (2) (a).

The Lomé Convention provides for free access for all the commodities of the ACP countries to the EEC market. However, these products are required to meet certain conditions to have originating status which are mentioned in protocol No. 1 of the Lomé Convention:

Article 1 1. For the purpose of implementing the Convention and without prejudice to paragraphs 3 and 4, the following products shall be considered as products originating in an ACP State, under the condition that they were transported directly, within the meaning of Article 5:

(a) products wholly obtained in one or more ACP States,

(b) products obtained in one or more ACP States in the manufacture of which products other than those referred to in (a) are used, provided that the said products have undergone sufficient working or processing within the meaning of Article 3.

Article 3 1. For the purpose of implementing Article 1 (1) (b) the following shall be considered as sufficient working or processing:

(a) working or processing as a result of which the goods obtained receive a classification under a tariff heading other than that covering each of the products worked or processed, except, however, working or processing specified in List A in Annex II, where the special provisions of that list apply;

(b) working or processing specified in List B in Annex III.

"Sections", "Chapters" and "tariff headings" shall mean the Sections, Chapters and headings in the Brussels Nomenclature for the Classification of Goods in Customs Tariffs.

According to the ACP point of view the rules of origin under the Yaoundé and Arusha Conventions were too stringent which implied that the ACP countries suggested that there should be a relaxation in the rules of origin.

The Community, however, was anxious to keep as much uniformity as possible in the rules of origin it applies to goods from third countries, whereas the ACP countries were anxious that various special situations should be allowed for. One of the aims of the ACP countries during the negotiations therefore was to seek a revision of the rules of origin. The rules were to be formulated so as to promote industrial cooperation of the ACP countries. In particular, the rules must grant the status of originating products to all goods which had been produced in one or several of the ACP countries. The Community had no difficulty in granting originating status to any product produced in one or more ACP countries. This means that the Community has undertaken to treat the ACP countries as one tariff area, i.e. to grant the attribution of cumulative origin to them. [33] This implies that joint production of export goods by ACP countries might be facilitated and regional integration between ACP countries could be encouraged. When the ACP countries sought to extend this principle to third developing countries generally, the Community rejected it since it was not prepared to extend it that far.

Another problem concerning the rules of origin was the percentage rule: "The percentage rule consists, where the product appears in List A, a criterion additional to that of a change of tariff heading for any non-originating product used". [34]

The ACP countries had suggested that a product should have originating status if the added value is 25% of the total value of the product. This was, however, unacceptable for the European Community because according to the Community this percentage of 25% often consists only of packing costs. This could imply that third countries could export their products to the EEC via the ACP countries and could thus benefit from the preferential treatment of the ACP countries. The EEC maintained therefore the position as defined during the negotiations, namely an added value requirement of at least 50%, which the ACP countries had to accept.

The ACP countries had also proposed a simple definition for "their vessels" so that products from the sea taken by their vessels would qualify as originating where 25% of the ownership of the vessel was vested in an ACP state or national. The Community did not accept this. In fact, the Community resolutely maintained the position as defined in the Yaoundé Convention. It was only at the final round of the negotiations that the Community made some concession by reducing the existing requirement of 75% in the Yaoundé Convention to 50%. The following agreement was reached:

33. "ACP-EEC Convention of Lomé", protocol no. 1 concerning the definition of the concept of "originating products" and methods of administrative cooperation, art. 1 (2): "...the ACP States are considered as being one territory".

34. Lomé Convention, protocol No. I, Annex I, "Explanatory Notes", Note 4—Article 3 (1) and (2) and Article 4.

"The term 'their vessels' shall apply only to vessels:
— which are registered or recorded in a Member State or an ACP State;
— which sail under the flag of a Member State or an ACP State;
— which are owned to an extent of at least 50% by nationals of States party to the Convention or by a company with its head office in one of these countries, of which the manager or managers, chairman of the board of directors or of the supervisory board, and the majority of the members of such board, are nationals of States party to the Convention and of which, in addition in the case of partnerships or limited companies, at least half the capital belongs to States party to the Convention or to public bodies or nationals of such States;
— of which at least 50% of the crew, captain and officers included, are nationals of States party to the Convention". [35]

Non-tariff barriers

The existence of non-tariff barriers such as quota or quantitative restrictions, sanitary regulations, levies, seasonal control, fiscal measures etc., was also of concern to the ACP countries. For free access to the EEC market to be meaningful, the ACP countries further demanded the abolition of non-tariff barriers since these might constitute a disguised restriction on trade or have the practical effect of impeding access.

The arbitrary nature and the strict way of enforcement of these measures restrict the access of ACP products to the Community market. Therefore, the ACP countries suggested that these measures should be abolished where they are no longer necessary or relaxed and harmonised at EEC level when they can be justified. The Community contended they had genuine difficulties since the administrative procedures having the effect of non-tariff barriers have not been harmonised at the Community level but remained as of now to be matters within the national competence of the individual member states of the EEC.

Some of the ACP delegates were very irritated about this because in the case of agriculture the ACP requests were rejected because of an existing Community policy while in the case of non-tariff barriers the ACP requests were rejected because of its absence. Some kind of solution had to be found, however imper-

35. Lomé Convention, protocol No. I, Annex I, "Explanatory Notes", Note 6.

fect. The Convention attempts to do this by providing for a consultation machinery with a view to reaching a satisfactory solution: [36]

> "Where new measures or measures stipulated in programmes adopted by the Community for the approximation of laws and regulations in order to facilitate the movement of goods are likely to affect the interests of one or more ACP States the Community shall, prior to adopting such measures, inform the ACP States thereof through the Council of Ministers. In order to enable the Community to take into consideration the interests of the ACP States concerned, consultations shall be held upon the request of the latter with a view to reaching a satisfactory solution".
> "Where existing rules or regulations of the Community adopted in order to facilitate the movement of goods or where the interpretation, application or administration thereof affect the interests of one or more ACP States, consultations shall be held at the request of the latter with a view to reaching a satisfactory solution.
> With a view to finding a satisfactory solution, the ACP States may also bring up within the Council of Ministers any other problems relating to the movement of goods which might result from measures taken or to be taken by the Member States.
> The competent institutions of the Community shall to the greatest possible extent inform the Council of Ministers of such measures".

Thus, there is some machinery for tackling problems arising out of the imposition of non-tariff barriers both at the Community level and at the national level of the member states of the EEC.

Stabilization of export earnings

> "With the aim of remedying the harmful effects of the instability of export earnings and of thereby enabling the ACP States to achieve the stability, profitability and sustained growth of their economies, the Community shall implement a system for guaranteeing the stabilization of earnings from exports by the ACP States to the Community of certain

36. Lomé Convention, arts. 5, 6.

products on which their economies are dependent and which are affected by fluctuations in price and/or quantity". [37]

Stabex is an answer to an issue that has divided the Community and the AASM for many years and that likewise on world level affects the establishment of harmonious and stable relations between producers and consumers of primary products.

Before the coming into force of the Rome Treaty, France granted price and sale guarantees to the products from its overseas territories. After the establishment of the EEC and the first association agreement, these guarantees had to be abolished because they were considered as a violation of the free trade principle. The AASM received production and diversification aid as a transitional measure. This proved, however, not sufficient to enable them to compete on the world market. So for years the associated states have demanded for a guarantee of remunerative, stable and equitable prices for their products. This request became even more justified as the relative advantage resulting from preferential treatment of the AASM on the common market has been weakened by the reductions of the common customs tariff and by the adoption of a scheme of generalized preferences.

However, the Stabex system is inseparably connected with the *sugar* problem. During the negotiations on the accession of the United Kingdom to the Communities, the British have asked for special measures to safeguard the interests of the sugar exporting countries from the Commonwealth. This implied that it was necessary for the EEC to share the burden of the Commonwealth Sugar Agreement under which, up to the end of 1974, Commonwealth sugar exporters benefited from a stable and privileged access to the market of the United Kingdom. The EEC accepted the British demand and the Commission seized the opportunity to extend it to the export of other primary products by the introduction of an ambiguous statement into Protocol No. 22 according to which the EEC was willing to safeguard the interests of all those ACP countries whose economies depend to a large degree on the exports of primary products.

To fulfil this obligation the Commission proposed, in its memorandum of April 1973, to stabilize the export earnings for a number of primary products exported by the ACP countries. This Stabex system was one of the main problems during the whole negotiations between the Community and the ACP countries for a

37. Lomé Convention, art. 16.

46

new Convention. The drawn out negotiations concerning the Stabex system were partly due to the fact that for a long time the ACP countries have requested an indexation of prices of their primary products to the prices of industrial products. They demanded that Stabex should guarantee to their main products, stable, equitable and remunerative prices in EEC markets in order to allow the ACP countries concerned to increase their export earnings in order to counteract any global deterioration in the terms of trade of primary products. The Community opposed, however, very strongly to include into Stabex the stabilization of real earnings, i.e. an indexation of prices.

The EEC was of the opinion that this problem could only be solved on a world level. According to the Community's point of view indexation would stimulate world wide inflation at that moment and furthermore such interference with the market-mechanism would lead to ruinous surpluses.

Concerning the products which should be covered by Stabex, the Commission proposed a list of eight products in its memorandum of April 1973. The ACP countries had proposed a much larger list of products. However, a compromise was reached on a list of 12 products or product groups consisting of 29 individual products. Processed products were also included. This was done with a view to support the expansion of processing in ACP countries which are producing raw materials.

One of the many issues during the negotiations in this field was about the criteria for the establishment of the list of products. The original criteria proposed by the Commission have been taken into consideration as well as those agreed to at Kingston where the ACP countries succeeded in getting more liberal criteria for the establishment of the product list.

The two classes of criteria taken into consideration were:
— "those agreed at Kingston, namely, the importance of the product to employment by the exporting country, deterioration in the terms of trade between the Community and the ACP country concerned and the different levels of development in the individual ACP countries"
— "the fact that receipts derived from any product are by tradition unstable owing to fluctuations in prices and/or quantities, and the dependence upon these products of the economies of the ACP countries". [38]

Although the Stabex scheme is intended for primary agricultural

38.   The Courier, *loc. cit.*, p. 25.

products susceptible to export fluctuations, the ACP countries asked moreover, for the inclusion of iron ore covered by neither criteria. The Community agreed to the inclusion of this product only by way of exception to accommodate Mauritania and for the sake of securing a general agreement. The inclusion of iron ore was accepted as a compromise in order to make a speedy end to the negotiations. However, the Community remained firmly opposed to mineral products being included under Stabex and this opposition has been recorded in a declaration of the Community annexed to the minutes of the negotiations.

Another difference existed on the question whether there should be a ceiling to the funds put at the disposal of the stabilization system. Agreement has been reached on an amount of no more than 375 million units of account for the five years period of the Convention, divided into five annual instalments of 75 million units of account. The question if the transfers have the character of an advance or a grant has been solved by accepting the principle that the transfer had to be repaid if certain conditions were met; this obligation does, however, not exist for the least developed countries. However, the Community's commodity imports from ACP countries of commodities covered by Stabex in 1973 which amounted to about 1,985 million units of account, is in sharp contrast to the small amount of money available for it. [39]

Satisfaction has been given to the ACP countries on the point of the utilization of the resources: they are free to decide how to use the transfers but the Commission has to be informed.

The scheme does not meet all the expectations of the ACP countries. Nevertheless, it is unique in the sense that it is the first of its kind and perhaps an important step forward towards the realisation of the aspirations of the developing world generally. Furthermore it should be emphasized that the scheme is of mutual benefit to the ACP and the EEC and probably more so on the long run to the EEC, since its effective implementation must necessarily ensure the maintenance of raw material supplies to the Community. This is so because if deliveries to the EEC are allowed to drop, then any funds which may be forthcoming for revenue stabilization will be that much lower as stabilization is only available on a moving average of past deliveries to the Community (see further chapter 4).

39. The Courier, *loc. cit.*, p. 28, table 2, Imports to the EEC (EUR 9) from ACP countries (1973).

The sugar protocol

The sugar protocol, as we saw already was the key to the Stabex system under the Lomé Convention. The ACP countries would probably not have been induced to sign the Lomé Convention without this sugar protocol. It was seen as a test of the good faith of the EEC by the ACP countries.

They saw the sugar protocol as a model for the kind of treatment they were expecting for other products. Sugar is one of the products which satisfies the criteria laid down for inclusion in the list of products specified under the Stabex scheme. However, it came in for special treatment because of other distinctive features. Sugar already played a very important role during the negotiations on the accession of the United Kingdom to the EEC and the obligation in Protocol 22 mentioned already to safeguard the interests of all the countries of which the economy depends to a considerable extent on the export of primary products, did particularly concern sugar. This is understandable seen in the light of the Commonwealth Sugar Agreement under which the United Kingdom has been obliged to buy sugar from Commonwealth countries at negotiated prices. This Commonwealth Sugar Agreement expired on December 21st, 1974. Sugar represents for a number of ACP countries a commodity of extraordinary economic and social importance. Partly for this reason, partly due to the high price of sugar, sugar has been the problem which has been negotiated last.

The ACP countries requested for long-term access for an indefinite period to the Community market for an overall quantity of not less than 1.4 million tons of raw sugar from the developing countries participating in the Commonwealth Sugar Agreement to which was to be added an appropriate quantity to meet the requirements of other ACP sugar exporting countries.

The ACP countries also demanded satisfactory arrangements over the question of price as well as a yearly review of the price. The sugar price was to take fully into account the world economic situation—in effect a price that would lead to substantial increase in their export earnings. The question of price remained a crucial negotiating issue to the very end of the negotiations. In return the ACP countries were prepared to guarantee the supply of individual quantities constituting the overall total. These quantities they demanded should be reviewed upwards to assure them of a share of the growth in Community consumption.

The Community had offered to guarantee the ACP countries to purchase yearly from them a quantity of 1.4 million tons of sugar, which should be renegotiated after five years. For this quantity the Community wanted to guarantee the minimum price which was also paid to the Community's beet-farmers. The ACP countries, especially Jamaica requested a much higher price because in 1974 the world market price for sugar was higher than the EEC price. According to the Community's point of view however, the world market price would probably decrease to a level which would be lower than the guaranteed prices of the Community. Furthermore, if the Community would pay a higher price to the ACP planters of sugar than to their own beet-farmers this would imply serious political risks.

The sugar regime which finally emerged from the negotiations is in Protocol No. 3. The agreement reached provides for the ACP exporting countries to supply and for the Community to purchase and import 1.4 million tons of sugar with the guarantee of a minimum price linked with the prices paid to Community producers. The sugar is sold on the EEC market at prices freely negotiable between the buyers and sellers. The Community will intervene by buying sugar at the guaranteed price if this price falls below a certain minimum level. The price to be guaranteed is to be negotiated each year inside the range of prices operative in the Community. This guarantee concerns sugar which it was not possible to market on satisfactory terms at prices freely negotiated between sellers and buyers. The protocol on sugar, contrary to the Convention proper which lasts for five years, is valid for an undetermined period. However, a clause provides for the possibility of withdrawal after five years and subject to two years' notice (see further chapter 7).

Industrial cooperation

Another new field under the Lomé Convention is the chapter on industrial cooperation. In the Commission's Memorandum of April 1973, there were no startling new ideas in the field of industrial cooperation. The wish to bring forward new and comprehensive necessary conditions concerning industrial cooperation into the new Convention came from the ACP side. At the request of the ACP countries this subject is dealt with in a separate title of the Convention which is largely based on a memorandum presented by the ACP countries during the joint ministerial meeting of July 1974, held in Kingston, Jamaica. In this memorandum, the ACP countries sought the commitment and assistance of the EEC to:

(a) promote the development and diversification of industry in ACP countries;

(b) promote new relations in the industrial field between the Community, the member states and the ACP countries, in particular the establishment of new industrial and trade links between the industries of the member states and those of the ACP countries;

(c) facilitate the transfer of technology to the ACP countries through training in industrial skills, access to industrial information and technology; and

(d) establish arrangements that would reconcile the interests of private industry and private investors in Europe with the exercise by the ACP countries of control over industrial sectors.

The place which industrial cooperation now occupies in the Convention is a reflection of the wish of the developing countries to play a bigger part in industrial production and trade in manufactures. In simple terms, the ACP countries wanted a radical change in existing economic structures: they wanted to see more and more of their raw materials processed in their countries rather than in factories situated in Europe so as to ensure a new and more international division of labour.

What emerged is a dynamic instrument in which the EEC has declared its willingness to assist the ACP countries to industrialise in particular by various measures of financial intervention under the financial and technical cooperation provisions.

The chapter on industrial cooperation is different from the other parts of the Convention in so far as these other sectors adopt an instrumental approach whereas industrial cooperation looks to the development of a whole sector in the economy of the ACP countries and makes use of a whole range of instruments of cooperation defined in various parts of the Convention and mainly in the title dealing with technical and financial cooperation. Some new themes have been developed as well like information, industrial promotion and the transfer and adaptation of technology. An institutional background has been given to the industrial cooperation by providing for an industrial development centre and a joint industrial cooperation committee which is created to ensure the fulfilment of the objectives under the provisions on industrial cooperation.

The main difficulty at the negotiations under the heading industrial cooperation originated in the wish of the Community to insert a general clause which would ensure suitable reception and working conditions for Community businessmen. Some of the ACP countries apparently saw in this signs of interference with their sovereign right to determine their own policies. On the other hand they wanted a guarantee from the Community and its member states that their firms and nationals would conduct themselves correctly.

Agreement has been reached on a somewhat watered down text by which the ACP countries shall take the necessary measures to promote effective cooperation with firms or nationals from the EEC countries who comply with the development programmes and priorities of the host countries, whereas the Community is to take steps to persuade their firms and nationals to participate in the industrial development of the ACP countries and shall encourage such firms and nationals to adhere to the aspirations and development objectives of the ACP countries.

The provisions for industrial cooperation are of particular importance for those ACP countries which, because of special circumstances, will not or hardly make an appeal to the EDF and which do not expect difficulties for their export products but on the other hand are in great need of aid for their industrial development.

None of the provisions of the heading industrial cooperation operate automatically. The way in which the framework is filled must therefore depend principally on the political goodwill, imagination and perseverance of those who carry responsibilities in this field. Thus one of the most important challenges in the Convention will be this framework which is provided to ensure some form of redistribution of industrial tasks (see further chapter 5).

Financial and technical cooperation

From the beginning of the negotiations on a new convention the ACP countries not only tried to maintain the level of aid received by the AASM under the Yaoundé Convention and to ensure the same level of aid to the new partners but to increase it substantially while at the same time improving the quality of Community aid to the ACP countries. Furthermore, they requested the right to determine the sectional direction of this Community aid and to have greater participation in its management and administration.

This was asked because for many of the ACP countries, Community aid has become a critical factor, especially for the least developed, landlocked and island countries and those ACP countries which are often affected by natural disasters. The ACP countries would also like to see that the participation of the Community in their regional schemes would increase.

52

The amount of the EDF

In the field of technical and financial cooperation, the main problem was to determine the amount of the Fund. The Community started from the principle that the states associated under the Yaoundé Convention should keep their acquired benefits and that the new partners should be given equal treatment. This starting point can, however, be interpreted in different ways. The ACP countries put forward the claim for financial aid to the amount of 8000 million units of account for the life of the Convention. The Community was only able to offer a global financial package of 3390 million u.a. for the life of the Convention. From the point of view of the ACP countries, this amount was inadequate. The amount offered was only half the amount asked for. The total funds of the EDF for the period of the Lomé Convention will be 269 per cent (at 1975 prices) higher than the funds of the EDF under Yaoundé II, while the total number of people covered has increased by 243 per cent which implies that the funds per caput have been increased from 11.83 to 12.75 units of account. However, in real terms, given the high inflation of recent years, the per caput level under the Lomé Convention will be more than 40% below the Yaoundé II level. [40] However, at the end of the negotiations, the ACP countries accepted the EEC offer for they recognized that it was a considerable effort on the part of the Community, having regard to its financial constraints at the time. In turn the Community accepted, however, the request by the ACP countries that the expiring date of the Convention had to be fixed five years after the date of signature, namely March 1st, 1980. This solution, which was already applied under Yaoundé II, means that the time needed for ratification could not work to the financial disadvantage of the ACP countries.

Responsibilities of the ACP countries

A very important change regarding the technical and financial cooperation concerns the increased responsibilities of the ACP countries in the management of this cooperation. This applies in particular to the power to take decisions concerning the projects submitted by the ACP countries. Under the Yaoundé system the project was transmitted to a Committee composed of representatives of the EC member states (the EDF Committee).

After a positive recommendation by this Committee the actual

40. "The Lomé Convention", OOI Briefing Paper, Overseas Development Institute, 1975, p. 5.

53

decision was taken by the Commission. In case of a negative recommendation the Commission could either take the project back or else ask the EC Council of Ministers to overrule its officials. At the beginning of the negotiations the ACP countries asked to participate in the decision making, meaning that they would have to participate in Commission's and Council's meetings.

This point of view had a certain logic as long as the ACP countries were still deliberating if some of them would participate in the EDF by a token participation.

Finally the ACP countries have agreed to the following arrangement: "Where the Community body, responsible for delivering an opinion on projects, fails to deliver a favourable opinion, the competent departments of the Community shall consult the representatives of the ACP state or ACP states concerned on further action to be taken, in particular on the advisability of submitting the dossier afresh, possibly in the modified form, to the relevant Community body. Before that body gives its final opinion, the representatives of the ACP State or ACP States concerned may request a hearing by the representatives of the Community in order to be able to state their grounds for the projects.

Should the final opinion delivered by that body not be favourable, the competent departments of the Community shall consult afresh with the representatives of the ACP State or ACP States concerned before deciding whether the project should be submitted as it stands to the Community's decision-making bodies or whether it should be withdrawn or modified". [41]

The increasing responsibilities of the ACP countries find further expression in the strengthening of the powers of national authorities in the implementation of the financial and technical cooperation and accordingly a diminution in the administrative, financial and technical responsibilities of the Commission delegate in the ACP countries. His powers formerly exercised in the beneficiary countries are now substantially curtailed and his role today is essentially in an advisory capacity. However, in order to give a new dimension to the various instruments of cooperation the ACP countries urged that the delegate of the Community should be not only of the EDF but also that of the Commission. Thus under the Convention there is now a delegate of the Commission covering all the areas in the ACP/EEC cooperation arrangements, mainly in the field of industrial cooperation and stabilization of export earnings.

In spite of the fact that the ACP countries now participate more

41. Lomé Convention, art. 54 (3).

effectively in aid administration and management, the ACP countries are not represented in the decision making committee. This is mainly due to the fact that the funds of the EDF consist of contributions of the member states.

The ACP countries also advocated the transfer of the functions of the EDF Paying Agents hitherto performed by the EC member states' banks to ACP national banks or national financial institutions approved by the ACP country concerned. The Convention also provides the consequential arrangements for effecting the transfer.

In the field of technical and financial cooperation two other points should be mentioned which though they figured already in the Yaoundé Conventions have received new emphasis in the Lomé Convention: regional cooperation and measures in favour of the least developed countries. [42]

A new scope and dimension is given to regional and inter-regional cooperation. On the insistence of the ACP, regional cooperation applies to relations either between two or more ACP countries or between one or more ACP countries on the one hand, and one or more neighbouring non-ACP countries on the other hand. Consequently, an ACP country or group of ACP countries participating with neighbouring non ACP countries in a regional or inter-regional project could request the Community to finance that part of the project for which it is responsible. Of the total Community financial aid 10% will be reserved exclusively for financing regional or interregional projects, to meet the objectives set out in the Convention. This differed from the Yaoundé II Convention under which no sectoral allocations were made, only expressing that the "desirability to promote regional cooperation between Associated States" should be taken into account in financing projects and programmes. [43]

Furthermore the special problems of the landlocked, insular or least developed of the ACP countries are recognized and special treatment is given to them. A list of 24 least developed countries has been drawn up. In favour of these countries special measures have been provided which may take the form of particularly favourable terms of financing, particularly favourable treatment in technical cooperation's schemes or priority application of certain other forms of aid.

42. Lomé Convention, arts. 47-48.
43. Yaoundé II Convention, art. 19 (2).

In the area of competition and terms of preferences for national firms of ACP countries, the ACP countries proposed substantial alterations to the rules and practices in existence. Thus, on the accelerated procedure for issuing invitations to tender for works contracts from which national firms of ACP countries derive maximum advantage, the ceiling for the value of such contracts was increased four-fold from 500,000 u.a. to 2 million u.a.. Suppliers in ACP countries are also given an automatic margin of 15% preference in all cases for the delivery of supplies. This is a very considerable improvement on the existing rules at the time where the preference was given on a case-by-case basis after the EDF Committee had delivered an opinion and the margin could be anywhere between 0% and 15%.

Contractors in ACP countries are also given a price preference of 10% for the execution of works costing less than 2 million u.a. It is important to stress in this connection that preference is not confined to the firms of the particular ACP country in which the works are being undertaken but extended to the firms of all the other ACP countries (see further chapter 6).

Establishment, services, payments and capital movements

One of the areas of the Convention which was negotiated towards the end of the negotiations is on establishment, services, payments and capital movements. The guiding principle of the ACP countries was that no commitment will be undertaken by them which would have the effect of, or might be construed as, preventing an APC country from taking such action as is necessary to meet its development needs. Further, the ACP countries insisted that any commitments undertaken by them must be on a reciprocal basis.

Accordingly, as regards establishment and services, the relevant provisions accord due recognition to the principle of non-discriminatory treatment on reciprocal basis. With regard to capital movements linked with investments and to current payments both the ACP countries and the Community undertake to refrain from taking action in the field of foreign exchange transactions which would be incompatible with their obligations under the Convention.

Institutions

The smooth and effective functioning of the elaborate economic cooperation instruments dealt with above and the further progress in the relations between the Community and the ACP countries will depend to a great extent on the readiness of both parties to implement the provisions of the agreement.

This readiness will find expression first of all within the institutional framework provided for in the Lomé Convention.

At the beginning of the negotiations the ACP countries were not prepared to discuss institutions, if any at all, until they knew the substance of the total offer made by the Community. The nature, form and content of institutions to be created was left to the final phase of the negotiations.

The preliminary and fundamental issue in this area was the name to be given to the economic cooperation arrangements which had been negotiated. The Community desired it to be known as a "Convention of Association". The ACP countries preferred it to be simply a "Convention of Cooperation". To the Commonwealth countries "Association" was politically unacceptable. According to their point of view at least the term gives the impression of an inferior status. Those of the ACP countries which were associated at the time of these discussions were, understandably, not sensitive towards retaining the term. Nevertheless, the solidarity of action which had characterised the approach of the ACP countries in the negotiations enabled them to adopt a common position and they rejected the term "Association". This was in itself a triumph for the ACP countries since it was in keeping with their principle that Community aid should be dissociated from any particular form of relationship with the Community. To the ACP countries, the term "Association" engenders, rightly or wrongly, an impression or feeling of a subservient position or an appendage status to the Community. And bearing in mind that the Convention is on the "basis of complete equality between partners" it was essential to remove any semblance of subordination of one party to the other, in the name given to the Convention.

With respect to the institutional provisions of the Convention, the ACP countries originally showed a certain reluctance towards maintaining those of the previous Yaoundé Conventions. Such was the case especially as regards the provisions of the Yaoundé II Convention for a Court of Arbitration of the Association and a Parliamentary Conference of the Association.

The ACP countries were opposed to the establishment of a Court of Arbitration, to which disputes, for which no appropriate solution could be found in the Council, had to be submitted. They preferred a more voluntary arrangement for the settlement of disputes and an *ad hoc* machinery for arbitration along the lines of the Arusha Convention. [44] According to the Yaoundé II Convention, parties had been obliged to submit: "disputes concerning the interpretation or the application of the present Convention" to the Association Council. According to the Lomé Convention: "any dispute which arises between one or more Member States or the Community on the one hand, and one or more ACP States on the other", *may be* placed before the Council of Ministers, or *may be* submitted (subject to the Council being informed) to a good offices procedure.

No provisions have been made for a Court of Arbitration. Instead: "If the Council of Ministers fails to settle the dispute at its next meeting, either Party *may* notify the other of the appointment of an arbitrator; the other Party *must* then appoint a second arbitrator within two months... The Council of Ministers *shall* appoint a third arbitrator". The decisions of the arbitrators are binding. Parties to a dispute, which have decided to avail themselves of their right to have recourse to a good offices procedure, are under no obligation, if such a procedure fails, to have recourse to arbitration.

The ACP countries were also opposed to the proposals for establishing a parliamentary conference as had existed under the Yaoundé Conventions. Such a conference would imply too strong a political tie with the Community and at any rate was inappropriate to the circumstances of many ACP countries. The Community, however, insisted and pointed to the broad support given by its Parliament to cooperation with developing countries.

As the ACP countries recognized the usefulness of a body associating public opinion to the implementation of the Convention, they proposed to create a Consultative Assembly, "composed on a basis of parity of members of the Assembly on the side of the Community and of *the representatives designated by the ACP States* on the other". [45] Unlike art. 50 of the Yaoundé Convention—"and *members of the Parliaments* of the Associated States"— art. 80 (1) of the Lomé Convention leaves it to the governments of ACP States to designate representatives. They may be members of parliaments, but also e.g. civil servants.

As had been the case under the Yaoundé Convention, a Council of Ministers, assisted by a Committee of Ambassadors, has been

44. Yaoundé II Convention, art. 51. Lomé Convention, art. 81, italics added.
45. Yaoundé Convention, art. 50. Lomé Convention, art. 80 (1), italics added.

created as the supreme organ for implementing the Lomé Convention. [46] The provisions—though broadly similar to those of the Yaoundé Conventions—show some interesting differences, however, which may be explained by the ACP countries' concern for a more equal relationship and for their reluctance to enter into a special arrangement which might negatively affect their solidarity with other developing countries.

Among the differences, we could mention the following. In order to be valid, the proceedings of the Council require the presence of *two thirds* of the accredited members representing the Governments of the ACP States. [47]

The missions of the Council are spelled out in more detail than had been the case in the Yaoundé Convention. Among them are: a periodic review of the results of the arrangements under the Convention; the publication of an annual report; exchanges of views on questions having direct repercussions on the matters covered by the Convention; and exchanges of views on other economic or technical questions which are of mutual interest. [48]

The Lomé Convention also provides for the possibility for the Council to delegate any of its powers to the Committee of Ambassadors. [49]

The articles on the institutional provisions of the Lomé Convention apparently have not given rise to the same amount of controversy as the articles on its policy-instruments. Whereas negotiations on the institutions took place at the very end of the convention-making process, they do, however, reflect the new type of relationship created by the Lomé Convention.

46. Lomé Convention, arts. 70-78. A Secretariat is provided for in art. 79.
47. Lomé Convention, art. 70 (3).
48. Lomé Convention, art. 74. Yaoundé II Convention, art. 44.
49. Lomé Convention, arts. 75, 77.

Part Two

THE CONVENTION: A NEW DEPARTURE?

Chapter 3

TRADE COOPERATION: PREFERENCES IN THE LOMÉ
CONVENTION, THE GENERALIZED SYSTEM OP
PREFERENCES AND THE WORLD TRADE SYSTEM.

by *Dr. Harry Stordel**

The Lomé Convention affords 46 countries in Africa, the Caribbean and the Pacific a comprehensive preferential entry to the
markets of the European Community. In addition to the special
preferences accorded to the ACP countries the Community grants
preferences to developing countries in general in the context of
the Generalized System of Preferences (GSP), agreed upon in
UNCTAD between the major industrialized countries on the one
hand and the developing countries on the other.

Special preferences accorded to a limited number of developing
countries can be meaningful to these countries only if they provide treatment more advantageous than that they receive under
the GSP together with other developing countries. Moreover, these
special preferences extend the departure in favour of developing
countries from application of GATT's most favoured nation principle and may also lead to increasing resort to this derogation in
world trade. Finally, the granting of such preferences gives rise to
a major innovation since, unlike previous contractual arrangements
of the Community with developing countries these preferences are
granted without reciprocity. The absence of reciprocity on a contractual basis will no doubt have a noticeable impact on the further development of the world trade system.

This chapter will consider these questions in some detail. It will
in particular examine the effects which the preferences accorded
under the Lomé Convention are likely to have on the GSP and in
particular on the EEC scheme of generalized preferences, as well as
on the world trade system as such. It should be noted in this
connexion that the Lomé Convention contains important innovations also in other fields of economic co-operation which may

---

* The views expressed in the paper are those of the author and do not
necessarily reflect those of the UNCTAD secretariat.

contribute considerably to the development of the world trade system.[1]

Preferences in the Lomé Convention

The trade preferences granted by the European Community to ACP countries replace those granted by the original EEC of the Six under the Yaoundé Convention and the Arusha agreement as well as the preferences granted by the United Kingdom to those developing countries of the Commonwealth which became members of the Lomé Convention. Generally all products originating in the ACP countries, with the exception of some agricultural products can enter the markets of the Community free from customs duties or charges having equivalent effect. Moreover, imports into the Community of such products are not subject to quantitative limitations or measures of equivalent effect. The agricultural products excepted from unlimited duty-free access are those coming under the common agricultural policy or to specific rules introduced as a result of the application of this policy. These products will, however, as a general rule enjoy more favourable treatment than the general treatment applicable to the same products originating in third countries to which the most favoured-nation clause applies. For these products, therefore, duty-free treatment applies when customs duties are the only form of protection applied by the Community. When protection extends to both customs duties and levies, the preferential treatment consists of partial or full reduction of customs duties or of the fixed component in variable levies. For selected agricultural goods subject to variable levies, the variable component of the levy may also be reduced or eliminated.

The agricultural products enjoying more favourable treatment rather than duty-free preferential entry are: beef and veal, fishery products, oils and fats, cereals, rice, products processed from cereals and rice, fruit and vegetables, products processed from fruit and vegetables, unmanufactured tobacco, certain sugar confectionery, cocoa preparations, preparations of flour meal and certain food preparations, flax and hemp, hops, live trees and other plants, bulbs, roots and the like, cut flowers and ornamental foliage, seeds, other products listed in Annex II to the Treaty and dehydrated fodder.[2]

1. Compare especially chapter 4, *infra.*
2. See Regulation (EEC) 1599/75 on the arrangements applicable to agricultural products and certain goods resulting from the processing of agricul-

According to estimates of the EEC Commission total imports in 1973 of goods originating from the ACP countries amounted to about $7.6 billion; of these only about $1.0 billion or 13.4 per cent consisted of goods coming under the common agricultural policy. Duty-free treatment will apply to 94.2 per cent of these agricultural imports with sugar accounting for 22.3 per cent. For the remaining 5.8 per cent the ACP countries would receive more favourable treatment than that applied to third countries in the form of reduced customs tariffs or reduced levies as explained above.

For the purpose of preferential treatment products originating in the ACP countries and imported by the Community are those which are wholly obtained in one or more ACP countries or which have undergone in one or more of these countries sufficient working or processing. Working or processing is considered sufficient if the products obtained receive a classification under a tariff heading other than that covering each of the products worked or processed. The exceptions to this rule are specified in lists A and B of the Convention.

The rules of origin provide for cumulative treatment in the sense that the ACP countries are considered as one area for origin purposes. The rules also provide for "Community content", i.e. products wholly obtained or worked and processed in the Community, will, when imported for further processing by one or more ACP countries, be considered as originating in these countries when determining the origin of the final products exported to the Community.

The rules of origin further specify that in order to be eligible for preferential treatment the products must be transported directly to the Community. Originating products may transit through third countries, provided that the crossing of the territory of these countries is justified for geographical reasons or needs of transport and that the products have not entered into commerce or been delivered for home use and have not undergone operations other than unloading, reloading or any operation designed to preserve them in good condition.

The preferential trade arrangements of the Lomé Convention

---

tural products originating in the African, Carribbean and Pacific states or in the overseas countries and territories. (Official Journal of the European Communities, Volume 18, number L. 166, 28 June 1975, pp. 67-80).

also cover quantitative import restrictions and measures with equivalent effect. Such restrictions apply to imports of products originating in the ACP countries only to the extent to which the member countries of the Community apply them among themselves.

Preferences in the EEC Scheme of Generalized Preferences

The EEC scheme of generalized preferences, introduced in 1971 in favour of all developing countries at a time when the Yaoundé Convention and the Arusha Agreement were still in force, is confined to limited preferential customs treatment. Preferential treatment does not extend to non-tariff barriers. The EEC scheme in particular does not contain any of the other measures provided for in the Lomé Convention such as the stabilization of earnings from exports of primary commodities of developing countries, industrial and technical co-operation, financial aid, etc.

The first limitation of the EEC-GSP scheme concerns the product coverage. The Scheme covers only manufactures and semi-manufactures in Chapters 25-99 of the Brussels Tariff Nomenclature (BTN). Also, the scheme includes only selected processed agricultural products. Preferential treatment is not extended to primary commodities, be they agricultural or industrial raw materials.

Serious limitations exist also for textile products covered by the Arrangement regarding International Trade in Textiles. Preferential treatment is granted only to those developing countries which were signatories to the former Long-Term Arrangement regarding International Trade in Cotton Textiles (LTA) and to those countries who undertook, vis-à-vis the Community bilateral commitments similar to those existing under LTA. Limitations concerning countries enjoying preferential treatment under the EEC scheme exist also for textiles other than cotton and for footwear as well as for jute and coir products.

Other limitations of the EEC scheme concern mainly the depth of the preferential tariff cut, the quantitative limits to preferential imports of individual products and origin requirements for certain products.

While the EEC scheme provides duty-free entry for manufactures and semi-manufactures, only a partial tariff cut is applied to processed agricultural products. The average preferential reduction of the Common External Tariff rates on all agricultural products covered by the 1975 scheme amounts to about 6.7 percentage points.[3]

Preferential imports of manufactures and semi-manufactures covered by the EEC scheme are restricted by *a priori* limitations comprising three types of superimposed constraints: (1) annual Community tariff quotas for "sensitive" goods and less rigidly applied overall ceilings for other goods; (2) arbitrarily fixed percentage shares of Community tariff quotas, which are separately applied by the respective EEC Member States, and (3) maximum amounts (often known as "buffers") to limit the proportion of the overall tariff quota or ceiling that a given beneficiary exporting country may supply on preferential terms during the year.

Preferential imports of processed agricultural products are moreover subject to a conventional safeguard clause of the type of Article XIX, GATT, without *a priori* limitation on preferential imports with the exception of few products subject to preferential tariff quotas.

Unduly stringent processing requirements are found in the origin rules. Moreover, cumulative origin extends only to selected regional groupings, and there is no provision of "Community content" in the EEC-GSP scheme.

Effects of the Preferences in the Lomé Convention on the GSP

In analysing the effects which the preferences of the Lomé Convention are likely to have on the GSP it is necessary to consider the relationship that existed between the special preferences granted by the precursors to the Lomé Convention and those granted under the EEC scheme of generalized preferences.

The EEC-GSP scheme was introduced following agreement in UNCTAD on the introduction of a generalized, non-reciprocal and non-discriminatory system of preferences by the major industrialized countries in favour of developing countries with the following objectives: to increase their export earnings; to promote their industrialization; and to accelerate their rates of economic growth.[4]

---

3. TD/B/C.5/34, Operation and Effects of the Scheme of Generalized Preferences of the European Economic Community, prepared by the UNCTAD secretariat, July 1975.

4. See resolution 21 (II) on preferential or free entry of exports of manufactures and semi-manufactures of developing countries to the developed countries, unanimously adopted at the second session of UNCTAD in New Delhi in June 1964.

The basic features of the GSP were laid down in the Agreed Conclusions on the Generalized System of Preferences unanimously adopted by the UNCTAD Trade and Development Board at its Fourth Special Session on 13 October 1970.[5]

As regards the special preferences, the Agreed Conclusions specified that developing countries which would be sharing their existing tariff advantages in some developed countries as the result of the introduction of the generalized system of preferences will expect the new access in other developed countries to provide export opportunities to at least compensate them.

When introducing its GSP scheme, the EEC did not grant any compensation to its associated countries enjoying special preferences, but it constructed its scheme in such a way that it affected the tariff advantages enjoyed by these countries only to a very limited extent. This was brought out *inter alia* in a study by the UNCTAD secretariat on the effects of the EEC-GSP scheme on the tariff advantages enjoyed by the African countries associated with the European Economic Community.[6] The study estimated that the products affected by the EEC scheme accounted in 1970 for a maximum of 1,8 per cent of the total imports into the EEC from the member countries of the Yaoundé Convention. The corresponding figure for the member countries of the Arusha Agreement was 3 per cent.[7]

These figures, although indicative of the limited scope of the GSP for the exports of developing countries, do not provide information about the extent to which the tariff advantages under the two association agreements were affected by the EEC scheme since they include the trade which enjoys duty-free entry under most-favoured nation treatment, i.e. the trade of products for which the Common External Tariff is zero. Excluding products for which the Common External Tariff was zero and considering exports of products which were at the same time granted preferential treatment under the Yaoundé Convention and under the EEC scheme, the study estimated that a maximum of 5 per cent of the preferential imports into the EEC from the member countries of the Yaoundé Convention was affected by the preferences under

5. See TD/B/332, Trade and Development Board, Fourth Special Session, 12-13 October 1970.

6. See TD/B/C.5/4, Effects of the Generalized System of Preferences on the tariff advantages enjoyed by the African countries associated with the European Communities, Report by the UNCTAD secretariat, January 1973.

7. Paragraph 6, op. cit.

the EEC-GSP scheme. The corresponding maximum figure for the member countries of the Arusha Agreement was 6 per cent.[8] However, even for these products the effects of the EEC-GSP scheme on the tariff advantages accorded under the two association agreements were evidently small, since the association agreements generally provided unrestricted duty-free treatment, in contrast to the limited nature of the preferences under the EEC-GSP scheme providing only small preferential tariff reductions of just a few percentage points for processed agricultural products and restricting preferential entry for manufactures and semi-manufactures by tariff quotas, ceilings, maximum amounts, etc.

In view of the fairly similar economic structure of the other developing countries which became members of the Lomé Convention in addition to those developing African countries members of the Yaoundé Convention or the Arusha Agreement, the effect of the EEC-GSP scheme on the tariff advantages accorded to the ACP countries under the Lomé Convention will likewise be rather limited. Again the reason is that the EEC-GSP scheme covers relatively few agricultural products and that in industrial products, it does not cover primary products including basic metals up to the stage of ingots. Since agricultural products as well as industrial raw materials and basic metals form the main export items of the ACP countries, generally only a small share of their exports of products enjoying duty-free or other preferential treatment under the Lomé Convention is also covered by the EEC-GSP scheme.

For the products enjoying preferential entry under both the Lomé Convention and the EEC-GSP scheme, the effect of the EEC scheme on the preferential tariff advantages under the Lomé Convention will again be smaller due to the small overlap in the product coverage of the two preferential schemes, and to the particularly favourable treatment accorded under the Lomé Convention compared to the limited nature of the preferences under the EEC-GSP scheme.

In addition to the question of special preferences one of the main problems for reaching agreement in UNCTAD on the features of the GSP had been the issue of "reverse" preferences, i.e. the granting of reciprocal preferential treatment by developing countries under the Yaoundé Convention and the Arusha Agreement to imports originating in the Community of the Six as well as the granting of preferential tariff treatment to products origi-

8. Paragraph 7, op. cit.

69

nating in the United Kingdom upon import into the Commonwealth developing countries.

Throughout the negotiations on the GSP the USA had consistently opposed reverse preferences and had been reiterating that developing countries granting reverse preferences would be excluded from enjoying generalized tariff preferences under its GSP scheme. In the U.S. preliminary submission to UNCTAD on the possible content of its GSP scheme developing countries granting special trade preferences were to be excluded from U.S. preferential treatment from the outset.[9] On the other hand, developing countries associated with the EEC had been opposed to any injection of the question of reverse preferences into the consideration of the generalized system of preferences and considered that in seeking elimination of reverse preferences in the context of the generalized system of preferences the USA was seeking reciprocity from those developing countries which extended preferences to some developed countries. The Community held the view that the association between African countries and the EEC in the field of trade was in the form of free trade areas in conformity with GATT rules, and that the reverse preferences had been given by the developing countries in that context.[10] Gradually the U.S. position became more flexible. In the Trade Act of 1974 which authorises the U.S. President to implement the GSP, developing countries granting reverse preferences may be designated beneficiary developing countries under the US-GSP scheme if they give assurance that the reverse preferences will be eliminated before January 1, 1976, or that action will be taken before that date to assure that the reverse preferences will have no significant adverse effect on U.S. commerce.[11]

It is difficult to judge which of the developing countries associated with the Community under an arrangement like the Yaoundé Convention or the Arusha Agreement based on reverse preferences, would have become eligible for designation as beneficiary country under the US-GSP scheme. The Lomé Convention

9. TD/B/AC.5/34, Add. 3, containing U.S. submission to OECD on generalized tariff preferences for developing countries (revised 21 September 1970).

10. See *inter alia*, TD/B/300/Rev. 1 and TD/B/329/Rev. 1, Reports of the Special Committee on Preferences on the first and second part of its Fourth Session, 1970.

11. Trade Act of 1974, Title V, Generalized System of Preferences, Section 502 (3).

does not require the ACP countries to grant reverse preferences to the Community. The abandonment of the concept of reverse preferences in the Lomé Convention on a contractual basis represents a major innovation in the position of the Community as regards its granting of special preferences.

While the Convention does not require the ACP countries to accord reverse preferences to the Community, it does not exclude the possibility that such preferences could be granted. This means, *inter alia,* that the African countries formerly associated with the Community under the Yaoundé Convention or the Arusha Agreement need not modify the preferential duty-free treatment which they have accorded the Community under these arrangements. [12] Operating under the assumption that the ACP countries will not be granting reverse preferences after 1 January, 1976, the U.S. President has included them in his list of beneficiaries under the US scheme. The absence of reverse preferences from the Lomé Convention enables the ACP countries to qualify for the generalized preferences under the US-GSP scheme, at least on that ground. To this extent the Lomé Convention has facilitated application of the U.S. GSP scheme to a large number of countries.

From the point of view of the beneficiaries of preferential treatment under the Lomé Convention the EEC-GSP scheme implies a certain sharing of preferential treatment with the other developing countries. From the point of view of the beneficiaries of the GSP only, the Lomé Convention, like its forerunners, creates discrimination in preferential treatment among developing countries to the disadvantage of those that enjoy such treatment only under the GSP.

This discrimination is two-fold: it concerns the product coverage which, as discussed above, is substantially larger for the beneficiaries of the preferences under the Lomé Convention, and it concerns the scope of preferential treatment of the products included in both, the GSP and the Lomé Convention. Here the beneficiaries of the GSP are discriminated against by the limitations on preferential imports from them or by smaller tariff cuts as compared to the unrestricted duty-free access granted to the beneficiaries of the preferences under the Lomé Convention, further enhanced by liberal rules of origin.

While all quantitative import restrictions and measures having

12. Hans-Broder Krohn, "Das Abkommen von Lomé zwischen der europäischen Gemeinschaft und den AKP-Staaten. Eine neue Phase der EG-Entwicklungshilfepolitik." HWWA, Europäische Gemeinschaft und Dritte Welt, 1975.

equivalent effect are completely eliminated under the Lomé Convention, with the exception of those which member countries of the Community apply among themselves there is no such provision under the EEC-GSP scheme. On the contrary, preferential imports are subject both to limitations as regards the application of the preferential tariff rate (tariff quotas, ceilings, maximum amounts) and to quantitative restrictions and other non-tariff barriers which apply to many products and in particular textiles. In its report on the operation and effects of the 1972 EEC-GSP scheme, the UNCTAD secretariat estimated that as a result of these constraints only 54 per cent of the 1970 exports from beneficiary countries of the EEC scheme into the Community of the Six of products covered by the scheme would have qualified for preferential treatment had the scheme been in operation in that year. [13] This estimate was based on a full utilization of preferential tariff quotas. Up to the present, however, the beneficiary countries have not been able to fully utilize these quotas. As a result of the limitations on preferential imports from major beneficiary suppliers (maximum amount limitation) and allocation of the tariff quotas in fixed percentage shares among the member States of the Community which do not correspond to traditional levels of import, the preferential tariff quotas have been utilized only up to 35 per cent in 1972. [14]

This discrimination extends to the rules of origin which make it possible for products to become eligible for preferential treatment. As a general rule, products considered as "originating from the country of origin" under the EEC-GSP scheme or the Lomé Convention are either those wholly produced in the exporting beneficiary country, or those which have, in the country concerned, undergone substantial processing. The principal criterion used for defining this "substantial" transformation is the change of tariff heading of the Common External Tariff (CET). Special rules have been made in the EEC-GSP scheme and in the Lomé Convention for cases where this change of tariff heading is not enough to justify a substantial transformation.

13. TD/B/C.5/3, Operation and Effects of Generalized Preferences granted by the European Economic Community, Study by the UNCTAD secretariat, January 1973.

14. UNCTAD, Operation and Effects of the EEC scheme in 1972, TD/B/C.5/34/Add. 1, Table IV. See also: Hajo Hasenpflug, "Ausgestaltung und Beurteilung des Allgemeinen Zollpräferenzsystems der EG gegenüber den Entwicklungsländern," HWWA, Europäische Gemeinschaft und Dritte Welt, 1975.

Many of the process requirements are less stringent under the Lomé Convention than under the GSP. For example, under the Lomé Convention, in the production of chocolate and other food preparations containing cocoa (CET heading 18.06) non-originating sugar may be used for up to 30 per cent of the value of the product obtained. Also non-originating cocoa beans, cocoa paste, cocoa butter and cocoa powder may be used since the rule of change of the CET heading applies. Under the EEC-GSP scheme non-originating sucrose must not be used in the production of chocolate, etc. of CET heading 18.06 and non-originating cocoa beans, cocoa paste, cocoa butter and cocoa powder must not exceed 40 per cent of the value of the product obtained if the latter is to qualify for preferential treatment. Moreover, to the extent that the process requirements are stringent under the Lomé Convention, they are considerably relaxed due to the provisions of "cumulative treatment" and "Community content" included in the Convention. In contrast to this, there is no provision of "Community content" under the EEC-GSP scheme and the partial cumulation granted under that scheme applies only to three regional groupings, i.e. the ASEAN countries, the Central American Common Market and the Andean Group.

In addition to preferential access to the markets of the Community, the Lomé Convention provides a wide range of other measures in order to accelerate the rate of growth of the trade of the ACP countries and to promote the development and diversification of industry in these countries. These measures include trade promotion activities and a framework for industrial co-operation which may open the way for effective industrialization of the countries concerned.

Although the objectives of the GSP include the promotion of the industrialization of the developing countries the EEC-GSP scheme provides little incentive in this field. This lack of incentive results largely from the uncertainty in the scheme as to whether a product eligible for preferential treatment will in fact benefit from preferential entry and for how long this will be the case. Uncertainty is inherent in the combined operation of the three types of *a priori* limitations or constraints referred to above. For most goods where these limitations are strictly or fairly strictly applied any prediction of whether a given shipment will in fact receive preferential treatment or whether the preferences will be discontinued through re-imposition of most-favoured nation duties following the reaching of the maximum amount, the Member State share of tariff quota, or the quota, is risky, to say the least. Fortuitous factors of timing, as well as the independent behaviour of competing exporters and importers will determine the actual outcome, which is thus a gamble of unknown odds. [15] Moreover, long-term planning for industrialization on the basis of the EEC-GSP scheme is not possible since, as set out in the Agreed Conclusions on the GSP, the grant of preferences under the GSP does not constitute a binding commitment, and in particular does not in any way prevent their subsequent withdrawal in whole or in part. The EEC-GSP scheme has therefore had little or no impact on decisions to invest, whether by governments or by private enterprise. [16]

The Lomé Convention does not have these shortcomings. It combines free market access with a comprehensive programme for industrial co-operation intended to promote the development and diversification of industry in the ACP countries and thus to build up the industrial export capacity which will allow to make full use of the availability of preferential market success. A programme for trade promotion follows the same objective. The Lomé Convention might therefore be considered as an example of what a generalized system of preferences could look like given the political will for an effective trade co-operation between developed and developing countries. The Convention could well serve as a guideline for improving the EEC-GSP scheme and the GSP schemes of the other preference-giving developed countries. A number of developing countries, recognizing the advantages of the Lomé Convention have already asked that its benefits should be extended to all developing countries.

There are, no doubt, political currents in the Community which would favour an extension of the preferences under the Lomé Convention to the developing countries as a whole. For the time being it seems, however, unlikely that the preferences under the Lomé Convention will be absorbed by the EEC-GSP scheme. As a protective measure the Convention provides *inter alia* in its Article 11 for consultations whenever contracting parties envisage taking trade measures affecting the interest of one or more con-

15. On the economic implications of tariff quotas, see paragraphs 86-94 of TD/B/C.5/3, Operation and Effects of the Generalized Preferences granted by the European Economic Community, Study by the UNCTAD secretariat, January 1973.

16. See, *inter alia*, TD/B/C.5/24, Experience of developing countries under the Generalized System of Preferences, prepared by the UNCTAD secretariat, March 1974.

tracting parties. The improvement of the EEC-GSP scheme would clearly be such a trade measure. A substantial improvement of the scheme can be conceived only if the Community agreed to increase the advantages of the ACP countries under the Convention in areas other than in market access. Given the limited export capacity of the ACP countries in the field of manufactures, further efforts of the Community for the industrialization of these countries might be a legitimate compensation for a wider sharing of the favourable market access conditions of the ACP countries in the Community by the beneficiaries of the GSP. It is, however, doubtful whether the Community will be ready to make such efforts at the present time. While on the one hand the Lomé Convention could serve as an example for improving the GSP, its very existence and the need to conserve trade advantages agreed therein, might therefore seriously impede substantial improvements of the EEC-GSP scheme.

The future development of the EEC-GSP scheme as envisaged at present is outlined in the resolution of the Council of the Community adopted on 3 March, 1975. The Council emphasizes that generalized preferences constitute a basic instrument of development co-operation. It indicates its desire to carry out continuous and gradual improvements to these preferences in accordance with the following guidelines:

> "— increased use of the present Community scheme, in particular by dint of measures for simplifying the scheme;
> — better administration of the scheme;
> — appropriate improvements and adjustments to the Community scheme, taking into account the export possibilities of the developing countries as well as the Community's economic possibilities".

In the resolution the EEC Council reaffirms its desire that these improvements should take particular account of the interests of the less developed developing countries with a view to improving their preferential access to the Community market. Recalling that the GSP was planned to cover an initial period of 10 years ending in 1980, the Council considers that in view of the aims of the GSP which are to increase the export earnings of developing countries, promote their industrialization and speed up their economic growth rate, it will be necessary to apply the generalized preferences for a further period after 1980.

According to the Information Memorandum of June 1975 on the Commission's proposals on the EEC-GSP scheme for 1976, the

Commission's approach involves only "modest" improvements. For processed agricultural products, the Commission is proposing an across-the-board cut of 10 per cent in the 1975 GSP duties, with a few exceptions. The 1976 EEC-GSP scheme will cover 231 processed agricultural products, imports of which from non-ACP beneficiaries are valued at 850 million U.A., as against 220 such products worth 600 million U.A. covered by the GSP on 1 January, 1975.

For industrial products other than textiles, the Commission is proposing a flat-rate increase of 15 per cent in all tariff quotas and ceilings, with only a few exceptions. The Commission has proposed as a temporary measure that the list of 13 products still subject to quotas should remain in effect with some changes in the system of special country ceilings intended to ensure a fairer distribution of benefits among the countries concerned by the scheme. The Commission has also suggested proceeding with the gradual introduction of a Community reserve in the remaining tariff quotas. The Commission feels that the system of quotas should eventually be replaced by the more flexible system of ceilings. Quotas and ceilings for industrial products other than textiles in the 1976 scheme will cover potential imports estimated at 2,650 million U.A., compared with 2,300 million U.A. in 1975.

Pending completion of the current bilateral negotiations under the Multi-fibre Arrangement, the Commission has proposed that the current arrangements for textile products be maintained for 1976 with a flat-rate increase of 5 per cent in the tariff quotas and ceilings expressed in tons. Guatemala, Paraguay and Haiti would be added to the list of beneficiaries for cotton textiles and Hong Kong for a number of products subject to ceilings. For jute and coir products the Commission has proposed that the GSP concessions should be maintained at the 1975 level pending re-negotiation of the agreements with India and Bangladesh, which expire on 31 December 1975. The quotas and ceilings for textile products will cover potential imports of an estimated 75,000 tons.

The value of potential preferential imports would thus increase under the EEC-GSP scheme for 1976 as compared to the 1975 scheme from 2,900 U.A. to 3,500 U.A., i.e. by about 20 per cent. Taking into account the nominal price increases due to inflation in the period under consideration, the real increase of potential preferential imports under the scheme would be around 10 per cent.

It appears from the above that at least for the more immediate future the impact of the Lomé Convention on the EEC-GSP scheme is not in the direction of substantial alignments of the product coverage and scope of preferential treatment under the latter to that of the Lomé Convention but rather in the direction of maintaining discrimination in the treatment of developing countries.

Preferences in the Lomé Convention and the World Trade System

The world trade system of the period after the second world war has been based largely on the General Agreement on Tariffs and Trade with its principles of most-favoured nation treatment, non-discrimination and reciprocity of concessions. This trade system has become subject to important changes over the past decade.

The establishment of economic groupings (customs unions and free-trade areas) such as the Community and EFTA; and the extension of other preferential trade regimes, have made considerable inroads in the general application of the most-favoured nation treatment. The principles of non-discrimination and of reciprocity have also been questioned in view of the contrast between the *de jure* equality and the *de facto* inequality as between developed and developing countries or within these groups of countries. The need to establish a more equitable international trade system in order to promote a rapid economic development of the developing countries has become more urgent than ever. The Declaration and the Programme of Action on the Establishment of a New International Economic Order, adopted by the General Assembly of the United Nations on 1 May 1974 at its sixth Special Session and the Charter of Economic Rights and Duties adopted by the General Assembly on 12 December 1974 are milestones towards a new world trade system.

The current multilateral trade negotiations in GATT recognize the importance and urgency of the trade and development problems of the developing countries. The participating countries are now seeking in a pragmatic way to elaborate and adopt negotiating rules and techniques which would facilitate solution of the trade problems of the developing countries and secure additional benefits for them. [17]

Substantial tariff cuttings on the most-favoured nation basis in the multilateral trade negotiations would diminish the preferential tariff rates under the Lomé Convention and thus affect the trade interests of the ACP countries. It is likely that this fact will limit

17. For details see *inter alia* the Tokyo Declaration of September 1973 on the opening of the negotiations, Press Release, GATT/1134.

the readiness of the Community to reduce its tariffs on products of particular export interest to the ACP countries. The preferences under the Lomé Convention may thus render a global liberalization of world trade more difficult.

A positive influence of the Lomé Convention on the world trade system may result from the principle of non-reciprocity which the Community has adopted in its commercial undertakings *vis-à-vis* the ACP countries. As discussed above in connexion with the issue of "reverse" preferences, the contractual preferential treatment provided by the Community to the products imported from the ACP countries does not require these countries to accord comparable treatment to the imports of products originating in the Community. Article 7 of the Lomé Convention explicitly sets out that in view of the development needs of the ACP countries the Community does not demand reciprocity in its trade regime with these countries. It is possible that the Lomé Convention may lead to a more general application of these principles on a contractual basis between developed and developing countries.

The preferential treatment provided by the Lomé Convention to the ACP countries represents a further step in world trade relations away from the principle of a general application of the most favoured nation treatment. Preferential treatment under the Lomé Convention comprises a larger number of beneficiary countries than covered in the preferential arrangements it has replaced. The preferential treatment also embraces a larger import market than the previous arrangements and, at least as far as the Yaoundé Convention and the Arusha Agreement is concerned, extends to a larger product coverage in the field of agriculture.

The departure in the Lomé Convention from the most favoured nation treatment cannot be justified, as was done by the Community in the cases of the Yaoundé Convention and the Arusha Agreement, on the grounds of formation of a free-trade area which is exempted under Article XXIV, paragraph 5, GATT from the basic obligation of the contracting parties to GATT to accord each other most favoured nation treatment. The preferential treatment of the ACP countries under the Lomé Convention would also not seem to be covered by other derogations from the most favoured nation treatment contained in the original provisions of the General Agreement such as Article I, paragraph 2 GATT, which *inter alia* covered the Commonwealth preferences. The departure in favour of developing countries from the most-favoured nation principle would seem to be justified, however, on other grounds, namely those which relate to Part IV of the General Agreement and those which relate to the promotion of a new international economic order as expressed in various resolutions of UNCTAD as well as of the General Assembly of the United Nations. These call for preferential treatment of developing countries so as to achieve a substantial increase in their foreign exchange earnings, diversification of their exports and acceleration of their economic growth. [18]

In part IV of the General Agreement the contracting parties of GATT have adopted a number of principles and objectives for the economic development of the developing countries. In this connexion they have envisaged the need for special measures to promote the trade and development of the developing countries. These principles and objectives are in particular concerned with the need for a rapid and sustained expansion of the export earnings of developing countries and in this connexion, *inter alia,* with a need to provide more favourable conditions of access for their products, as well as to attain stable, equitable and remunerative prices for their primary products. These principles are also concerned with the need for a dynamic and steady growth of the real export earnings of developing countries so as to provide them with expanding resources for their economic development. The contracting parties of the GATT have agreed in this context on the principle that the developed contracting parties of the GATT do not expect reciprocity for commitments made by them in trade negotiations to reduce or remove tariffs or other barriers to the trade of developing countries (Article XXXVI par. 8.)

The non-reciprocal preferential treatment accorded under the Lomé Convention as well as the stabilization of export earnings from commodities of the ACP countries, the provisions on industrial co-operation, financial and technical co-operation, etc., would seem to be a step towards the realization of these principles. In particular these principles would seem to justify the deviation from the most favoured-nation treatment to the extent that the discrimination which results from the preferences under the Lomé Convention affects the developed countries.

In applying the principle of non-reciprocity in the trade field as well as with regard to others of its main features the Lomé Convention can be considered as a step towards a more just and equitable international economic order. There remains however the discrimination of those developing countries that do not belong to the group of the ACP countries. In order for the Lomé Convention

18. See *inter alia* General Assembly resolution 3202 (S-VI) Programme of Action on the Establishment of a New International Economic Order.

to affect favourably the world trade system as such, it would need to be followed by similar action of the Community and other developed countries with regard to the developing countries as a whole. The Lomé Convention could then act as a catalyst for taking concrete measures in the field of market access, stabilization of the export earnings of developing countries, industrial cooperation, etc., in favour of developing countries to make further progress in the establishment of a New International Economic Order as proposed by the General Assembly of the United Nations at its sixth Special Session and in line with the Charter of Economic Rights and Duties of States adopted by the General Assembly on 12 December, 1974.

Chapter 4

EXPORT EARNINGS FROM COMMODITIES: EXPORT EARNINGS STABILISATION IN THE LOMÉ CONVENTION.

by *Dr. Bishnodat Persaud**

Compensatory financing for shortfalls in export earnings has been receiving increasing attention in the international discussion of the regulation of the export trade in commodities of developing countries. The inclusion of an export earnings stabilisation scheme (Stabex) in the Lomé Convention has therefore attracted international attention. Stabex is one of the new and important features of the association arrangement between the EEC and developing countries.

Prior to the Lomé Convention, the only international export earnings stabilisation scheme in existence was the IMF Compensatory Financing Facility. Developed market economy countries are attracted to the idea of compensatory financing for shortfalls in export earnings because it does not interfere with the operation of market forces and because it does not, as is the case with price regulation arrangements, lend itself directly to price raising policies. However, while most countries see compensatory financing in a supplementary role to price stabilisation commodity arrangements, the United States and West Germany would like the main thrust in commodity stabilisation policy to be compensatory financing. Whether compensatory financing is to play the major or supplementary role, the agreement on Stabex represents an interesting advance in compensatory financing provision, and is worthy of close examination to see the extent of the scheme, its economic implications and the possibilities it offers for extension on a global scale.

* The views expressed in this chapter are not necessarily those of the Commonwealth Secretariat and should not therefore be associated with the Secretariat. The author wishes to acknowledge the assistance of Prof. Hans Singer in the development of his ideas on the commodity problem through comments and discussions on this and other papers prepared before.

81

Provisions of Stabex

Stabex is concerned with stabilising for each ACP country, the nominal export earnings in the EEC market of each of a number of eligible products. The products concerned fall into twelve groups and included in these are twenty-nine individual items. The product groups are as follows:

1. Groundnut products
2. Cocoa products
3. Coffee products
4. Cotton products
5. Coconut products
6. Palm, palm nut and kernel products
7. Hides, skins and leather
8. Wood products
9. Fresh bananas
10. Tea
11. Raw sisal
12. Iron ore

For a product to qualify for a country, export earnings from it to all destinations must be at least 7.5 per cent of total export earnings in the year previous to the applicable year. Stabex however incorporates special provisions for least developed, land-locked and island states and for the thirty-four states listed in the Convention as belonging to this category, the qualifying proportion is 2.5 per cent and in the case of one product—sisal—the qualifying proportion is 5 per cent.

A country becomes eligible to receive a transfer for a product if for a calendar year, nominal export earnings fall by at least 7.5 per cent below a reference level established by calculating an average of the export earnings for that product in the EEC market, for the previous four years. The transfer would be the whole amount of the shortfall. For the least developed, land-locked and island states, the shortfall must be at least 2.5 per cent of the reference level. A further concession made in relation to the economic circumstances of countries, is that in the case of five very poor countries—Burundi, Ethiopia, Guinea-Bissau, Rwanda and Swaziland, reference levels and transfers are made in relation to exports to all destinations.

Countries which have received drawings are to make repayments when export earnings exceed the reference level and when such excess is due to an increase in unit values above the average for the reference period. The quantity exported must at least be equal to the reference level and repayment must not exceed the increase in unit value multiplied by the reference quantity. However for twenty-four least developed states repayments are not required. Repayments must be completed in a period of five years and if amounts are outstanding at the end of this period, then taking into account the economic circumstances of the country concerned, the EEC might either waive repayment or require the outstanding amount to be reconstituted within a specified period.

The amount of money provided by the EEC for Stabex for the five year period of the Convention is 375 u.a. and this fund is divided into five equal annual instalments with the flexibility that the amount disbursed in a year could be increased by an advance of 20 per cent of the following year's allocation.

The Need for Export Earnings Stabilisation

Developing countries tend to have a high dependence on export earnings from one or a very small number of commodities. The nature of demand and supply of these commodities tends to result in unstable export earnings and these are regarded as having adverse consequences on balance-of-payments, public revenues, economic planning, ability to maintain imports of essential capital and consumption goods, maintaining critical consumption levels and on the incentive and ability of producers to undertake innovations and finance needed inputs.

Commodity arrangements with price regulation measures are sometimes employed to bring about stabilisation in earnings, but these have the disadvantage that they are difficult to negotiate and administer. In fact the record of price stabilisation commodity arrangements is poor indeed. Among exporting countries there tends to be a preference for price stabilisation arrangements since stabilisation is achieved through market processes and not through transfers which may tend to be seen as a form of aid and which whether so seen or not, could be provided with funds which may be diverted from aid sources. There is the other important advantage for exporting countries, that the price regulation measure could be used, with or without supply management, to raise long-term average prices.

From the economic standpoint there is the problem in commodity arrangements that price stabilisation need not result in earnings stabilisation since it does not provide for the situation where earnings level is affected by production shortfalls. Importing countries tend also to be concerned with the disadvantages for them of increased average prices which could result from the operation of price stabilisation measures and also of possible market distortions which could follow from regulated prices which are inappropriate in relation to long-term demand and supply.

Even though commodity exporting countries may have a preference for price stabilisation measures, because of the problems involved in setting up and administering commodity agreements and the delays that are possible in establishing a large programme of commodity agreements, they are showing keen interest in compensatory financing. Most of these countries regard adequate provision for compensatory financing as urgent in the short-run and important normally. Even if there are established in the long-run a large number of commodity agreements, there might still be residual earnings fluctuations to be evened out and in the case of some commodities, compensatory financing may be the only appropriate stabilisation measure because of perishability or sharply conflicting interests between different exporting countries. In the integrated programme for commodities recommended by the Secretary-General of UNCTAD, compensatory financing is one of the important elements but it is seen as playing a complementary role to commodity arrangements.

In view of the above considerations there is now considerable interest in the establishment of adequate provision for export earnings stabilisation for developing countries.

The Commodity-by-Commodity Approach

Unlike the IMF facility, Stabex is concerned with the stabilisation of earnings for individual products and not total export earnings and eligibility fordrawings does not depend on the existence of a balance-of-payments deficit. It is the case with Stabex that a country may be receiving drawings from it while total export earnings may be booming because of buoyant conditions in other commodities. The commodity-by-commodity approach of Stabex has the advantage that it could be used to remedy the difficulties faced by each commodity. It was the intention of the EEC in proposing the scheme, that at least part of the drawings should accrue to producers of the commodity which is facing an earnings shortfall. However the scheme which has emerged does not have the requirement that governments should use the proceeds to finance internal stabilisation schemes although such a possibility is not excluded. The absence of such a provision makes utilisation of the scheme to prevent fluctuations of earnings having adverse effects at the level of producers optional.

The Reference Period and Inflation

A problem with Stabex is the determination of the reference level of earnings on the basis of the average of the previous four years. This could result in an inappropriate reference level especially in a period of high inflation since the reference level would be trend level of earnings for a year which is about two years before the applicable year. Thus a fall in nominal export earning of 10 per cent below the reference level could mean a much higher fall in real earnings because of high inflation in the intervening period between midway in the reference period, and the current year.

In order that the norm would be appropriate in relation to the current level of earnings, the moving average used to determine the norm should be centred on the current year. The IMF uses a five year moving average with a judgemental forecast made for the two post-applicable years and although such forecasts are given maximum limits, their use involves a more appropriate method than a reference period based wholly on past years, especially in view of current high rates of inflation which are likely to continue at abnormal levels for some time. An improvement of Stabex would therefore be the use of a more up-to-date reference period.

The Stabilisation of Real Earnings

A serious issue is whether stabilisation should not have been based on real earnings rather than nominal earnings. This is a different issue from the appropriateness of the reference period. It is concerned with whether the trend in the import purchasing power of earnings should not be taken into account. Although nominal export earnings may be stable or may even be increasing, in terms of the purchasing power of imports, there may be a decline because of adverse terms of trade. Should such declines in real earnings determine eligibility for transfers?

Because of the nature of their demand and supply, many commodities exported by developing countries tend to suffer from adverse terms of trade for long periods. In view of high dependence on a narrow range of commodities, such declines could pose serious adjustment problems and a scheme which takes into account real earnings would therefore be more appropriate in relation to the trade problems of developing countries. It should be noted however that an adverse net barter terms of trade need not mean a decline in real earnings since export volumes could be increasing. Thus a scheme which stabilises real export earnings need not mean much larger financial requirements. The value of real income stabilisation is that if a country has a high dependence on one commodity and that commodity is experiencing not only an adverse net barter terms of trade but also an adverse income terms of trade, then the decline in real earnings involved and the adjustment that might be required to move to the production of more favourable commodities, could be assisted by such a scheme. Provision should be made in such a scheme for repayment to be made only when there is an increase in real earnings.

The Triggering of Transfers

The use of a sharp cut-off point of 7.5 per cent for the determination of eligibility for transfers also results in the anomalous situation where a 7 per cent shortfall results in no transfer whereas an 8 per cent one brings about a transfer of the whole 8 per cent. A graduated system would operate more fairly and discourage the deliberate creation of a larger shortfall where there is developing the possibility that a shortfall may not be large enough to lead to qualification for a transfer.

Diversion of Exports

One possibility which might have to be watched is the encouragement that could be given to the diversion of exports to other markets because of the assurance of a level of export earnings from the EEC market regardless of the volume of exports. From this point, a global compensatory financing scheme is better than a regional scheme, such as Stabex. The regulations make provision against such an abuse of Stabex, but diversion could still be encouraged covertly or under the guise of increased sales to other markets for other reasons. It remains to be seen to what extent diversion might be encouraged. One disincentive which exists but which might not, however, be adequate is that diversion would reduce reference levels and thus the levels of transfer possible in later years.

The Adequacy of the Fund

A serious problem which might develop is the inadequacy of the total provision for the five-year period. The fund of 375 u.a. seems small in relation to the size of the trade involved. There is also the consideration that during the negotiations, while the product coverage was extended considerably from early proposals, the fund envisaged was not similarly expanded. There is also the fact that the first year or two of the scheme would use a reference period which would be greatly influenced by the very high commodity prices of 1973 and 1974. Should the fund or the annual allocation prove inadequate, transfers may be rationed among those qualifying. However it seems more likely that the EEC would provide the additional sums required in such an eventuality.

Special Measures for Poorer Countries

An advantage of export earnings stabilisation schemes is that they are more amenable to incorporating special measures for the poorer and less fortunate countries than price stabilisation arrangements. They do not also result in additional burdens to poor importing countries through increased prices. Stabex has provided special measures for the least developed, land-locked and island states with a high level of concessionality to the least developed in the fact that they are not required to make repayments. There are no such special measures under the IMF facility because of the tendency of IMF policy to avoid differential treatment to different groups of members.

Repayment Conditions for Other Countries

The interest-free condition of the transfers is a liberal provision compared with the IMF facility in which interest charges are 4-6 per cent per annum. The discretionary policy regarding the treatment of outstanding transfers after five years, provides the opportunity for the entry of extraneous political influences. There should be a more definite policy and the fact that a country has not been able to conclude repayment in a period of five years would in many cases indicate incapacity to make repayments and consideration should be given to the adoption of a definite policy of waiving transfers which remain unpaid after this period.

Additionality

If the Fund provided for Stabex would in the absence of Stabex have been used as aid, then the conditions for disbursement under Stabex become criteria for aid distribution for the funds involved. The question which arises then is whether the criteria involved is in any way better than those normally used for ordinary aid. Transfers under Stabex for any country would be greatly influenced by the size of its trade with the EEC in the eligible commodities. Countries with larger trade volumes or larger per caput exports would tend to receive a larger share of the transfers and since these countries are likely to be in a better economic position, then the criteria involved are likely to be less appropriate than those used for aid distribution. The higher concessionality involved in transfers to poorer countries would only to a limited extent help to ameliorate this problem.

Although Stabex funds are from the EDF, it does not follow that Stabex is using funds diverted from ordinary aid. It is possible that the adoption of an export earnings stabilisation scheme would have helped to increase the total amount of funds available for assistance to the ACP and that at least, partly, the funds provided for Stabex are additional.

Compensatory financing represents a separate need apart from aid and it is important that it should be conceived in a way which would allow additional provision for it by developed countries.

Stabex as a Model for a Global Scheme

After agreement was reached on the establishment of Stabex, the EEC felt that Stabex might be suitable as a model for a global export earnings stabilisation scheme. However attention became focussed later, on the possibility of a liberalised IMF facility serving the international requirements for compensatory financing. It is doubtful however whether the IMF framework is a suitable one satisfying in the near future all international requirements for compensatory financing. The changes required might come about too slowly. The IMF is essentially concerned with temporary balance-of-payments assistance and it might be sometime before it could accommodate a scheme which would relax the balance-of-payments criterion, be less restrictive on the maximum levels of drawings, adopt special measures for poorer countries, provide assistance which would go beyond the short-term to take into account cyclical movements, take into account the trend in real earnings and provide assistance to remedy sectoral problems. Some liberalisation of the I.M.F. facility took place recently (December 1975). However these changes are far from meeting these requirements.

In view of this, it might become necessary to think of a global scheme outside the IMF framework and Stabex might attract attention as offering such a possibility. In fact at the Seventh Special Session of the UN General Assembly, the Swedes proposed a global Stabex-type arrangement. An essential difference was that the Swedish scheme would compensate for shortfalls in aggregate earnings from all commodities except fuel.

The commodity-by-commodity approach of Stabex has the advantage that it could provide assistance for sectoral problems and with improvements along the lines mentioned here, a global Stabex scheme, could provide a suitable supplementary scheme to the IMF facility for compensatory financing.

In the absence of a global scheme in which Stabex could be incorporated, the ACP countries are at an advantage relative to other countries exporting the products covered by Stabex, and to the extent the governments of ACP countries allow the proceeds of Stabex to benefit the production of the products concerned, then this could lead to some misdirection of the distribution of production. Some of these products from the ACP already enjoy preferential access in the EEC, and Stabex thus adds to this advantage. However the total effect is limited by the small margins of preference and the modest character of Stabex, and any evaluation must take into account distortions resulting from other preferential arrangements. The extension of Stabex on a global basis in terms of export earnings of all developing countries in all markets, would remove the special advantage provided by Stabex to the ACP.

Conclusion

There is considerable international interest in the stabilisation of export earnings of developing countries. While a few developed market economy countries would like to see the main thrust in commodity stabilisation policy in compensatory financing for shortfalls in export earnings, many countries see compensatory financing as supplementary to price stabilisation arrangements. This is the role seen for compensatory financing in the integrated programme for commodities recommended by the Secretary-General of UNCTAD.

Stabex is a welcome addition to the IMF Compensatory Financing Facility, which is the only other export earnings stabilisation scheme in existence. Stabex unlike the IMF scheme uses the commodity-by-commodity approach and its transfers could therefore be used to assist sectoral problems. Stabex also has the advantage of providing transfers on a more liberal basis—interest-free drawings, grants for the least developed countries, and concessions also for land-locked and island states. Differential treatment according to economic circumstances has not yet been incorporated in the IMF facility.

Improvements are possible in Stabex. A more up-to-date reference period is required if inflation is to be taken into account adequately. The moving average should be centred on the applicable year and forecasts of earnings should be made for the subsequent years in computing the moving average.

Because of the high dependence in developing countries on a few commodities and the possibility of declining net barter and income terms of trade for these countries, stabilisation should be based on real income. This might lead to larger drawings and the need for a larger fund but not substantially so, since the volume of exports tends to increase with time for many commodities. Repayment should also be based on an increase in real earnings.

Eligibility for drawings should be on a more graduated basis and the possibility of diversion to other markets has to be watched.

The Fund provided may only partly be additional to the ordinary aid programme. To the extent that it is not, then Stabex involves other criteria for aid distribution which may not be as efficient since countries with larger export earnings would benefit more. It is necessary that funds provided for compensatory financing schemes should be additional to those provided for the ordinary aid programme.

Finally since the IMF facility may not be able to incorporate all the requirements of a satisfactory compensatory financing scheme—attention to sectoral problems, higher concessionality for the poorer countries, longer repayment periods, less restriction on levels of drawings—it might be necessary to think of another global scheme. The Swedes have already recommended a global Stabex-type arrangement. Stabex could be the basis of such a scheme if it could be extended to cover more products, all developing countries, earnings in all markets and the improvements mentioned above.

Chapter 5

INDUSTRIAL COOPERATION IN THE LOMÉ CONVENTION

by *Dr. Joshua C. Anyiwo*

The Lomé Convention is an agreement on cooperation in several areas between an industrialized Community (the EEC) and a group of non-industrial or industrially developing countries (the ACP); the industrial cooperation of the Convention is aimed to promote a better international division of labour on lines advantageous to the ACP. Against this background I shall review industrial cooperation in the new Convention, namely: first the conception of industrial cooperation and the circumstances leading to a need for such cooperation between the ACP and the EEC; then the type and scope of the industrial cooperation needed by the ACP and other industrially developing countries of the world; and against this background the extent to which the industrial cooperation of the Lomé Convention attains its principal objective and satisfies the needs of the ACP.

Finally, I shall attempt to anticipate and briefly touch upon any special problems that appear inevitable either from misconceptions in the roles to be played by the ACP and the EEC, or from an ill-advised implementation protocol for some aspects of industrial cooperation in the new Convention.

Perspective on Cooperation

Perhaps one of the major hindrances to meaningful cooperation among nations is the often erroneous perspective on cooperation demonstrated by many people. It could not be that a singular perspective on cooperation is not conceivable; nor could it be that such a perspective is inaccessible to any of the bodies seeking cooperation with another. On the contrary, it does seem that improper perception of cooperation arises mostly from inadequate attention, and a dispirited approach, to cooperation in general.

Definitively, cooperation in the context of this chapter, is the combination of bodies (persons, nations, firms, etc.) for the purpose of production, purchase or distribution, for the joint benefits of those bodies. By this conception, cooperation is seen to possess three principal properties namely:

(a) it possesses a subject area;

(b) it involves the design of a system for the combination of the interests of the cooperating bodies in the area of cooperation; and

(c) it redounds to a joint realisation of benefits by the cooperating bodies.

Unfortunately, however, developing countries tend to conceive of cooperation as a one-way flow of aid from an already developed body to a developing body. In fact, the extreme viewpoint in which the developed body in a cooperation venture is expected to "divine" the needs of the developing body, set the latter's priorities for it and virtually undertake a "child-rearing" responsibility for the developing body, is not uncommon among many developing countries. Such misconceptions of cooperation have virtually completely prevented meaningful cooperation among developing countries and have also limited the benefits to developing countries of cooperation between them and developed countries.

Among the developed countries, on the other hand, cooperation is often ill-employed (and thus ill-conceived) as disguises whereby the cleverest of the cooperating bodies exploits the other parties. Especially with respect to cooperation with developing countries, it has become a common supposition in many quarters that many developed countries employ the guise of such cooperation arrangements to ensure continuous supply of needed raw materials from the developing countries. It is, therefore, not improbable that even after a scholarly theoretical design of a good-spirited system of cooperation between developed and developing countries, the former may not make any genuine efforts to contribute to the meaningful development of the latter; rather each body may seek ways to outwit the other.

A proper conception of cooperation must recognise a group of equal partners who having identified areas in which they need one another's help and having jointly worked out a system of arrangements whereby they can organise their different resources, seek genuinely to redistribute their joint resources towards joint and equitable realisation of benefits for all concerned.

In a cooperation venture there cannot, therefore, be any senior or junior partner; no "leader" or "follower" partner, although leadership abilities must be recognised as part of the resources to be contributed by those who possess them. And, all partners must contribute as equally as possible in the design and implementation of the processes of this "mutual aid towards mutual benefits".

Turning our attention now to Lomé we see the Lomé Convention as a modern example in international cooperation between developed and developing countries. None of the partners in the Lomé Convention, the EEC and the ACP, should be considered superior or inferior to the other; each has something important to offer towards the joint realisation of benefits by all.

The subject areas of Lomé are social, economic and industrial development; the full spectrum of man's physical development.

A good design of the system for the combination of the interests of the cooperating bodies must comprise the set of all the institutions, protocols and processes necessary and sufficient for effecting meaningful redistribution of resources among the EEC and ACP countries; and this must include intra-ACP and intra-EEC cooperation as well as cooperation arrangements within individual partner nations, for instance, between government and private sector. The titles of the convention represent an attempt at such a design of the desired system of cooperation; this attempt must, however, be continually reviewed to ensure that it meets and continues to meet the intended objectives.

The general objective of the Lomé Convention is the joint realisation of benefits by the EEC and the ACP countries; the creation or the beginning of the creation of a new international order of more equitable distribution of physical, human and other resources towards global well-being of man.

Lomé will, therefore, have failed if any party to the Convention should, years from now, exhibit no benefits from the implementation of the Convention. Lomé will have failed, if the gap between the rich and the poor among the ACP and EEC countries should widen rather than narrow.

Industrialisation in the ACP: Present State, Main Obstacles and Major Needs

It has been noted often (during the course of the negotiations leading to the new ACP-EEC Convention and at some other instances) that industrialisation is a major component of the development strategy of ACP countries and that all ACP countries without exception have given high priority to the industrial sector in their development plans and in their programs for future development both at national and at regional levels. What have been the achievements by the ACP in the area of industrialisation during their post-independence years?

In anticipation of the answer to the above question I readily suggest that the framework within which we may begin to understand and realistically review the industrial achievements of the ACP countries must include the bold realisation that: the ACP countries remain essentially a technologically backward society, and, therefore, a non-industrial or, at best, an industrially developing group of nations.

Against this background knowledge we should have no difficulty understanding the observation commonly made in many developing nations of Africa, the Caribbean and the Pacific that in these countries industrialisation has thus far failed to provide any major impetus for development, structural change and employment; and that although the range of industries established in these countries has widened in the last decade, these nations continue to import a higher proportion of most of their requirements of consumer, intermediate and capital goods than other regions.

A number of reasons have been suggested to explain the small impact that industrialisation has so far made in the ACP countries, and the various problems limiting the process of further industrial development in the ACP. I shall now review these and attempt to elicit from them some fundamental causes.

Main Obstacles to Industrialisation in the ACP

Among the many obstacles to industrialisation in the ACP countries which have been constantly noted are the following:

(i) that traditional approaches to industrial development, which no longer meet the needs of the present situation, continue to be employed: the contributions of the private sector to industrial development, supplemented by the activities of individual governments and multilateral institutions, have not adequately advanced industrial development in many developing countries;

(ii) that much industrial development in the ACP has been confined to "enclave" activities having minimal linkage effects with the rest of the economy, and a low level of permanent absorption and diffusion of technology and skills;

(iii) that attempts by ACP countries to re-define the parameters within which industrial development should take place have frequently involved greater public sector control and participation; that this has created fears among foreign private investors, making them less willing to take risks or to provide capital or skills for further development;

(iv) that the penetration of international markets for the sale of the industrial products of the ACP countries is beset by numerous marketing problems such as the difficulty for ACP industries in meeting the product standards demanded by consumers in the developed countries, market restrictions imposed on local subsidiaries of multinational companies, etc. and

(v) that poor loan terms granted by the developed countries have often adversely affected the balance of payments of the developing ACP countries and have accordingly amplified their debts considerably; that this impacts seriously on the adaptation and utilization of imported foreign technology which is usually capital intensive.

Upon further consideration of these and similar obstacles to industrialisation in the ACP countries one readily notes that they all point to a few basic causes. I suggest three such causes as follows:

(a) a presently low level of the "industrial mentality" in ACP societies:

By this I assert that industrial revolution is dictated, and industrial development guided, by what I have referred to as the "industrial mentality". Industrial mentality is a psychological orientation of the mind which puts the latter in an adventurous frame within which the mind becomes truly the architect of its own fortune, deliberately designing its own trajectory of development and systematically "conquering" obstacles confronting it in the process; the industrial mentality is that agency by which scientific and cultural development are deliberately projected into a technology for the satisfaction of apparent needs; and, industrial mentality is acquired by long exposure to and practice in practical industrial problem solving situations.

(b) an initially low economy from which a capital intensive development must be fashioned:

The initial low level of economic development of the ACP countries compels them to be strongly reliant on foreign financial aid for most of their industrialisation efforts. This inevitably results in the ACP countries often sacrificing initiative, objective and priorities, as the provider of the developmental capital often dictates the pattern of the development.

(c) the disadvantageous "late-comer" position of ACP countries in the area of industrialisation:

The ACP and other developing countries have historically been classified as perpetual consumers and non-producers of industrial products. The psychological impact of this classification, among other things, will ensure that penetration of international markets for industrial products by the ACP, in the role of "Seller", will be a steeple-chase.

In the implications of the above three realities, I believe, may be traced and derived all the impediments to rational industrialisation in the ACP countries.

Major Needs Towards Industrialisation in the ACP

The major needs of the ACP countries towards rapid and rational industrialisation easily reduce to a need for measures which will remove the major causes of the obstacles to industrialisation in those countries. I have suggested three such major causes; the corresponding measures needed for their removal may adequately be summarized by the following principal need:

"a need to create a sound base for sustained, self-motivated and self-reliant industrial development in the ACP countries".

Quite clearly such a sound base would include:
(i) measures for the rapid acquisition and development of the critically needed industrial mentality for sustained, self-motivated industrial development;
(ii) measures for the improvement of the presently low economic position of the ACP countries, for instance through soft loans, with no strings attached, from the developed countries and world organisations, or through reviewing the relative importance of the abundant raw material resources in the ACP countries (as the crude oil cartel has successfully done), thereby forcing changes in the international economic order along lines favorable to the ACP and other developing nations; and
(iii) measures to aid ACP nations' penetration of international markets for industrial products as "Sellers" not just "Buyers".

Industrial Cooperation in the Lomé Convention

A desirably high degree of complementarity appears to exist between the resources of the ACP Group and those of the EEC, towards enhanced meaningful industrial cooperation between the two bodies. For example, while the EEC possesses a high level of technological know-how, it is from the ACP Group that the EEC must seek raw materials with which to sustain its industries. On the other hand, loaded with a large variety of raw materials, the ACP is nonetheless, essentially a non-industrial group seeking rapid industrialisation and aspiring to a restructured and more favorable

96

international division of labor. Within our perspective on cooperation, industrial cooperation between the ACP Group and the EEC must, therefore, involve extension of EEC's technological know-how to the ACP, with appropriate and complementary extension of ACP resources to the EEC.

Title III of the Lomé Convention details the objectives and terms of the industrial cooperation arrangement between the EEC and ACP. From that title we observe that the following five major areas have been emphasized: ACP manpower development, industrial projects planning and implementation, industrial information and promotion, industrial trade promotion and transfer of technology. I shall consider each of these areas in turn, examining in the process the provisions indicated for their realisation.

ACP Manpower Development

Inadequacy of general education, especially the lack of technical and vocational training, is a recognized and critical obstacle to industrialisation in ACP countries. Manpower shortages, particularly in the category of skilled workers and foremen which form very strategic links in the chain of industrial production, are often acute in virtually all ACP countries. It is not surprising, therefore, that cooperation in the area of manpower development for ACP countries has been emphasized in the Lomé Convention.

The provisions for ACP manpower development are not quite clearly articulated in the Convention. It would appear, from the Convention, that the training programs will be handled by a division of the proposed Center for Industrial Development which will be jointly operated by the EEC and ACP. However, in recent discussions top officials of the EEC seem to indicate that the Training Division of the EEC Commission will undertake the responsibility of organising all the needed training programs.

Nonetheless, it is clear, from Title III of the Convention, that ACP countries, either separately or in convenient regional groups, must articulate and submit to whatever body is responsible for the training programs a clear and precise program of their manpower development needs. Based on such programs and operating through the designated body for training, the EEC will contribute to the organisation and financing of the training of the ACP personnel, at all levels, in industries and institutions within the EEC. In addition, the EEC will contribute to the establishment and expansion of industrial training facilities in ACP countries.

Industrial Projects: Planning and Implementation

Another area where inadequacy of technological know-how and a low level of trained manpower critically obstruct industrialisation in the ACP countries is the area of planning and executing industrial projects, ranging from small local projects to large scale regional projects. The general objective of ACP-EEC cooperation in this area includes facilitating the planning and execution of industrial projects within ACP States as well as promoting the development and diversification of industry in those States.

Proper industrial planning involves, of course, the recognition and provision of the appropriate environment necessary for meaningful industrialisation; and this includes such social and economic infrastructures as transport, energy, communication, industrial research and training, as well as effective linkages between upstream production (e.g. agriculture, mining, fisheries and forests) and industries.

Further, as meaningful industrial project implementation must necessarily include full participation by local nationals, it would be necessary to elicit the participation of nationals of ACP States, for example through deliberate encouragement of those nationals in the establishment and development of small and medium-size industrial firms within the ACP States.

All these needs are recognized by the EEC and ACP, and are provided for in the industrial cooperation agreement of the Lomé Convention.

The Convention distinguishes two types of industrial projects namely: regional projects (which involve more than one ACP State) and local projects (which involve just one ACP State). ACP countries, either individually (for local projects) or in regional groups (for regional projects), are expected to indicate as clearly as possible their priority areas for industrial cooperation and the form they would like such cooperation to take. Then the ACP State or States, guided by industrial information and promotional services available from the Center for Industrial Development, must take such steps as are necessary to promote effective cooperation in the particular projects within the framework of the convention, with either the EEC or individual member states thereof, or with firms or nationals of the EEC member states who comply with the development program and priorities of the host states. The EEC and its member States undertake only to endeavour to set up measures to attract the participation of European firms and nationals in the industrial development efforts of the ACP state or states concerned, and to encourage such firms and nationals to

98

adhere to the aspirations and development objectives of those ACP States.

EEC financing may be available for some of the projects, especially the regional projects.

Industrial Information and Promotion

Paucity of information, often on the most elementary questions, can be quite an important obstacle to cooperation of any kind. Especially in a cooperation scheme such as the Lomé Convention where external operators (primarily the European private sectors) play a crucial role, it becomes almost mandatory to establish measures aimed at cross-feeding information between ACP countries, the EEC and the external operators. For example, potential European investors should be able to readily obtain basic social and economic data on ACP countries regarding conditions affecting establishment and work (legal provisions and regulations, investment codes, cost of factors of production, etc.), availability of finance, information on surveys, projects and industrial establishments. And ACP countries should also be able to readily obtain such information as would facilitate their contacts with the European world of finance and industry as well as such steps as are necessary to identify and prepare industrial projects.

Given the availability of pertinent industrial information, it would be necessary, in the framework of a cooperation agreement such as Lomé, to find the partners with necessary finance, technology and marketing potential, bring them together and promote agreement between them, for instance through organised meetings and missions in specific industrial sectors, including individual contacts. These measures aimed at facilitating and intensifying direct contact between persons and institutions in EEC and ACP countries for the purpose of stimulating effective transfers of capital, technology and marketing facilities for industrial projects, constitute the essence of industrial promotion.

Obviously, industrial information and promotion are essential to meaningful industrial cooperation. The Lomé Convention recognizes this reality and has emphasized its actualisation.

The Convention includes the establishment of a Center for Industrial Development as a new and strictly operational instrument which will be jointly managed by the ACP and EEC. In fact, this Center is expected to be the nerve center for the actualisation of the industrial cooperation in the Lomé Convention. Its functions focus mainly on industrial promotional efforts. Thus, it is principally through this Center that it is hoped to arouse European private sector interest in industrial cooperation with the ACP, and to persuade them to take positive actions.

Industrial Trade Promotion

Industrialisation of ACP States must necessarily involve those States in the role of marketers of industrial products. To obtain full benefit from the trade and other arrangements of the Lomé Convention it would thus be necessary to undertake specific trade promotion for ACP industrial products aimed at aiding ACP countries to increase their share of international trade in those products.

Again, the Lomé Convention recognizes this need as an essential part of an industrial cooperation arrangement between the EEC and ACP countries.

Art. 34 of the Convention makes provisions for carrying out trade promotion schemes by the EEC, aimed at seeking recognition and acceptance in European and foreign markets of products manufactured in ACP States. This will naturally involve efforts by the EEC to familiarise industrial producers in ACP States with European market regulations and requirements (such as standardisation, health rules, quality standards, etc.), and to help them to conform. In addition, it is proposed to draw up programs jointly between the EEC and ACP States designed to stimulate and develop trade of industrial products among ACP States and between the EEC and the ACP.

Transfer of Technology

Technology is the basic ingredient to industrial growth. The EEC has technology and the ACP Group needs to acquire technology to facilitate its industrialisation. Thus, effective transfer of technology between the EEC and the ACP is crucial to meaningful industrial cooperation between them.

There are essentially three steps in the transfer of technology and they are independent of who are involved in the transfer, although variations in the detailed processes involved in each of those steps may exist depending on the peculiarities of the transferer and transferee. The first step is that of access to technology; the second is the transfer process proper; and the third is adaptation of the transferred technology to the local needs of the transferee.

The EEC approaches the question of transfer of technology between it and the ACP Group with schemes for protecting technology transfers based upon the reality of European market econ-

100

omy system. The ACP Group, on the other hand, approaches this area of cooperation from a longstanding realisation that so far the transfer of knowledge has taken place on terms very unfavorable to developing countries, at an unduly high cost, and in conditions unacceptable to developing countries.

The Lomé Convention, in this area, attempts to marry these two different viewpoints. It accepts the reality of European market economy system as fixed but then introduces possibilities of financial and technical cooperation closely linked with training schemes and the execution of specific industrial projects as part of the general scheme for industrial cooperation. The Convention also includes provisions for effecting a transfer of technology from Europe to the ACP States. It essentially involves the following two aspects:

(i) financial and technical assistance to the ACP States at the following successive states of technology transfer:

(a) information on availability of technology,

(b) selection and purchase of appropriate technology,

(c) adaptation of the technology

(d) formation and functioning of local ACP potential for research and technology adaptation,

(e) recourse to European technological research capacity.

(ii) cooperation agreement between ACP States and European firms involving long-term management contracts; sub-contracting with technological facilities, etc.

General Comments on Industrial Cooperation in the Lomé Convention

The EEC and ACP countries can create, and have indeed created, the framework within which industrial cooperation between the two groups may be effected. But neither the ACP nor the EEC as a group can ever substitute itself for the "operators" who actually implement the cooperation.

The private sector in both the EEC and ACP as well as the separate governments of both groups are the real "operators". They are the ones who by their attitudes and responses to the expressed needs for cooperation can forge real partnerships which will ensure the success or failure of industrial cooperation between the ACP and the EEC.

I shall now further examine the protocols, proposed in Title III of the New Convention, for actualizing the objectives of the industrial cooperation agreement, especially with regard to the real "operators", and also touch upon a few general problems of industrial cooperation between developed and developing countries.

ACP's Quest for a New International Division of Labor

By this the ACP countries strive towards truly being "the architects of their own fortunes", essentially in order to extricate themselves from the present evolutionary cycle of international order in which the developing countries appear doomed to a subservient role as perpetual international consumers and non-producers; for in that role, there is no hope that the social, economic and industrial development of presently developing countries can ever approach the level attained by the presently developed countries of the world.

A new international division of labor along lines favorable to the developing countries is a legitimate desire, recognized by the United Nations as requiring urgent attention, towards world peace and prosperity.

How does industrial cooperation in the new EEC-ACP Convention refer to this issue? How are the "operators" in this industrial cooperation poised to play their parts?

In Title III of the new Convention the legitimate wish of the ACP countries to assert greater ownership control of their raw materials and to process as much of it as possible at home is recognized and accepted; and in response the EEC undertakes to cooperate with the ACP to promote the development and diversification of the industries in the ACP States necessary to that end. Furthermore, in recognition of the difficulties that would face the ACP in finding markets for ACP industrial products, the EEC has undertaken to actively promote the marketing of ACP industrial products in both EEC and other foreign markets; and to cooperate to bring about a better distribution of industry both within and among the ACP States.

The EEC private sector which will play a critical role in effecting this cooperation does, however, appear to have strong reservations in the practicality of this agreement. According to them, what seems entirely acceptable as a general objective can make for acute distress in particular industries in the EEC resulting in serious socio-economic hardships for Europeans. They realistically emphasize that the transfer of industrial capacity from the EEC to the ACP countries will continue to be a difficult and slow process. The EEC private sector rather suggests other avenues for evolving this international division of labor, such as: extension, instead of reduction, of European enterprises; transfer of some EEC factories

102

to ACP countries with adequate compensation, as well as favorable adjustments in ACP import and expatriate quota rules; the method of subcontracting; and the encouragement of "EURO-ACP" companies, etc.

ACP countries legitimately find it necessary not to compromise their sovereignty. Mindful of their broader national objectives, they must study the EEC private sector's attitude, fears and suggestions in greater detail in order to evaluate their several impacts as well as the extent to which their acceptance satisfies ACP's present objectives.

Nonetheless, the questions remain: Is the EEC as a body really fully able to make good its undertaking to, as a matter of urgency, actualize the ACP's quest for a new and favorable international division of labor? Does the ACP as a group have clearly articulated ways and means of monitoring and directing their quest for a new international order favorable for their development?

On my part I have noted that the incentives in this exercise to the EEC are not obvious. It would clearly be a matter of conscientious sacrifice on the part of the EEC (perhaps undertaken on the understanding that they would derive complementary benefits in other areas of cooperation) for the EEC to provide meaningful cooperation with the ACP in the latter's quest for a "place under the sun", especially since such a demand would implicitly entail the withdrawal from someone else of some or all of his "place under the sun".

Transfer of Technology

In the minds of many ACP nationals and from the viewpoint of developing countries in general, the Lomé Convention may not have adequately addressed the aspirations of developing countries towards more favorable transfer of technology, as well as towards a secured protection against abuse in the operations connected with the transfer of techniques, especially the price and restrictive clauses.

Nevertheless, it would really be naive for developing countries to expect that the technological resources, which have taken the developed countries years of hard work and heavy financial investment to accumulate, could overnight be handed over to the former free. The realisation of such a demand must await fundamental changes in basic human attitudes; for instance, in which global cooperation, rather than international competition, is emphasized.

It is reality and will remain so into the foreseeable future, that developing countries must pay a price for the acquisition of the

103

technological resources of industrial countries, in just the same way that industrial nations must pay a price for the raw material resources of developing countries. The ACP approach to the transfer of technology must therefore be formulated against the background of this reality. Pertinent questions should be: What is a fair price for the purchase of technology as a resource, vis-à-vis the present and projected prices of other resources vital to man's total development? Are there alternatives to direct purchase of patents, technological techniques, etc., which the ACP could exploit to speed up its industrialisation; and so on?

It is the strong opinion of the present author that problems in the transfer of technology arise mostly as a result of misunderstanding, among nationals both of the developed and developing nations, of the concept and processes of the transfer of knowledge. Briefly, I stress once again that effective transfer of knowledge critically involves a mentality re-orientation attainable through contact and deliberate experimentation. I maintain that even if all the technological know-how of the industrialised world were now made available to the developing countries, it would be many years before sustained, self-motivated industrialisation in the latter would be anything but moderate. Developing countries must invest heavily in research and development as a mentality orienting agency for their nationals; they must permit and encourage their nationals to experiment in project development in order to acquire and sustain technological know-how; they must educate their general public towards a technological society in order to hasten the generation of those social attitudinal changes which constitute part of the environment needed for sustained self-motivated development. Developing countries must increase effective contact between their nationals and those of the developed countries, in all fields; staff exchange programs between indigenous ACP organisations, for instance, and appropriate European and other foreign organisations must be encouraged, as must intra-ACP transfer of knowledge; and in each case the emphasis should be not merely to copy the industrialised world but to understand their problems and the ways they have tried to solve them in order that the developing countries may determine how best to identify and tackle their own problems.

When monetary prices must be paid for technology, the ACP Group must attempt at international levels to quantify technological know-how as a resource and to relate its value to that of other essential resources in human interaction. The use of multi-national corporations should be encouraged, although efforts must be made

104

at international levels to define the structure and operation of multi-nationals and to limit the undesirable influences of such corporations; for multi-national corporations can be an effective alternative organ for the transfer of technology and for general international cooperation.

In the light of the foregoing, it seems that the approach of the Lomé Convention to the transfer of technology is not after all unrealistic. But, whatever price the ACP Group pays for European technology it must demand in proportion for its own resources. Soon the irrationality of the industrial world over-pricing their own resources and under-pricing the resources of the developing world would become obvious; then will the path have been opened towards a new and rational international economic order.

Cooperation Within the Parties to the Convention

In the new EEC-ACP convention the ACP countries stand as a bloc just as stands the EEC. However, in the implementation protocols, the freedom for each of the 55 countries involved to exercise independent options within the broad terms of the Convention is quite clear. The success of industrial cooperation in the new Convention would thus depend to a large extent on the magnitude and seriousness of antecedent cooperation among the ACP States as well as among the EEC Member States.

Equitable distribution of industries, elimination of unnecessary duplication or multiplication of functions, pooling and distributing resources for common good, and many other such considerations towards rational industrialization must be areas of serious attention for agreement among the ACP countries. Each ACP country must, for instance, be prepared to sacrifice desirable industries if the concentration of such industries in other ACP countries is determined to be of greatest value to the ACP bloc. I strongly recommend the employment of methods of systems analysis in planning cooperative industrialization in the ACP bloc.

In their negotiations with the EEC the ACP countries demonstrated unmistaken ability to work together towards a common purpose. But the drafting of a Memorandum of Agreement can often be a mere academic exercise. In real situations of competitive economic planning and infrastructural development, will rationality prevail over internal political conditions sufficiently to ensure that the aspirations of industrial cooperation in the new Convention are pursued?

Among the EEC, inter-governmental cooperation, cooperation between government and private sector, and cooperation within the private sector will be called for. Although the mere fact of the continued existence of the EEC is indicative of the ability of EEC Member States to cooperate successfully in these areas, it may still be asked if in dealing with developing countries, where, occasionally, interests may be divided, governments and private sectors of the EEC can continue to cooperate, as may be incumbent upon them, for the success of the new EEC-ACP Convention?

Aspects Bordering on International Politics

Perhaps the greatest fear entertained by private sectors of the developed countries in industrial cooperation between developed and developing countries is the security of foreign investments in these developing countries. Foreign investors generally believe that an attractive overall investment climate in the developing countries, beyond such specific investment incentives as tax concessions or the existence of national investment guarantee schemes, is critical to meaningful industrial cooperation with these developing nations. But details of what these foreign investors consider to constitute a favorable investment climate often appear to threaten the sovereignty and independence of the developing countries; as though with their technology these foreign investors want to hold the developing nations to ransom.

In the new EEC-ACP Convention provision is made to guarantee risk capital for major investments. Furthermore, ACP countries are enjoined to be as specific as possible in defining their needs and objectives, while the EEC undertakes to encourage its private sector to adhere to the aspirations and development objectives of the ACP countries.

In reviewing some discussions between representatives of the private sector of the EEC and those of ACP countries it is but too obvious that what is sought by all is a detailed specification of the rules of the game, preferably as an international legal document binding on all nation-States. The Economic and Social Council of the United Nations appears to be suitably placed to play an active role in formulating such international ground rules on foreign investments.

Another avenue for effective industrial cooperation between developed and developing countries, and one which is favored by the private sector of the EEC, is the route of multi-national corporations. Multi-national corporations have distinct capabilities which can be put to the service of development. Their ability to tap financial, physical and human resources around the world and to combine them in economically feasible and commercially profitable activities, together with their capacity to develop and apply new technology and skills, to translate resources into output and to integrate product and financial markets throughout the world, has proved to be outstanding. But while the role of multinational corporations is largely economic in character and influence, it has become uncomfortably apparent that multinational cooperations can also influence, for good or ill, the mode of life, the socio-cultural fiber and political development within a country, as well as relations among countries.

It would be unfortunate, however, to sacrifice the numerous beneficial influences of multinational corporations for their limitations; the limitations as well as capabilities of multinational corporations in meeting total world development objectives need to be clearly understood. International cooperation is needed in this area with a view to formulating, if possible, clear international policies on the operation of multinational corporations. The United Nations has rightfully taken a lead in this matter; some guidelines have indeed already been proposed[1] which will be of great interest to ACP and EEC countries in the operation of their new Convention, especially with regard to industrial cooperation.

Besides the aforementioned political problems that could be generated by the real "operators" in the process of industrial cooperation between the EEC and ACP, one must, although at the risk of being immediately branded a pessimist, also consider the impact of international political tensions on the operation of the new EEC-ACP Convention. For example, most, if not all, of the ACP and other developing nations of the world strongly condemn the repression of their kind in certain parts of the world (such as in South Africa and Rhodesia) and the possible expansionist potential of such countries. Any relationship between the EEC (or any of its Member States) and the declared "enemy countries" of the developing nations of the world, which is interpreted by the ACP countries as furthering repressionism, is bound to generate political tension between the ACP and the EEC. Can industrial cooperation between the EEC and ACP be made as nearly independent of political relations between them? We must remain aware of that question.

1. The Impact of Multinational Corporations on Development and International Relations. U.N. Publication, New York, 1974.

The Institutions in Title III

Two institutions, the Industrial Cooperation Committee and the Industrial Development Center, are provided for as agencies by which industrial cooperation in the new EEC-ACP Convention will be implemented.

Essentially, the Industrial Cooperation Committee is the monitoring agency for the total industrial cooperation effort between the ACP and the EEC; in that role, it can impart a decisive drive to the underlying policy. The Industrial Cooperation Committee also guides and supervises the Industrial Development Center, which will jointly be managed by the EEC and ACP and which is expected to be the nerve center for the actualisation of the proposed industrial cooperation.

This new institutional approach is welcomed by the private sectors of both the EEC and ACP, although with some reservations. The private sectors seem unanimous in urging that the proposed institutions should operate merely as centers for reflection, exchange of methods and elaboration of new forms of economic relations, but should not become a compulsory channel for industrial cooperation between the EEC private sector and ACP countries. Private sector opinion seems to be that the establishment of a compulsory channel for industrial cooperation can only help to stymie the cooperation efforts, and that direct contacts between the different States and the representatives of the European private sector are the best way to realise an efficient form of economic collaboration between the ACP and the European private sector.

Further, the private sector appear to favour the inclusion of experts in the Industrial Cooperation Committee in order to lend to the Committee meetings the necessary technical support.

While indiscriminate rigidity is undesirable, it is very likely that at least initially most ACP States will look to the proposed institutions for help in formulating their needs and in searching for best-qualified partners in industrial ventures. For facility in these respects, a strong Center for Industrial Development, including a strong and efficient multinational team of experienced industrial liaison officers, and adequately equiped with modern information processing capability, is indispensable.

For the monitoring, supervision and guidance of the total industrial cooperation effort, a strong multinational team of systems engineers operating within the Industrial Cooperation Committee is highly desirable.

Whatever view we hold of the significance of the Lomé Convention to ACP development in particular and to world cooperation and development in general, it must remain an indisputable fact that in the exercise of negotiating the Lomé Convention, and in the several discussions on, and analyses of, the Lomé Convention that have been undertaken worldwide since February 1975, some significant knowledge has been gained that is beneficial to the ACP Group, the EEC and the world in general, towards a better understanding of the elements of meaningful global cooperation and rational development.

We have learned a few important facts about cooperation in general and industrial cooperation in particular, especially between developing and developed countries.

First, it has, for instance, become obvious that a concerted approach must be adopted in the implementation of the new EEC-ACP convention of Lomé, both between the EEC and the ACP and within the EEC and the ACP Group. Experiences must continually be exchanged, risks and tasks shared, and deliberate effort made to understand one another's problems.

In the ACP Group this calls for increased intra-ACP cooperation as critical to the success of the Lomé Convention and essential to the general development of the ACP Group. Regional integration, equitable distribution of industries, elimination of unnecessary duplication or multiplication of functions, pooling and distributing resources for common good, and many other such considerations towards rational development are areas demanding serious attention for agreement among the ACP countries. For this, rational methods of systems analysis must be employed over emotional methods based on political and selfish aspirations.

Among the EEC, inter-governmental cooperation, cooperation between government and private sector and cooperation within the private sector will be called for.

Between the EEC and the ACP Group, the need for certain basic structural and attitudinal changes in European countries must be understood, and the type of the environment needed in the ACP countries for meaningful ACP-EEC cooperation must be articulated.

Secondly, it must be remarked that it would be utterly wrong and shamefully unfortunate, if industrial cooperation in the Lomé Convention were interpreted, either in the EEC or in the ACP countries, simply as the transfer of European industrial patterns into ACP countries. Such a simple-minded attitude would inevitably lead to unplanned industrialisation of ACP countries; and, because European industrial patterns cannot always fit into the circumstances of ACP countries, industrial cooperation based on this naive approach is bound to create social and economic problems in ACP countries of a nature and dimension alien to both the EEC and the ACP.

Thirdly, we observe that industrialisation is a capital intensive development; and that the success of any industrial cooperation arrangement will, therefore, depend to a large extent on the financial resources available. The amount of the European Development Fund provided for the Lomé Convention does not appear to be sufficient for the desired impact of the convention, although the orientation of the fund is praiseworthy.

Fourthly, we have recognized that as industrial development cannot be undertaken independently of general social and economic development, industrial cooperation would be meaningful only if undertaken as part of a more general cooperation arrangement involving trade, technical, financial and other areas of cooperation.

Finally, as I have attempted to point out in my earlier discussions, a memorandum of agreement on cooperation does not operate automatically. There are human elements among its "operators". The imagination, goodwill and perseverance of those human elements involved will determine whether we have created another beautiful theoretical design or a practical beginning of a new and rational way of life for all mankind. We are faced with a challenge which we cannot afford to be unequal to.

Chapter 6

FINANCIAL AND TECHNICAL COOPERATION: THE EUROPEAN DEVELOPMENT FUND AND THE LOMÉ CONVENTION

by *Dr. Ir. J.J.C. Voorhoeve**

This chapter surveys the development assistance which the European Community (EC) offers to developing countries. The emphasis is on financial development cooperation with those countries that are associated with the Community, but the possibilities for expanding this aid to non-associated countries are also explored.

The European Aid Program

The European Economic Community was designed before the colonial period had come to an end. The Community's founding fathers paid little attention to relations with what was to become the Third World, but the Treaty of Rome was flexible enough to allow the member-states and the Community institutions to acquire most of the tools needed for playing a significant role in development cooperation. Today, the EC has a whole array of development instruments: (i) an historically based cooperation policy with the African, Caribbean, and Pacific partners in the Lomé Convention; (ii) an emerging cooperation policy with other developing countries; (iii) a global food aid policy, and (iv) a global commercial policy.

The opportunities offered by these instruments are still far from being used fully because of reluctance to integrate politically and a certain hesitance to development cooperation in general. Nonetheless, Europe has recently performed more successfully on the development stage than in other sectors of policy integration. However slow the pace, the Community is moving to a world-wide cooperation policy.

The European aid program is financed by the European Development Fund (EDF), the Community budget, and the European Investment Bank (EIB). The EDF provides grants, loans, and risk

* The views expressed in this paper are those of the author and are not to be attributed to the World Bank Group.

capital to developing nations which are associated under the Lomé Convention. The Community budget provides mainly food aid and emergency relief. The EIB grants loans mostly for development purposes within the EC, but is increasingly also involved in development projects in non-member states.

The European Community's aid programs add up to a substantial and growing contribution to the total bilateral and multilateral aid effort. As shown in table 1, it disbursed almost half a billion units of account[1] in 1974, which is, in real terms, almost one and a half times the amount provided five years ago.

The share of Community aid in total multilateral aid from all international agencies has also increased, rising from 3.3 percent in 1970 to 10.4 percent in 1974. Relative to Official Development Assistance (ODA) from bi- and multilateral sources, the Community's share was 5.3 percent in 1974. The size of the Community's aid program is comparable to that of the medium-sized donors among the OECD countries.

The Community aid program is supplemental to the national efforts of the member states. As table 2 shows, seven of the nine EC members which are DAC donors accounted for almost 5 out of 11 billion dollars in 1974, or 43.0 percent of the total ODA flow to developing countries.

Relative to the member states' own aid programs, the Community's program is not very large. Its share is rising, however; it amounted to 12.3 percent of their national aid disbursements in 1974.

The terms of the Community's aid program compare very favorably to other aid institutions. The share of grants in total ODA has risen from 79 percent in 1970 to 97 percent in 1974. The average grant element in total ODA reached 93 percent in 1974. The least developed countries received only grants totalling 21 percent of total ODA from the EC in 1974.

European development assistance is concentrated on the poorest developing countries. The groups with a Gross National Product (GNP) per capita below $200 per year receive over 60 percent of EC aid. This stands in sharp contrast with the flow of resources from other donors. Countries below $200 p.c. comprise 55 percent of the LDC population (excluding Communist Asia), but they received 46 percent of all bilateral and multilateral flows in 1974.

The original concentration of EC aid on African countries,

1. Equivalent to U.S. $1.00 up to 1971; $1.0857 in 1972; $1.1912 in 1973, and $1.2448 in 1974.

112

which form only a small part of the needy, has been reduced recently. In 1974, South Asia has become a major recipient of EC aid.[2]

The European Development Fund

The major institution for Community aid is the European Development Fund. Created in 1958, it has been replenished three times, most recently in the context of the Lomé Convention. Table 3 portrays the total resources made available to associated developing countries.

The rise of resources in nominal terms has been very large; the fourth EDF is almost 8 times the first in current dollars. Part of this is inflation, however, because in real terms the increase amounts to 282 percent.

The third European Development Fund was replenished in 1975 under the Lomé Convention. The nine Common Market states agreed to channel over 4 billion dollars through the EDF and EIB to at least 46 developing countries from Africa, the Caribbean, and the Pacific during 1975-1980.[3] Table 4 shows the composition of EDF IV.

Comparison with the Second Yaoundé Convention

The widely acclaimed Lomé Convention is indeed a substantial improvement on the Second Yaoundé Convention, not only regarding the volume of financial aid but also in number of recipients, lending policies, and trade arrangements.

The *volume* of financial aid has increased from 1000 million u/a for 1970-74 to 3,550 million u/a for 1975-80. Aid per capita increased from 11.3 u/a to 17.2 u/a in nominal terms, while the population of the recipient countries rose from 81 to 197 million.[4] If aid per capita is adjusted for inflation, however, a slight decrease in real terms may have occurred.[5]

---

2. This subject will be further analyzed below.

3. See annex 1 for a list of these countries and a categorization by region and level of development.

4. Excluding Nigeria with 69 million inhabitants.

5. Depending on actual disbursements, inflation, and parity changes. On the basis of DAC's ODA deflator, aid per capita available in 1969 under the second Yaoundé fund was slightly larger in real terms than the aid available per capita in 1975 under the Lomé Convention.

Regarding lending *policies*, the following changes are noted:

a. A new fund for stabilization of export revenues around a medium-term trend. This major innovation has been analyzed in chapter 4 and is not further treated here.

b. More emphasis on industrial cooperation between the EC and ACP states.

c. More emphasis on regional cooperation among borrowers.

d. More emphasis on aid to the poorest countries which have the worst prospects and are disadvantaged in aid receipts and technical assistance.

e. More emphasis on agriculture and rural development.

f. A greater say of borrowing countries in the utilization of funds, particularly through the new consultation procedures for country programming.

g. More emphasis on development of small- and medium-scale enterprises.

h. A fund for micro-projects from which small grants can be rapidly disbursed to finance rural development projects which spring from local initiative.

i. A rise in the percentage of funds available for soft loans, and an increase in their grant element.

As for *trade arrangements*, the most important changes are the afore-mentioned Stabex scheme, free access to the Common Market for almost all (99.2 percent) imports from the ACP countries, non-reciprocity in trade preferences, and a commodity agreement on sugar containing mutual supply and purchase obligations at an indexed minimum price (compare chapters 2-4, supra).

No analysis of Europe's development aid is complete without paying attention to these trade relations. As the largest trading block, which is much more interdependent with the economies around and below the Equator than the USA, the European Community has always placed much emphasis on trade in its relations with the Third World.

Comparison with the World Bank Group

The European Development Fund and the European Investment Bank may be considered as regional development institutions. The donors are Western European countries and the recipients are mainly African countries, but recently also a number of small Caribbean and Pacific states. The two institutions lie midway between national-bilateral and universal-multilateral institutions.

The World Bank Group, consisting of the International Bank for Reconstruction and Development (IBRD), the International Development Association (IDA), and the International Finance Corporation (IFC), is financed by both developed and developing nations and operates on all continents.

The recipients of EDF and EIB aid have no voting rights in decision-making within these institutions. The shareholders are the Common Market members. However, formal consultation exists within various common association institutions, and informal consultation outside them. If an aid request is refused, the prospective borrower has the right of a hearing. In the World Bank Group, lenders and borrowers have voting rights according to their capital subscriptions. While the OECD states have a majority of the votes in the Bank, decisions are, in practice, mostly made by consensus.

The EDF and EIB offer a range of financial assistance which is different from the World Bank's. It runs from grants to normal loans at market rates, with in-between loans on special terms (40 years, 10 years grace, and highly subsidized interest rates). Most of the aid is granted. Under the Second Yaoundé Convention, only 19 percent of total EDF/EIB resources available for associated states was loan aid. Under the Lomé Convention, loans will amount to about 27 percent of total EDF/EIB aid. By comparison, World Bank Group finance ranges from IFC loans with interest close to market levels, through IBRD loans at lower than market rates, to very soft IDA credits bearing only a 3/4 percent service charge. World Bank finance is almost exclusively loan capital, and the grant element of its total ODA flow is lower than that of the EDF/EIB flow to associated states.

A major difference between the World Bank Group and EDF/EIB is simply size. Average annual commitments by the World Bank Group were $3279.2 million in the five year period from 1970 to 1974. Commitments by the EDF and EIB, plus the Community's budget, were on average $421.2 million during these years.[6]

Aid from the World Bank Group consists mainly of project finance. Program loans and emergency assistance are exceptions. By comparison, EDF channels a relatively large share of its resources into non-project aid, e.g. to assist in natural and economic disasters. Relative to its smaller resource flow, EDF also finances more technical assistance than the World Bank Group. There are also important differences in the distribution of funds over economic sectors. Since 1959, EDF has channeled significant shares of its resources into education, health, and rural development. The

6. DAC Statistics.

World Bank Group has greatly expanded its lending in these "social" sectors since 1968. E.g., agriculture and rural development accounted for 31.5 percent of total IBRD/IDA commitments in fiscal year 1975.

EDF has a different approach to aid requests. While the World Bank makes a thorough investigation of the proposed project's impact on the entire national economy, for which it uses sophisticated economic methods, taking into account many socio-economic variables, the EDF puts more emphasis on financial and non-economic considerations.

The Community emphasizes regional integration projects and offers technical assistance for their design and implementation. One-tenth of the EDF funds for 1975-1980 have been earmarked for integration projects. The World Bank Group also encourages integration, but puts no special emphasis on this. The World Bank is available for assistance to economic integration projects if opportunities arise.

Geographical Expansion

With the signing of the Lomé Convention, the EC has expanded its special aid relationship with the 19 African and Malagasy states of the Yaoundé Convention to 21 Commonwealth states and six other African countries. The Lomé Convention also enables others to join, subject to the approval of the EC-ACP states. Although the original 46 ACP states comprise about half the U.N.'s Third World members, they form the "smaller half" by far and contain only about 14 percent of the Third World's population.[7] It should be noted, though, that 24 of these countries are among the world's least developed.

Since the beginning of the EC, aid lobbies in member states have advocated expansion of Europe's aid to other than associated developing countries. These advocates gained some formal ground at the Paris summit of 1972. The Paris Communiqué removed the legal and political barriers against expansion and thereby decided the issue between regionalists and globalists in favor of the latter— at least in principle.

In practice, the globalists have not yet made much headway. When Britain expressed its desire to split aid 50-50 inside and outside the association, and establish a new EC fund for non-asso-

7. Including OPEC members, but excluding the less-developed centrally planned economies.

ciable states, it met strong opposition. The globalists succeeded in 1974, however, in making the EC take the initiative for the U.N. Emergency Operation for the countries most severely affected by the oil and commodity crisis of 1973-74. Commitments by the Community plus those of individual member states reached $723 million by the end of 1975. As the lion's share goes to India and Bangladesh, a clear gesture has been made towards non-associated states. In the past two years, non-associated countries have received a considerable share of total EC aid: 32 percent in 1973 and 36 percent in 1974. This is due to the global nature of the food and emergency aid programs. It has to be seen, however, whether the EC will keep up in the future the effort of 1974 and replace part of the food and emergency assistance with long-term development finance for non-associated countries.[8]

For the time being, the EC aid policy seems to maintain the established geographical priorities, which are, in descending order: (1) associated African, Caribbean and Pacific states; (2) Mediterranean states; (3) South Asia; and (4) other developing nations.

In the Mediterranean, Greece and Turkey have received EIB loans in the past. Greece has requested the EC to provide a large amount of new financial aid and envisages complete membership of the EC. New association agreements have been concluded with the Maghreb[9] countries under which the EC will make available 339 million u/a in financial assistance. The Commission has also opened negotiations for agreements on economic cooperation and possible financial assistance with the Machrek[10] countries. Several countries in the Middle East, Asia, and Latin America have concluded trade agreements with the Community, but the Community does not provide them with long-term development finance.

Harmonization of National Programs

Harmonization of national aid programs is a declared objective of the European Community.[11] Not much has yet been achieved in

8. During the renegotiations for British membership, it was accepted in principle that the Community would provide substantial aid to non-associated countries. The Commission followed this up by proposing in 1975 a program for food aid, financial and technical assistance, and emergency relief for non-associated (mostly Asian) countries for the period 1976-1980.

9. Algeria, Morocco and Tunisia.

10. Egypt, Lebanon, Syria and Jordan.

11. Council Resolution dd. July 16, 1974.

117

this respect. The common stance taken during the 1975 IMF/World Bank meetings and in the 7th Special U.N. Session is regarded by many as the exception rather than the rule.

In the past, the European Commission has launched several initiatives for coordinating member states' aid programs, although the Treaty of Rome did not grant explicit authority for this. As most member states regard development cooperation with the Third World as an element of foreign policy and not as a separate sector of external relations, themes of "high politics" predominate. This has forced the Commission to concentrate on the technical and "low"-political side. Generally, the Commission has selected for joint action only non-controversial subjects. Consequently, the EC aid program has settled at the level of a common denominator and has taken the shape of a supplementary program which is not closely related to most member states' aid programs. The Commission's efforts to have at least some regular meetings among EC aid organizations have not been unsuccessful, but these meetings have generally remained information exchanges. Coordination of activities has been achieved for individual projects but not for general lending programs.

As in so many other policy sectors, integration is, in theory, very desirable. Close harmonization of national policies, through the Council of Ministers, with the Commission active as policy planner and mediator would promote the following:

a. Increased European leverage over international development cooperation, which would emphasize the European point of view and could encourage other donor states to take joint international action.

b. Meeting the expectations of those developing countries which look to a new Europe as an alternative to the established Powers.

c. Elimination of confusion in developing countries which have to deal presently with eight European entities (the seven DAC donors, plus the Brussels administration).

d. Integration of aid policies with commercial, agricultural, industrial, and other policies that are already determined on a European scale but do not yet reflect external development goals adequately.

e. Improved availability of aid to developing nations by (a) pooling technical assistance, (b) untying bilateral aid at least among the Nine, (c) coordinating the lending programs to individual recipients, (d) bringing new approaches from fellow-donor states into existing national development programs, and (e) mutual encouragement of member states to new initiatives and larger programs.

f. Establishing the necessary joint program size for effective action against the toughest development problems, especially in the food-deficit areas of the world.

In addition to these five factors which are based on external needs, there is an internal motive which gives impetus to harmonization—the perception in Europe and the U.S. that the Nine should integrate their foreign policies. [12] Foreign policy cooperation is a declared European aim, and aid harmonization can provide a relatively powerful stimulus to that purpose. Concertation would reinforce Europe's external identity and promote the habit of joint action on matters which are not as sensitive as military security, but will certainly increase in importance. As such, development aid harmonization would help to develop Europe itself.

The Federal Republic of Germany believed so strongly in the benefits of coordinating and eventually merging the national aid programs that it made in 1976 such "communitization" a precondition for its approval of new aid commitments, such as a program for nations other than those covered by the Lomé Convention. Whether this precondition will contribute to "communitization", or rather cause stagnation in Brussels' aid activities remains to be seen.

12. The validity of this perception is outside the scope of this chapter, and is essentially a political judgment.

Chapter 7

AGRICULTURAL COOPERATION AND THE LOMÉ CONVENTION

by *Theodor J. Dams*

In the preceding chapters, we focused attention on the interpretation and significance of the four most important titles of the Lomé Convention, separately.

In this chapter, I intend to deal with an area of cooperation—agricultural cooperation—which is affected by a variety of provisions throughout the titles of the Convention.

As annex I shows, 16 of the 46 ACP countries have a predominantly agricultural structure of economy with a low exportable surplus. Twenty-seven ACP countries heavily rely for their GNP on the export of agricultural commodities.

This analysis therefore tends to approach agricultural cooperation as an integral part of economic development as a whole. More specifically, it departs from the following four general considerations.

(1) The nine member countries of the European Community are supposed to develop into an economic unit; this implies that the Community should pursue integrated and coordinated economic and monetary policies and should face third countries with one voice.—Anyone who analyses the degree of integration within the Common Market can only come to the conclusion that this goal is far from being realized, especially since 1969 (revaluation of the exchange rates with the deterioration of the common agricultural market) and above all since the fall of 1973 (oil-price increases and their results on the balance of payments in the respective countries).

(2) The Common Agricultural Policy of the EC has made a substantial contribution to the internal integration process of the Community, as well as to GATT-decisions towards a more liberal international trade; at the same time the Common Agricultural Policy has been a heavy burden with regard to the measures pursued to protect domestic agriculture.

(3) The Lomé Convention is essentially *one* aspect of three activities of the European Community:

120

(a) The Lomé Convention is a policy of *regional* cooperation with developing countries; (b) there is a *global* policy of the Community towards all developing countries (general system of preferences, food aid, UN-special funds, etc.); (c) the harmonization and coordination of the national development policies of member countries of the European Community is another task.—The agricultural sector is touched upon in *all* three areas mentioned above; an analysis confined to the Lomé Convention would therefore result in an incomplete coverage of the Common Agricultural Policies. Furthermore, it must be taken into consideration that the solutions in the agricultural sector of the Lomé Convention could give new incentives toward future international negotiations, and toward a new orientation of the project and program approaches financed by Official Development Aid (ODA). In consideration of these facts, it therefore seems necessary that the three approaches of the European Community mentioned above should be treated in this chapter.

(4) Agriculture in the Lomé Convention cannot be related solely to the Common Agricultural Policy of the European Community; the Convention opens new roads for the development of agriculture in the ACP-countries and for negotiations in the broader framework of the United Nations.

Development of least developed countries

With the increase of oil prices (Fall 1973) and the severe food shortages (since 1972) on the world market, the situation of some developing countries has become precarious.

In Article 48, 24 countries are listed as "least developed countries" or as landlocked or island ACP States. Although the listing procedure of the Convention differs from that of the UN one finds 16 ACP countries on the United Nations list of "least developed countries". Since a low per capita income is nearly always to be associated with a predominantly agricultural structure of the economy, the provisions of the Lomé Convention with respect to agriculture are therefore of particular interest to a world-wide policy of economic development. Among them, we could mention the safeguarding of export earnings from agricultural commodities; and the promotion of agriculture with special consideration of the social-economic relationships (the pre-conditions for the agricultural development and the consequences for the adjustment process of agriculture in relation to the growth of economy as a whole).

Moreover, in some years crop failures in several ACP-countries have caused food shortages. In these cases, in the framework of the food-aid program of the European Communities, some ACP-countries have received a relative priority in the deliveries. The food aid of the EC will continue, as long as these countries are not in a position to feed a growing population from their own agricultural resources. Empirical analysis has shown that in a large portion of the ACP-countries the rate of growth of the population is higher than that of their agricultural production, a fact which in the last decades has led to a lower degree of self-sufficiency in food (table 5).

The two-pronged approach of the Lomé Convention (development of the agriculture of the ACP-countries and guaranteeing agricultural export earnings) is entirely correct from the viewpoint of agricultural policy. But, an important prerequisite is a consistent development planning of agriculture in these ACP-countries, whereby the diversification of the production structure with the help of stabilizing the export earnings from agricultural exports can be achieved.

Agricultural trade

With regard to entry of agricultural products from ACP countries in the Common Market, article 2 (2) of the Convention provides for only limited import facilities.

So, for example, all the products in Annex II and all other products covered by an agricultural market organization will only receive more favoured treatment in comparison with the same imports originating from third countries. The priority of domestic production remains guaranteed through the market organization of the Common Agricultural Policy; therefore, the Lomé Convention will generally not affect the market organization of the Common Agricultural Policy. In the case of changes of the Common Agricultural Policy in the direction of an increased protectionism, this would lead to a further limitation of agricultural exports concerned from the ACP-countries to the EC. In other words, the protectionist character of the Common Agricultural Policy of the EC also applies to imports from the ACP-countries. Measured in relation to the total agricultural exports of the ACP-countries, the percentage of exports to the Common Market is very small; estimates leave it at under 10%, although the possibility of increasing it is given. In relation to the total ACP-exports to the EC, the percentage of agricultural products affected by common market regulations (excluding sugar) is estimated at 4-6%,[1] and at 16-18% if sugar is included.

It should also be kept in mind that EC-imports from ACP-countries make up only 5% of total EC-imports. In quantitative terms, only a small volume of the agricultural products, covered by common agricultural market organizations, are thus subject to import restrictions.

The problem of sugar imports from ACP-countries was solved only at the end of the negotiations.[2] The conflict between the common market organization for sugar in the EC, where the sugar-beet growers enjoy substantial protection, and the interests of the ACP-countries, where the export of cane sugar is often the only source of foreign exchange, is clear. Only four weeks before the end of the negotiations the Jamaican Minister of Commerce, P.J. Patterson, complained bitterly about the attempts of some member countries of the EC to uphold their opinion that "Europe of the Nine" could produce sufficient sugar for its own needs by growing sugar-beets.—The solution to this question was a key point in the negotiations as a whole. P.J. Patterson remarked: "We can look upon the sugar question as a test of the sincerity of the European Community..., we will stand as a group against any attempt to divide the ACP-countries by the handling of this question".—The central issues of the negotiations regarding sugar were the fixing of both import quantities and prices.

The outcome of the negotiations—as laid down in protocol nr. 3 to the Convention—can be summarized as follows.

a) The Community "undertakes for an indefinite period to purchase ... specific quantities of cane sugar...".[3] The Convention is valid for an indefinite period; no changes may enter into force until a period of five years has elapsed from the date on which the Convention enters into force, namely 1 March 1980 (Protocol No. 3 on ACP sugar, Article 2).

b) The agreed export quantities and guaranteed prices still apply in the event of disequilibria in the common sugar market of the EC. Accordingly, there are no "preventive measures" to limit ACP

---

1. Compare chapter 2, supra p. 39 footnote 24
2. Compare chapter 2, supra p. 49.
3. The quantities agreed upon amount—according to article 3 of the Protocol—to 1,2215 mill. tons annually for the next five years. They are 13% less than demanded by the ACP countries.

imports to EC countries should there be excess supply on the EC market. This means that the EC must take into consideration sugar supplies originating from ACP countries when planning its stabilization purchases. By providing for fixed delivery quantities and the same prices, the common agricultural policy has the effect of guaranteeing the fixed rates of incomes both to farmers in the ACP countries and the EC.

c) The export price of sugar is determined according to the intervention price fixed annually by the Council of Ministers of the European Community. In other words, a price determined by the EC along political lines, adjusted for rates of inflation determines the export earnings of the ACP countries from the export of sugar to the EC.

The protocol has thus established a hitherto unknown link between EC agricultural protection and the export earnings derived from sugar exports of the ACP countries. It provides the first important example of an indexing of the returns received by developing countries from their exports according to the internal market price of these goods prevailing in the EC. The protocol merits particular consideration, because such a policy of indexing has been a pressing issue of the developing countries for quite some time.

The extent to which the ACP countries can deliver the export quantities agreed upon in the long run is difficult to determine. In any case, the export volume for the first half of 1975 was placed at only half of the quantity allowed according to the protocol (a delivery period of four months would mean the export of 75% of the half-year quota listed in the Protocol, or, the equivalent of 309,800 tons of white sugar).

As of 30 June 1975, the equivalent of 331,865 tons of white sugar were delivered to the EC. The share of exports to the EC as percentage of total domestic production varies considerably among ACP countries. For example, in Mauritius it is 90%; in the Caribbean countries, the annual share fluctuates appreciably due to climatic conditions. The export potential of Uganda, Kenya and Tanzania is presently unknown as they have not exported sugar (although they were signatories of the Commonwealth Sugar Agreement). Even detailed statistical studies hardly present well-founded analyses of the export potential of sugar. Another critical problem must be mentioned: In the event that excessive supply prevails on the EC market, it will be necessary to re-export the sugar originating from ACP countries. In this case, the higher earnings of the ACP countries derived from sugar exports would remain unchanged; these "re-exports", however, would increase the supply of sugar on the world market, and in turn lead to a lower world market price. Such an effect would possibly mean lower returns from sugar exports for developing countries not signatory to the Convention.

In the crop-year 1975-76, the sugar harvest in the EC was lower than normal. The ACP countries thus did not encounter difficulties in exporting sugar to the EC. The situation will be quite different in "normal" crop-years, however; on average the EC produces the equivalent of 11.0-11.1 million tons of white sugar from its own harvests, and the ACP countries an additional 1.22 million tons. Assuming an annual consumption of the equivalent of 10.0-10.1 million tons of white sugar (excluding possibilities of increasing consumption), 2.22-2.32 million tons would have to be re-exported by the EC countries. In this connection the question may be advanced, if it were not more practical for the ACP countries to supply the world market directly—yet maintaining the same price guarantees. The proposals put forth by the EC Commission to include sugar by increasing the Community's food aid programs merit particular consideration in the light of the preceding arguments, although the quantities envisioned would not result in an appreciable relief of the market (proposal of 6 March 1974: Maximum limit of 40,000 tons during the period 1974/75-1976/77).

Stabilizing the export revenues

Since UNCTAD III (and, of course, since Yaoundé I and II) the question of increased participation of underdeveloped countries in world trade has been an issue of intense discussion. The Lomé Convention is, as it were, the intermediate link between several world-wide oriented Conferences.—For a limited number of developing countries this Convention represents an attempt to organize the relationship between "trade and aid" preeminently from the aspect of international trade. The discussion includes both the quantities to be exported, as well as the revenues. The "one-sided free trade area" with its provision to waiver the determination of originating products with the ACP is an attempt to increase the countries export potential. In addition, the stabilization of the export revenues is considered a necessary (but not sufficient) requirement for economic growth in the ACP. "Stabex" is a new orientation of development policy, where the instruments of trade policy find new meanings especially for those countries whose economic structures are primarily based on agriculture.[4]

The original intention of the ACP countries to compensate possible reductions in export revenues through the indexing of export and import prices was not realized (with reference to increased inflation, dangers of over-production etc.); instead of stabilizing the respective product prices, the compensation-effect is in fact one of offsetting the losses in foreign trade when certain limits are exceeded and the commodity has a certain share of total exports.

Financial aid provided by the EC

The European Community grants financial aid with the objective of "eliminating structural imbalances in the various sectors of the ACP States' economies".[5] These measures are aimed at contributing towards the economic and social development (Art. 40 (1)), in particular by improving the living conditions of the population. In fact, several modern aspects of development policy, particularly in the fields of agricultural and rural development, have been realized in the financing of projects and programs.

At this point it appears appropriate to discuss some of the new policies for the promotion of agriculture that were presented by the World Bank and at the World Food Conference (Nov. 1974), and have since been endorsed by the developing countries and discussed during the negotiating of the Lomé Convention.

Due to a variety of obstacles and difficulties agriculture in some of the developing countries does not reach the production targets set by national planning authorities and international institutions. Among them is the insufficient participation of the population involved in "easier, well-formulated projects"; in the first period, the "most dynamic farmers have been mobilized and it will take much longer to mobilize the others, especially the smaller and weaker farmers" (World Food Conference 1974).

Therefore, at the World Bank Conference in Autumn 1973 in Nairobi/Kenya, a new target was fixed: Whereas during the past decade the agricultural production of small farmholders increased by only 2.5 percent per year, between 1985 and the end of the century it is to reach 5 percent annually. This requires *financial* and *organizational* measures as well as *institutional pre-conditions.*

The World Food Conference held in Rome in 1974, docu-

4. Compare chapter 4, supra.
5. Compare chapter 6, supra.

mented the following: The slow growth of agricultural production in several developing countries, especially since 1972 (and partly even its absolute decrease), is also attributable to the fact that many *small* farmers are not able to increase production without their accruing "social and institutional changes in the organization of rural communities". In this connection, "the conference calls on governments to bring about appropriate progressive agrarian reforms ... and other institutional improvements in rural areas aimed at ... organizing and activating the rural population ... for participation in integrated rural development and at eliminating exploitative patterns of land tenure, credit and marketing systems where they still prevail..." (from Resolution II. para. 1).

The targets *set for* the Second Development Decade (1971-80) and the results during the first half demonstrate an urgent need for new strategies in this field of agricultural policy. They bring me to the following critical reflections:

a) Success in agricultural development depends mainly on the motivation and mobilization of the masses of the rural population.

b) The innovation process can only be initiated if a number of political, social, and economic pre-conditions are met.

c) The necessary participation of the rural population requires a new "Institution-building" process which must be supported by the people concerned.

d) Even if economic objectives in agriculture are reached, the planning process must still take into account the social consequences of these results. "Socio-economic development" is, indeed, more than "economic growth".

e) Unemployment and underemployment have to be reduced in rural areas as they constitute constraints for a better allocation of production factors in agriculture. Therefore, it is necessary to define the leading economic sector of the development process.

In their implications for a strategy of agricultural development policy these reflections show the need of *integrated rural development projects* in which the economic, sociological, social and political problems are taken into consideration.

Considering the fact that (according to data from the World Bank) two-fifths of the population in developing countries classified as the poorest in the income distribution are not affected by the official development aid (ODA), such rural projects are a means both of increasing agricultural production and of improving the distribution of incomes.

In view of this discussion, the importance of Article 46 of the Lomé Convention for the policy measures with respect to the development of agriculture and rural areas becomes evident: "1. The financing of projects and programmes comprises the means required for their execution, such as capital investment in the fields of rural development ... schemes to improve the structure of agricultural production ... micro-projects for grassroots development, in particular in rural areas..." The use of the concept "grassroots development" here speaks for itself!

Together with the provision in art. 48 that: "In the implementation of financial and technical cooperation, special attention shall be paid to the needs of the least developed ACP States", a double concentration thus appears possible: on the least developed countries and on the poorest parts of their populations.

This new orientation constitutes progress, provided two conditions are met:

a) The security of integrated planning, so that agriculture can contribute its full share toward the growth of the economy as a whole and the improvement of living conditions.

b) The participation of so-called non-governmental organizations (Article 49, 2, b and Protocol No. 2, Article 14 ff.), so that Producers' cooperatives can initiate and undertake projects.

"Development from below" is institutionally assured through the "decision from above" taken at the Lomé Convention. This strategy still has to be developed on the national level by a number of ACP countries. In view of this analysis, the Lomé Convention may be regarded as a solid formulation for the promotion of agriculture and the development of the rural areas in the least-developed ACP countries.

Food Aid

From 1968 to 1974, the European Community and member states have granted food aid—to an amount of approximately 1 billion units of account—to developing countries stricken by natural disasters or most severely affected by food shortages.

In the case of grains, the Community had subscribed, during the Kennedy-Round negotiations, to the Food Aid Convention within the framework of the International Grains Agreement renewed in 1971. The total amount of food aid for grains increased from 1,035,000 tons in 1969 to 1,278,000 tons in 1975. The share of the Community rose from 30-50% in the same period, the remainder being provided bilaterally by member states.

In the case of milk products (skimmed milk and butter oil) decisions were taken unilaterally by the Council of Ministers on proposal of the Commission in July 1968 and April 1969. Such aid has been provided exclusively by the Community.

At these times, food aid was geared towards the development of CAP and the disposal of agricultural surpluses, rather than towards solidarity.

In an effort to show EC responsibilities towards the needy countries, during the food crisis, the Commission—in March 1974—submitted a three year indicative program for a common food aid policy to the Council of Ministers.

Although the Council of Ministers has so far restricted itself to the annual fixation of schedules for implementing food aid programs, the concept of forward planning has been adopted by the 1974 World Food Conference in Rome. According to operative paragraph 2 of Resolution XVIII, the Conference:

> "Recommends that all donor countries accept and implement the concept of forward planning of food aid, make all efforts to provide commodities and/or financial assistance that will ensure in physical terms at least 10 million tons of grains as food aid a year, starting from 1975, and also to provide adequate quantities of other food commodities".

According to the EC Commission, the following points are important for the concept of food aid:
1) Food aid is a way of showing the international responsibility of the Community ("own identity and personality of the Community").
2) Food aid is an important instrument for cooperation between the Community and non-associated countries and a form of compensation for the countries not included in the Lomé Convention! (44% of the food aid is for Southeast Asia, 16% for Africa).
3) Notwithstanding the efforts of international organizations, the EC should develop and carry out "its own policy under its own rules" for food aid.
4) The Community has the technical means at its disposal to maintain a certain elasticity in its production of agricultural commodities according to the needs of the developing countries.

With respect to the Commission's concept of planned production of food aid, the following critical remarks could be forwarded.
1) Food aid cannot serve as a geographical "counterbalance" to the regional concept of cooperation with the ACP countries.
2) The "planned production of agricultural surpluses" can set dangerous precedent for the formulation of a common agricultural

policy. Food aid should be separated from the agricultural policy of the European Community, and its members. Financial aid destined for the purchase of food stuffs should be granted directly to the countries, which in turn would buy the necessary commodities at prices prevailing on the world market (perhaps from other developing countries with surpluses).

3) Integrated planning in the recipient countries is a prerequisite for the efficient application of food aid; in other words, food aid should be used in such a manner that it provides the greatest possible contribution to economic growth (development of infrastructure, promotion of own agricultural production etc.). It is therefore necessary to grant *additional* aid in the form of transfers of capital and know-how.

4) A "planned increase in production" solely for the purpose of food aid would be very expensive. In view of the fact that the financial transfers of the industrialized countries are dropping in real terms (probably in the future—as in the case of the Federal Republic of Germany—also in nominal terms), it only seems appropriate that these financial measures be used for the promotion of agriculture in developing countries.

The issue of food aid demonstrates the long-range conflict between the agricultural policies of the industrialized countries and the interests of the developing ones.

Harmonizing and coordinating national development policies

The Lomé Convention only embodies a part of the development-cooperation policies of the Communities and their member states. Another part results from the obligations under articles 110-116 of the EEC Treaty with respect to a common commercial policy.

Otherwise the EC member states and ACP countries are free to take their own decisions regarding development projects and programs on a bilateral level. Attempts to coordinate the development policies of the individual EC countries have proven to be very difficult, because of the vast differences in orientation.

The EC has not even been able to coordinate the respective policies regarding regional and agricultural structures within the Common Market, and even greater difficulties are to be expected in coordinating the development policies of the various countries.

It would be worth-while, however, especially with regard to agricultural projects, to attempt a so-called "joint aid programming". Such programming would involve a concentrated and co-ordinated use of development aid without requiring the individual countries to give up their geographical distribution of aid. In any case, the integrated agricultural and rural planning could thereby become much more efficient.

The recommendation has been made to begin with "joint aid programming" in the ACP countries with such a procedure. Accordingly, a program of aid from the Community should be made for each ACP State for the duration of the Convention. The harmonization of the Community aid and the individual national aid programs should begin already with the finding and planning of the projects, and without limiting the authority of the ACP States.

Thus, it is a most important objective of the EC to coordinate the development policies of its member countries, particularly in the agrarian sector.

Concluding remarks

It is hard to estimate the importance of the Lomé Convention for the agricultural sector. Considerable progress has been achieved in the areas of trade policy and the financing of projects in agriculture—particularly when compared with the former Conventions negotiated with associating countries.

The Lomé Convention has relatively little influence on the Community's common agricultural policy. This policy is based on Articles 39 and 40 of the EEC Treaty and concentrates on maintaining the incomes of the European producers. It may therefore reasonably be expected that noticeable changes in this area will not take place. The share of the agricultural exports (excluding sugar) from ACP countries is relatively small when compared with these countries' total volume of exports to the EC. It is reasonable to expect that the returns from international trade will increase to the benefit of the ACP countries when they themselves first process the tropical agricultural produce and then export the finished products to the EC. The relaxation of the rules with respect to the concept of "originating products" can promote a "division of labor" among these countries. Just how far this would initiate a stronger adaptation process of the Community's agro-allied processing industries remains to be studied. In any case, the possibilities in this area are much greater than in the more limited one of agricultural market organization. The question at this point is above all, whether or not the ACP countries are in a position to increase production on a sustained basis; this applies especially to sugar. The new situation provided for in the Lomé Convention will only become reality when the new potential of these countries' increased participation in international trade is combined with a consistent policy of promotion of agricultural projects, which in turn must effect changes in the production structure of the EC countries. The Lomé Convention provides the possibility of taking into account these new points of development policy, albeit in modest proportions.

Chapter 8

THE LOMÉ CONVENTION AND THIRD COUNTRIES:
AS SEEN BY OUTSIDERS

According to the preamble of the Lomé Convention, Contracting Parties are *"Resolved* to establish a new model for relations between developed and developing States, compatible with the aspirations of the international community towards a more just and more balanced economic order".

In the Lomé Convention—both during negotiations and in the articles agreed upon—more attention has been given to the aspirations of the international community than in the two previous Yaoundé Conventions. The enlarged European Community showed more openness to the world and the ACP countries more solidarity among themselves and with the non-ACP developing countries, than the community of the six and the AASM countries had shown on previous occasions.

In this chapter, the Convention will be evaluated by observers from three representative third countries: the United States—the major trade-partner of the EC from the "first world"; India—a leading Asian state having important relations with the EC, from the "third world"; and Hungary, a member of CMEA, belonging to the "second world" which for historical and ideological reasons has not been prominent in development cooperation.

AN AMERICAN POINT OF VIEW

by *I. William Zartman*

It is difficult to present *an* American point of view about something like the Lomé Convention without someone mistaking it for an attempt to present *the* American point of view. But it is also difficult for an academic who has epistemological and ideological doubts about the sociology of knowledge to present a point of view that has something distinguishably American about it; at best it is a point of view of an outsider, a non-participant in the Convention and a private citizen at that.

There are two ways in which a phenomenon such as the Lomé Convention can be viewed. One is the point of view of the philosopher or art connaisseur, consisting of a number of judgments on the various provisions of the agreement. Unless the judge is partial to one side, the best marks will be given to those provisions which give the most to both sides, the Nash solution of the bargaining problem.[1] But "most" can have an infinite number of referents. A state of affairs can be judged according to some future ideal; yet if this alone is the basis of comparison, the whole imperfect world will be found wanting. It can also be understood an outcome of certain past realities; yet in this light alone, everything becomes inevitable because everything has a past cause. Neither point of view gives a very understanding basis for evaluation. Phenomena such as the Lomé Convention are moments in an on-going process, not simply objects or situations, to be judged like a picture, as good or bad. Although this may appear rather abstract and evident, there are still a number of observers of the Convention, as of its predecessors signed at Yaoundé, who subject it to a static judgment, usually negative, indicating that the Convention does not give "enough" or that it is part of a fixed relation of dominance between one party and the other.

The other way to evaluate the Lomé Convention is from the point of view of the social scientist or historian, looking at the event as a moment in an on-going historical process that began earlier and continues afterward. Three such contexts are available: one relating to North-South economic relations, another to Eur-

---

1. See I. William Zartman, *The 50% Solution* (New York: Doubleday Anchor, 1976), pp. 13, 25.

African political relations, and the third to inter-African political relations.

The economic context for evaluating the Lomé Convention appears to be closest to the official American point of view, although an exact classification is difficult to make since the US Government has been rather discreet on the issue. Officially, the American position favors free trade in principle and welcomes developments in line with that position. Thus, the Lomé Convention can be interpreted as a way-station on the path from the highly preferential arrangements of the colonial system to a trading world open to the free and unhindered market forces of supply and demand. The Rome and Yaoundé predecessors of the Convention had established free trade areas between the individual Associates and the EEC, and the Arusha Convention provided reciprocal preferential treatment for the European and East African Communities. Lomé eliminates this preferential notion by reducing the EEC to most-favored-nation status, a derogation of the free trade notion, to be sure, but at least a substitution of equal status for preferential status.

It has been clear enough in general American policy statements that the US is pleased at the removal of reverse preferences. To some extent this is a position of self interest. The United States was able to penetrate the markets of its Southern trading partner, Latin America, without the benefit of preferential tariff arrangements because of its general economic strength, and it can only benefit from a chance to compete on equal terms for the African market. It is probably quite unlikely that such competition make very rapid inroads into those countries whose trade is heavily dominated by Europe, notably some of the former French and a few of the former British colonies, since trading habits can be stronger than economic laws. In other countries, however, and frequently the most attractive ones, the American trade share has already increased and can be expected to increase even more under competitive conditions. But the US position is not only one of interest; it is also grounded on a belief that increased competition provides better conditions of choice and price, and therefore assures the best goods at the lowest cost for developing countries, as well as others.

In the other direction, the Lomé Convention maintains the free trade conditions of its predecessors by guaranteeing free access for ACP goods to European markets. This provision too may be regarded as part of a move toward free trade, not via most-favored-nation treatment, but through a generalized system of preferences

(GSP) for developing countries' goods. Nothing in the Convention prevents the EEC from extending this same treatment to the rest of the developing countries, after consultation with the ACP countries.

The third major provision of the Convention, the Export Stabilization arrangement, can also be viewed as a step in a general evolution, both compatible and contradictory with American policy. STABEX also represents a point in a transition, from reliance on free market mechanisms for given levels of income for raw materials to reliance on a generalized systems of cushions and guarantees to maintain those levels. The latter is also a part of American policy, for in his 1 September 1975 speech Secretary Kissinger built on the STABEX notion to propose such a Development Security System out of the IMF. Nonetheless, such provisions are scarcely part of a system of free trade, which would rely on market forces alone.

Thus, within the context of three elements of economic evolution, Lomé can be considered quite literally a step in the right direction and, furthermore, just about the maximum step that is compatible with its nature as a continent-to-continent agreement. The Lomé Convention has grown out of a series of agreements covering first 18 and then 21 or 22 African members, joined to 6 Europeans; it now covers all 37 independent Black African states at the time of signing, is open to other Africans as they become independent, and ties them to 9 Europeans; to these 37 are joined 9 other members from outside either continent. Any further extension of membership would make the agreement a semi-global rather than a continent-to-continent one. In general, this evolution, both in economic terms and, more implicitly, in membership, appears to be viewed favorably by American policy.

A second evolutionary *context* in which to view the Lomé Convention concerns *inter-African relations*. Since the wave of independence has spread across the continent, Africa has been engaged in a number of important debates over the nature of its political relations. On the continental level, the debate was between those who sought a rigorous ideopolitical definition of Africanity to include codes of foreign policy conduct and a tight institutional framework, and those who regarded membership in Africa to be a geopolitical matter with freedom of interpretation and implementation left to the members. On the intercontinental level, the debate was between those who sought rapid diversification of relations among the developed world and those who sought to combine newly-won sovereignty with the benefits of some spe-

136

cial relationship with the former metropole. Generally if not exclusively, former British colonies tended to be on the first side of both debates, while former French colonies tended to be on the second, adding a problem of communication to the differences of opinion.

The continental debate was resolved initially by the creation of the Organization of African Unity (OAU), which provided an institutional framework and a list of principles but left their interpretation and implementation to the member states. The same year, in 1963, moves were made to resolve the intercontinental debate, when major English-speaking African states, impressed with the absence of political constraints in the Yaoundé Convention signed that year, opened the first step in negotiations with the EEC. What for the French states was post-colonial continuity was of course diversification for the English states. Negotiations with East Africa broke down in 1965, and implementation of the Lagos Agreement with Nigeria broke down upon signature in 1966, leaving Nigeria more adamant than ever against European association. But after East Africa negotiations recommenced and reached agreement, in 1968, and Britain met EEC authorization to recommence its negotiations the following year, the picture began to change.

Thus, an all-African cooperation agreement with Europe lies at the crossroads of trends in European and African relations in the 1960s and 1970s. Schematically, Britain's move to Europe started Commonwealth Africans moving toward the position of non-Commonwealth Africans, where they met the Yaoundé Associates moving in the other direction, away from past close ties with the members of the EEC. A contractual relationship that is something less than Association is the result. The Africans saw that Europe was no longer interested in separate African groups (since, in the worst interpretation, division no longer led to rule), so the Associates no longer had an incentive to maintain separate status; put otherwise, Europe was no longer interested in granting special privileges to a few when for a little bit more they could have better relations with the many. Yet it is interested in some special attention to Africans—few or many—in part because European states still consider such relations a family affair, with the former colonies viewed as students or apprentices now off on their own, and in part because Europe is dependent on Africa for its supplies of copper, coffee, cocoa, and uranium, among others.

One other consideration placed Lomé at the crossroads of these trends: just as the Europeans had an interest in including all Africa in a broad agreement, so the former Associates had a special interest in winning the potentially most important state in Africa located squarely in their midst—Nigeria—away from a position of principled hostility to a major element in their foreign policy. Nigeria, in turn, has tended to see a role for itself as a leader of the surrounding states of West and Equatorial Africa, replacing with greater legitimacy the leadership which it perceives to have been previously exercized in the area by the metropole. The price of Nigerian adherence to the pro-European postition was to let it write its own terms, resulting in the 8-point Abidjan Declaration ratified by the OAU in 1973 and used as the basis for negotiating the Lomé Convention.

Thus, in this second context, of inter-African political relations, the Lomé Convention is the clear result of a general trend of coordination and harmonization of African positions, of nearly as great importance as the previous landmark in the same trend, the OAU itself. The point cannot be made too strongly: ever since the beginning of the first Yaoundé Convention, Europeans have looked to a single Eur-African agreement that would break through the colonial barriers between English- and French-speaking countries; ever since the late 1950s, when a visiting mission from newly independent Guinea found itself looked down upon by ever-so-slightly less newly-independent (but British colonized) Ghanaians and in turn scorned the pretentions at independence of a country that still had pictures of the British Queen (as Commonwealth head) on the walls, there has been a strong barrier to effective communication and cooperation between the two ex-colonial groups. This condition has been broken (even if not yet totally destroyed) by the single stand, joint negotiations, and common accord in the Lomé Convention.

The third context in which to evaluate the Convention concerns the *evolution of postcolonial relations*.[2] Here there is much less consensus over interpretation, and the meaning derives from the theoretical perspective from which the facts are understood. Two such perspectives are available. A currently popular one is the dependency approach. It considers that the attainment of political sovereignty masks the reality of continued dependency on world economic structures, and that calculations of power and interest within this relationship explain African underdevelopment. Impa-

2. This argument is developed in I. William Zartman, "Europe and Africa: Decolonization or Dependency?", LIV *Foreign Affairs* 2:325-43 (1976).

tient with the apparently slow progress of African states toward development and the real difficulty of new nations to overcome the growing gap that separates them from the industrial states, dependency analysts believe that the cause for this situation lies in the constraints of international politics and economics, not in the policies and resources of the new nations themselves.

The basic mechanism of these constraints is seen in the ability that international economic and politics predominance gives the industrial states to coopt African leadership into an international social structure that serves the world capitalist economy. By conditioning the upper layer of African society into consumption, reading, vacation, style and other value orientations focussed on Europe, the dominant politico-economic system removes the need for direct intervention and indirect colonial rule. The more the new elite "develop", the more their expectations rise, the more "modern" they become, the more they become "programmed" to look North, think Western, and alienate themselves from their national society locked in its underdevelopment. Since mass development is such a monumental task in the best of conditions, and since it is even more difficult against the wishes and interests of the dominant capitalist structures, these alienated Westernized elites have little difficulty in repressing the spread of development and maintaining themselves in power as a political class, and with them the predominance of their European cooptors.

The other approach can be called the decolonization theory. It considers Eur-Africa (and other North-South) relations to be part of a process of replacing various forms of bilateral metropolitan influence with multilateral relations. In this process, political independence is only the first step and the "last" step of complete independence is probably never attainable—or desirable—in an increasingly interdependent world. Each layer of colonial influence is supported by the others, and as each is removed it uncovers and exposes the next underlying one, leaving it vulnerable, untenable and unnecessary. The specific order of the layers may vary from country to country, depending on local conditions, but the most common pattern is political (sovereignty), military, social (demographic), economic, and cultural. In this pattern, the transfer of sovereignty removes the need and justification for the stationing of metropolitan troops; military evacuation removes the security for settlers and commercial populations; foreign repatriation reduces the support for effective economic operations; and economic diversification brings new cultural influences. Thus, decolonization has its own logic, wherein each step creates pressures for the next and reduces the possibility of counteraction in retreating postcolonial forces.

Even in these summary forms, it is evident that the dependency "theory" is based on a number of sweeping and untenable assumptions, such as the fixed equations between being modernized and thinking Western, or between dependency and underdevelopment, or between motivation and simplistic notions of interest. It is also evident that the approach is as static as the approaches discarded at the beginning of this essay, providing at best a snapshot of events but not taking into account either past change or present possibilities. The strength of the decolonization theory is that it recognizes change and finds an explanation for it in the relationship between successive elements of that change. At the same time, it also provides an ideal type or model against which to compare events, not only in the direction of their evolution from bilateral dominance to multilateral interdependence, but also in the pace at which this evolution takes place, balancing needs and capabilities, providing regular spacing between the removal of various layers, and using each remaining layer of metropolitan presence and influence to build up the capabilities that will replace it.

From the evolutionary point of view of decolonization, therefore, the Lomé Convention is a welcome development. Neither a neocolonial consolidation nor an institutionalization of dependency, it is a natural step in the process that both dilutes and multilateralizes postcolonial ties, while building the capabilities of the ACP states. If the ACP countries did not receive satisfaction on the amount of aid (they never have, in any of the preceding conventions), most of the other eight points of the Abidjan Declaration were met fairly and the provisions for STABEX and the end of reverse preferences were radical departures from the previous agreements. In effect, the Lomé Convention represents a victory, ten years later, of the Dutch and German points of view in the debate over the first Yaoundé Convention. Since the Franco-Belgian point of view prevailed in general in the Yaoundé negotiations, each side has had its turn, and in an order that represents evolutionary progress.

If this sounds as if previous Association conventions were negotiated among the European members rather than between Europe and Africa, that is at least partially accurate. In the absence of verbatim records of the ministerial meetings in Kingston (July 1974) and Brussels (October 1973, February 1974, January 1975) and of the drafting sessions with the Commission in Brussels, it is hard to make a full comparison with negotiations on the earlier

140

Conventions of Association.[3] Nonetheless, a few observations can be offered on changes in the ways outcomes were achieved, to complement the preceding comments on changes in the outcomes themselves.

First, Lomé marked a shift from the characteristic process of Yaoundé wherein Africans posed their problems and Europeans invented the solutions. (This is not to say that the solutions were adequate to the African problems in their broadest sense, but only to identify their source). Already in the Lagos Negotiations of 1964-66, the Nigerians showed a greater control of the agenda than had the Yaoundé Eighteen by bringing up answers to their own problems. Not only did this show experience and initiative, but it also forced the decision to accept or reject on the Europeans. In the Lomé negotiations, this shift in roles continued. The most notable example is Title III on Industrial Cooperation, which was an African answer to African problems. When proposed, it took the Europeans by surprise, was accepted by the Commission before full instructions were available, and then caused some second thoughts among the members. It would be easy to dismiss this difference between the two rounds of negotiations as merely evidence of Nigerian participation, but it is more likely that it also represents a change on power relations, a growth in experience, and an indication of further shifts as decolonization proceeds and European responsibility for Africa diminishes.

Second, Lomé negotiations showed a striking degree of solidarity among the Africans and their partners, despite the threefold increase in their numbers over the Yaoundé negotiations. In previous negotiations, both sides were rather badly divided, but the Europeans turned this to their advantage by negotiating an agreement among themselves and then presenting the result to the Africans with admonitions not to challenge a carefully bargained accord lest it come apart. Rich with this experience, the Africans at Lomé stuck together, both among themselves and with their partners from the Caribbean and the Pacific. On one hand, except for one occasion at the Brussels meetings of July 1973, they refused regional groups or spokesmen for fear that the Europeans would divide and conquer. On the other hand, negotiations were carried on by nine working groups among which the 46 ACP states were divided, so that they were forced to speak for each other and

3. Cf. I. William Zartman, *The Politics of Trade Negotiation Between Africa and the European Economic Community* (Princeton: University Press, 1971) and additional references cited therein.

trust others to speak for them. The Nine were impressed with the solidarity of the ACP states and with their unshakable adherence to the views of the Group of the 77. Such solidarity is certainly a sign of the times; that it is a trend toward a permanent state of affairs would probably be too much to say, for unity of demands must produce unity of rewards if it is to last.

Third, certain characteristics were observed in the use of the means of persuasion during the negotiation of the Association Conventions, but comparable judgments about Lomé must await further data. In previous negotiations, the Africans were generally observed to have made use of nonvolitional statements of contingent gratification and deprivation—predictions and warning—and the Europeans used volitional statements—promise and threat. A shift on the part of the Africans to greater equality in the means of persuasion could only come upon a shift in the sources of power. Signs of such shift are evident but more analysis of the negotiatory exchanges is necessary before conclusions can be drawn.

The Lomé Convention has been examined in three different contexts by an American, with specific reference to offical American policy in the most relevant of the three. In each case, it has been found to be an understandable outgrowth of past events and at the same time a step in a progression that has frequently appeared desirable. But nothing in this world is perfect, and it would be misleading to leave the impression that Lomé is an exception or that even if there is some improvement to be made, nature will take its course. In each case, the general trend of events suggests major areas where efforts are now needed.

In the economic context, although the evolution toward different trading systems is evident, the fact nonetheless remains that even under favorable conditions, Africa has not achieved a major penetration of the European market or improved its terms of trade. (The same thing is evident in the case of investment, where Africa has received an absolute increase from the 1960s to the early 1970s, but a relative decrease in the proportion of world investment). Trade expansion has not been a notable result of the previous conventions and does not appear to be an assured outcome of Lomé. If anything, African economies may be putting more attention to import substitution than export expansion, a point which requires greater consideration and discussion.

In the African political context, Lomé continued the previous conventions' tradition of registering a notable failure to institutionalize inter-African cooperation. There are still individual free-trade-and-most-favored-nation areas between each ACP state and the EEC; despite some stated principles, there appears to be nothing in the Lomé Convention that will contribute to the acceleration of African economic regionalism any more than there was in the Yaoundé Convention (only Arusha made a small contribution to the strengthening of an African region, which in this case needed all the contributions it could get). Studies generally agree that African economic nationalism is a political matter and not an economic advantage.

In the context of decolonization, the next round lies outside the Convention. Aid is one way to increase the flow of resources to the developing world; investment, under the proper conditions, is another. African states need not only to work to increase investment, but also to increase pressure to Africanize the personnel in the firms that are established in their country. Remnents of one layer that are now anachronistic, given the progress in other areas, are the remaining metropolitan military—all French—stationed in a few countries and the new Soviet troops which have nothing to do with the defense needs of their host countries; African states should act in unison to press their colleagues to eliminate these vestiges. Above all, African states need to take advantage of all the possibilities offered by Lomé and all other means to diversify production, replace imports, create trade, bridge national markets, and increase the development that goes with decolonization.

Indeed, in sum, the most positive aspect of the Lomé Convention lies in its trends, away from African status as a European game preserve and on to a position of greater independence and self-reliance, tempered by compensatory asymmetry. But in the end, these two characteristics—self-reliance and compensation—are contradictory and at the final outcome of the trend, the two groups of partners on both sides of the Mediterranean must chose which will predominate. European controls over decisions affecting Africans have been greatly reduced in the Lomé Convention, and thus self-reliance has been increased. But the actual size of the compensation has also been reduced if other elements than total figures are taken into account: effects of inflation on the EDF, percapita EDF allocation, effects of GSP and lowered European tariffs on African trade creation, various restrictions on STABEX. The Lomé provisions are clearly a step in the right direction, and no one who has actually read them could seriously claim that they represent reinforced European regionalism or a reaffirmation of imperialism. It is hard to pretend that Lomé represents too great a European role in Africa; whether the step in the right direction is big enough or not, the trend would indicate that the Lomé Convention (or at most its extension by one term) is likely to be the last of its type, that self-reliance is likely to win out over compensation (if only willy-nilly), and that any new Eur-African relations of a multilateral type are likely to find their form within the global framework that will represent as much of a dilution of Lomé as Lomé did of Yaoundé.

AN INDIAN POINT OF VIEW

by *K.B. Lall*

It is a tribute to the skill and the vision of those who negotiated the Lomé Convention that even those who are not parties to it have not only lent their support but have also welcomed the new concepts and the new tools incorporated in it. They have viewed the Convention as blazing a new trail in the evolving relationship between the developing and the developed world.

For instance, India's Prime Minister, Madame Indira Gandhi, in the course of her address to the Commonwealth Heads of Government assembled at Kingston, from April 29 to May 6, 1975, observed as follows:

"We welcome the decisions of the Lomé Convention where a number of Commonwealth countries' points of view has received some understanding. We would like to regard the Lomé Convention as a precursor to similar arrangements with other regions".

At the same conference, Forbes Burnham, Prime Minister of Guyana, viewed the Lomé Convention as "only a beginning—an outline that had to be filled in and refined by negotiation of further areas of agreements as well as by practice".

While welcoming the Convention, the non-signatory developing countries desired some of its new concepts to be applied over a wider field. Prime Minister Burnham warned that "the 46 ACP countries must not allow themselves to be an elite and thus to become a factor for division" in the developing world. He asked for the new approaches to be "globalised as soon as possible for the benefit of the developing countries and of the international community as a whole".

India's Foreign Minister, Mr. Yashwantrao Chavan, described the Lomé Convention as "a significant development" and shared Prime Minister Burnham's hope that "the Lomé approach must be globalised for the benefit of all developing countries".

Prime Minister Wilson responded by declaring that "I have made clear to our own Parliament that we intend to build on Lomé in respect of Asian countries so powerfully represented at this Conference".

The conclusion reached by the Commonwealth Heads of Government meeting at Kingston is summed up in paragraph 38 of its final Communique. It runs thus:

"Heads of Government welcomed the conclusion of the Lomé Convention drawn up by the European Economic Community and 46 countries of Africa, the Caribbean and the Pacific. They welcomed the increased cooperation within the Convention between Commonwealth and non-Commonwealth countries in these areas. They expressed the hope that the principles underlying the Lomé Convention could usefully contribute to the further development of relations between the EEC and other industrialised countries, on the one hand, and developing countries, including the Asian and other Commonwealth countries, on the other".

It is not possible to comprehend fully either the maturity or the depth of this conclusion except in the context of a conjuncture of historical, political and economic circumstances which made it incumbent on all the parties concerned to evolve new principles of partnership between nations, based on political equality and rooted in the diversity of their economic situation. A full understanding of the context which made it possible for the Lomé Convention to be negotiated and concluded is essential to the faithful implementation of its provisions and to the extension of its principles to the broader relationship between the developing and the developed world.

Let us, first, look at the background of the Lomé Convention. It was preceded by the first Yaoundé Convention which came into effect on June 1, 1964, and the second Convention, which came into effect on January 1, 1971. Protocol 22 annexed to the Treaty of Accession required the enlarged Community to negotiate a wider arrangement embracing 20 Commonwealth countries of Africa, the Caribbean and the Pacific. At the same time, Protocol 23 provided for transitional arrangements in respect of the application of the general tariff preference scheme and a Joint Declaration of Intent was adopted on the development of trade relations with certain Asian countries.

In October 1972, at the Paris Summit, the old Europe, the Europe of the Six, which had evolved an exclusive relationship with 19 countries in Africa, along with its three new partners, emerged as a full-fledged power on the world stage, affirming its right to have "its voice heard in the world's affairs", expressing its determination to make a contribution to international relations "commensurate with its human, material and intellectual re-

146

sources", and proclaiming that its mission is to be "open to the world". The Summit showed Europe to be ready to come to grips with the realities of the Seventies, its internecine struggles cast into the dust bin of history, its colonial heritage thrust into the past, ready to assume, no doubt gradually, its global responsibility as an economic power of great consequence.

At the same time, 46 sovereign States in Africa, the Caribbean and the Pacific, as also a number of independent countries in Asia, stood ready to forge a new relationship with the Nine, transforming earlier bonds, based on domination, into new links based on political equality and wide-ranging co-operation.

In the meanwhile, the developing world as a whole had evolved a common sense of identity, an ineradicable aspiration to unity, and firm foundations of solidarity. It is with some pride as an Indian that I trace the origins of the spirit of identity, unity and solidarity to the Asian Relations Conference convened by our first Prime Minister, Pandit Jawaharlal Nehru, in New Delhi, in March 1947, 5 months before India herself attained political independence.

And yet, there was a tremendous diversity of underdevelopment situations in different countries. Many of them exported only raw materials and some had only one product to export. Some very very poor; the economic structures of others gave hope for the future. Each was keen, however, to build its own future by its own efforts. None was prepared to accept inequality. It was necessary that the external environment must adjust available means to varying needs, under conditions of full partnership amongst equals.

These, then, were the main elements—historical, political and economic—of the conjuncture in which the Lomé Convention came into being. It is interesting to note that the conjuncture of these very elements led the Community to make fresh moves and negotiate new instruments to regulate its relationship with other developing countries.

Of these elements, the political environment was the most dominant. If Europe had not declared its readiness to be open to the world, and had, on the contrary, striven to develop an exclusive relationship, the ACP States might have been apprehensive of diminution of their sovereignty. Equally, if the Third World had not developed its sense of solidarity, long before the conclusion of the Lomé Convention and other instruments, it would not have been easy for the rest of the developing world to lend its support to measures designed to suit the particular needs of the ACP States.

147

The political environment exerted a tremendous influence on the ACP negotiators. You would recall their sustained opposition to any provisions in the Convention which could carry with it the tint of regenerating, in the economic field, a colonial relationship that had died on the political field. This is why the ACP negotiators had set their face against reverse preferences. This is also the reason why the ACP negotiators took every care to preserve the possibility of developing closer economic links with developing countries who were not signatories to the Convention. It is important to notice that, while assuring most-favoured-nation treatment in their imports from the Community, they took care, in Article 7 (2) (b), to exempt from it the "trade or economic relations between ACP States or between one or more ACP States and other developing countries".

I would like to pay my tribute to the ACP negotiators for their perception of the value of closer co-operation amongst developing countries as a whole. It is this perception on their part which has persuaded those developing countries which are not signatories to the Lomé Convention to welcome the privileged relationship between the ACP States and the Community and which will continue to persuade them to lend support to the solution of the problems of ACP States in their relations with the rest of the industrial world.

Cooperation between ACP and non-ACP States is founded in their common interest in forging a more equitable relationship between them, on the one hand and the industrial world, on the other. The successful conclusion of the Lomé Convention must be viewed in this context as a partial advance towards their common goal. It is the joint interest of all the developing countries to defend this advance and to extend and widen it further. Any attempt to take a narrow view or to bar equivalent provision to other developing countries in a similar situation, or to withhold like treatment for like products, will defeat the common purpose.

Fortunately, the declaration made by the Nine at the Paris Summit to be open to the world, the steps taken by the Community in pursuance of the Joint Declaration of Intent, and the thoughts set forth by the Commission in its "Fresco of Community Action" provide a frame for the Community to develop a set of measures appropriate to the needs of other developing countries. The entire developing world, including the ACP States, will be interested in this development.

I recall with pleasure the welcome which the ACP negotiators had given to the attempts made by the Community to overcome some of the trading difficulties of the non-ACP States through an extension of the generalised system of preferences in 1974 and 1975. The keen interest shown by the ACP negotiators in some of the forward-looking provisions of the Commercial Cooperation Agreement between India and the Community, concluded towards the end of 1973, is not without significance. It is not too difficult to detect its impact on some provisions of the Lomé Convention.

It is because of our common interest in the treatment meted out to the developing countries by the industrialised world that all of us follow with such keen interest the improvements, which have been effected in some of the trade agreements that had been concluded by the Community earlier, the progress of negotiations with Maghreb and Machreq countries, the effort to conclude commercial cooperation agreements with other ASEAN countries, and the development of a dialogue with Asian countries and with our friends from Latin America and the Arab world.

You are aware of the various proposals for the organisation of industrial cooperation with non-associated developing countries. Measures of financial cooperation are already at a very advanced stage in the process of decision-making. Unfortunately, a combination of extraneous factors has slowed down the pace, but it is clear that the Community is engaged in the task of concerting its means with a view to deploying at an early date a coherent set of measures in its relations with non-ACP States. The Community and the entire developing world have an equal interest in imparting a fresh impetus to this movement.

The evolution of the Community's relationship with ACP States must proceed in tandem with the evolution of the Community's relationship with the rest of the developing world. The two sets of relationships are not only complementary to each other but also mutually reinforcing.

It is true that concern has been expressed in some quarters about the divisive potential of one or two provisions in the Lomé Convention. I find it difficult to read a divisive intent even in its Article 2 (2) (ii). To my mind, this has no bearing on the operation of the generalised scheme of tariff preferences in favour of developing countries. At any rate, the world community has committed itself, in the Resolution adopted on September 19, 1975, at the Seventh Special Session, to effect the widest possible improvements in this system and, at the same time, to find ways and means of protecting the interests of countries which enjoy special advantages in consideration of their special needs.

In fact, many of the provisions of the Lomé Convention lend

themselves to wider application. Who can, for instance, say that the economic structures of Srilanka or Bangladesh do not call for equivalent provisions being applied to them? Who can urge that non-signatories do not stand in need of protection of their export income? The Community by itself cannot, of course, protect the export income of every developing country. This must be the common responsibility of the entire industrial world. In fact, the problem for some of the poorest countries is wider and deeper. It is not merely their export income but their terms of trade which need both protection and improvement.

There is yet another constructive feature of the Lomé Convention. I have in mind its Title III and Title IV, dealing with industrial cooperation and with technical and financial cooperation. If these are too narrowly interpreted, the provision of technical services and equipment goods may be limited to the resources available with the Nine. A narrow interpretation will tend to increase the expense and limit the advantages for the beneficiary states. There is a variety of social and economic considerations relevant to economic activity in developing countries and which have not been faced in Europe for over a 100 years.

What can be done to make the experience of those developing countries which have faced these problems in the recent past available to the ACP States? I am sure you all know that we in India have lived with these problems and overcome them; and we are ready to share our experience with our friends, signatories of the Lomé Convention.

India already has a major technical and economic cooperation programme, spread over many developing countries. We also have a number of firms of reputed consultants, who have successfully prepared feasibility studies and detailed project reports and have developed the infrastructure and erected factories in many parts of the world. We have adapted technological processes to the requirements of countries in the early stages of industrialisation. Our industrial machinery is simpler, less expensive and more appropriate to the conditions that obtain in developing countries. We would like our friends from the ACP States to have the freedom to make their own choice. I am sure it is not beyond the ingenuity of the Community institutions to implement the provisions of Title III and Title IV of the Lomé Convention, and to use the instrumentalities of the EDF, the EIB, and the Centre for Industrial Development in such a manner as to make it possible for the ACP States to have easier access to our experience, our skills and our goods.

Such a move will be thrice blessed: first, it will give to both ACP and non-ACP States a vested interest in their respective relations with the Community; second, it will reinforce cooperative trends in the developing world; third, it will help promote better understanding between the developing and the developed world.

To conclude, the Lomé Convention is born out of the old links which the member States of the Community had with different parts of the developing world in the days gone by; it constitutes a point of departure for the new order, expected to be fashioned with the help of the Community's spokesmen in the forthcoming dialogue at Paris.

HUNGARIAN POINT OF VIEW

by *Tibor Palánkai*

The association agreements of the European Economic Community are as old as the Treaty of Rome. At that time the colonies of member states, mostly in Africa, were declared associated territories. Following independence two Yaoundé Conventions in 1963 and 1969 were signed by the majority of the former African colonies. In 1968 three East African States also entered into associated relationship with the EEC.

The EEC is largely based on a market model of integration which meant *regional liberalization of trade* within the given zone. The Convention of association signed between the EEC and developing countries in Africa also aimed at liberalising trade.

Parallel with the creation of the customs union in the EEC free trade in industrial goods was introduced between the EEC and the associated African states. The liberalization of a considerable part of trade had thus occurred already in the course of the first Yaoundé convention, the second only reinforced this once again.

Free trade between the two zones was not however complete. A weakness of the articles of association was that they only partially covered trade in agricultural products, though the majority of the associated African countries could be regarded as agricultural producers and such products made up a large proportion of their export incomes. The African associates were accorded preferences for only a small proportion of products covered by the common agricultural policy. With one or two exceptions, it amounted to only a few percent on the export lists of the associated countries. Nor did the EEC fully liberalize the import of tropical agricultural products. Some of them were subjected to high consumer taxes by EEC countries. Liberalization under the Arusha agreements was even less complete. On the other hand the articles of association allowed the Africans, as developing countries, to subject EEC imports to duties or quantitative controls, going as far as the right to increase these, or reintroduce barriers to trade that had already been abolished.

The associated countries were also granted *financial aid and credits.*[4]

These funds were used mainly to finance investments in the

4. Compare Table 3.

infrastructure and in agriculture. The EDF took part in some very important investments but considering the development needs of the associated countries their importance was not really large. Nor were the amounts made available by the Development Fund particularly large even when compared with the total aid provided by the member states. Taking the period of association as a whole the sum amounted to 7 per cent of the total state aid provided by the Six, and roughly 20 per cent of state aid given to the associated African countries.

The articles of association *did not essentially change the patterns of the earlier colonial division of labour.* On the contrary, its structure, and the dependence and outflow of revenues of the associated countries, were wisely preserved in a new neocolonial form.

Association produced mainly certain *short-term advantages* for the African countries concerned. The markets of the other EEC countries were opened to them in addition to those of their former mother country, allowing them to increase selling their traditional export goods. Considering their limited resources for development EEC funds and technical assistance were far from unimportant for the countries concerned. Some of the governments wished to encourage private investment by Common Market companies as well, and they continued to need technical aid from West-European countries in a great many fields. Their interest in association was however largely derived from their dependence. The heritage of the earlier division of labour made association a need which it proved very difficult to do without.

Looking *at long-term development interests* one could hardly judge association to be fully to the advantage of these African countries. Being extraordinarily backward countries they were primarily interested in establishing the foundations of industrial and economic development. Only helping, in limited areas, the liberalization of trade in most fields essentially endangered such an endeavour. This was particularily true in relation to the developed West European countries. It is obvious that EEC countries with a per capita annual national income of 2,500 to 3,000 dollars and associated countries with an annual per capita income 100-150 dollars were not batting in the same league. This huge difference in power was really not compensated by possible unilateral customs protection. In such conditions association in the long term made it more difficult to protect their growing but weak domestic industries. It preserved the monocultural economic structure, and limited these countries to the role of suppliers of raw-materials and food to Western Europe. No substantial change occurred in the structure of exports, or their economy as such, of the developing countries concerned during the years of association.

The nearly twenty years have proved also that association did not lead to any considerable growth in their trade or export incomes.[5]

Association has not improved the position of the countries concerned within the world economy either. Because of the backwardness, insufficient competitiveness and export-structure of the associated countries, the concessions given them proved ineffective. As raw-material exporters they would have enjoyed low EEC tariffs in any case. Tariff concessions granted to industrial products had no practical significance, their industries being minimal.

The new Lomé Convention, included forty-six countries in Africa, the Caribbean and the Pacific. In addition to the earlier associated countries, twenty-one Commonwealth countries and six other African countries take part. The Arab and a few other countries excepted, just about every country in Africa is covered by the Lomé Convention.

The ACP countries include a group of the poorest countries of the developing world.[6]

In the Lomé Convention there are *a number of new elements* compared with the former Associations. Liberalization of trade continues to be important.

A major change is that the developing countries have managed to eliminate *the principle of reciprocity.* They are able to decide over the import of EEC goods in terms of their own economic interests, though they must not be discriminated against in the context of imports from other developed countries. This allows for complete protection at home, and does not force them to discriminate against imports from third countries, and is therefore to the advantage of the developing countries.

The section referring to the encouragement of industrial cooperation is a new element in the Convention as well. It expresses the desire of ACP countries to change the conventional division of labour between developed and developing countries. However, it is also interpreted as a way of encouraging the participation of foreign private capital, including the multinational corporations, in their economies.

5. Compare Chapter 6, *supra.*
6. Compare Annex 1.

The Stabex, export income stabilization system, is something new as well.

The Lomé Convention established the total aid to be given over the five years at 3,390 million units of account.[7] The ACP successfully fought for a right to have a say in the management of the European Development Fund. The scope of financing has been extended as well. Investments can be used for industrialization, energy, mining, agriculture, tourism, the infrastructure, cooperation in technology, communications systems and marketing.

Joint action by the developing countries secured them concessions from the EEC in a number of respects. The Lomé Convention is the first major international agreement in which developing countries obtained new conditions, though limited, as part of efforts to create a new international economic order. There are a number of elements which show a tendency to transform the forms and structure of the former traditional international division of labour.

It should be stressed however that it would be a mistake to overestimate the importance of the Lomé Convention.

First: In spite of all that *it did not* in the last resort *create a qualitatively new relationship between the EEC and the ACP developing countries,* nor did it basically change the economic position and development prospects to the latter. Their economic and trade dependence continues to be basically unchanged, since 69 per cent of their largely monocultural exports (in 1974) are still directed towards EEC markets. In spite of unilateral liberalization the most backward countries cannot really compete with the large companies of the EEC. Regarding modernization and structural change the market-forces of the EEC though larger, can still not be regarded as a major factor.

Second: The Lomé Convention *does not mean a major transfer of resources* within the given zone from developed to developing countries either. The roughly 3,400 million units of account made available over five years mean only an annual per capita of 3.4 units of account for aid. Bearing in mind the extraordinary backwardness and huge development needs, these are only of marginal importance. The European Development Fund only provides 375 units of account for export stabilization. All the ACP countries can share in this but, with the exception of the Twenty-four least developed countries, the others must refund credits once

7. Compare Table 3, and chapter 6, *supra.*

their export-income rises above the average of the four previous years. It is questionable whether large-scale technological transfer will really take place under the heading of industrial cooperation. *Third*: Taking into account their extreme underdevelopment, it can be argued that the concentration of limited resources and their planned exploitation is of particular importance in the interests of more rapid economic development of the countries covered by the Convention. This cannot be done without increased state intervention and regulatory power, and the growth of the state sector. As against this the whole Lomé Convention system *is suffused by support for the growth of private enterprise* in the ACP countries. This, to a certain extent, results in asymmetry between the development needs of the countries concerned and the socio-economic development model urged by the EEC. This is expressed by the stress on market liberalization though it is proven that free-trade zones are hardly likely to create industries in backward countries, and can certainly not create bridges over huge gaps of development between zones. A point is also that the Lomé Convention provides for special support of small and medium national firms. The Convention also prescribes that there must be no discrimination in the conditions for private firms in the EEC which wish to invest, or establish branches, in ACP countries. EEC private firms largely benefit from the use of funds made available through aid.

Fourth: The Lomé Convention is only a new form for *a wider European regionalism.* It can be considered as a means to maintain and strengthen a Western European sphere of political and economic influence in the area, particularly against the United States. It is also important from the point of view of security of supply of some food, basic raw materials and energy for Western Europe. The Lomé Convention at the same time in some respects turns the developing member countries against the other ones and it is also aimed at separating them from orientation towards the socialist world.

The Lomé Convention, thus, is only a small step forward from the old links, and is basically preserving the traditional capitalist division of labour, maintaining dependence and the former possibilities of exploitation. It is taking the interests of developing countries concerned into account in some respects. But the Lomé Convention is also a compromise in which the EEC is not restricted in pursuing its own interests.

Of course I should like to stress that it would be unjust to look at every present problem in these developing countries in the light of their association relationship, or to examine their long-term development objectives and prospects only on the basis of their relationship to the EEC. Development and the closing of the gap depend on many other factors as well. Among them, three are of special importance.

First: The acceleration of general economic development, the modernization of the economy, and the transformation and diversification of largely monocultural structures in developing countries is in the first place determined by socio-economic conditions at home. Long-term economic development basically depends on the extent to which it proves possible to mobilize limited socio-economic sources, concentrating them properly, and exploiting them effectively. Conditions and potentials differ, which makes the selection of growth sectors for development particularly important, always ensuring proportionate growth of the country as a whole. This cannot be done without a modernization of social conditions; bearing in mind the considerable survival of pre-capitalist elements, radical social reform is needed in most places. Overcoming backwardness in no less extent also depends on the speed and effectiveness with which the cultural and educational standards of the population can be raised. This is of equal importance from the point of training and education of labour force, and of improvement in social standards. The dynamism of developments at home, and a closing of the development and structural gap naturally depends on outside factors as well. Conditions at home however considerably affect the effectiveness of international cooperation and aid. Lacking the right domestic conditions even a well-directed and large transfer of technologies and resources would fall on infertile soil.

Second: Regarding outside conditions of development, trade and economic dependence must be lessened and done away with, and exploitation must come to an end. That is the prime task. This equally presupposes the taking possession and control, of their national resources, as well as adjustment at home to changes in the world economy, and differentiation in their international economic relations. Developed capitalist countries will naturally, in the future as well, continue to be the major trading partners of developing countries, in the long-run, and this particularly applies to those within the Lomé Convention. The form, structure and character of this relationship is therefore most important for these countries which are largely dependent on world economic conditions. In this respect the countries of the Lomé Convention secured themselves partially favourable terms. Their importance, cannot of course be unambiguously established in advance, since one might well doubt that the aims of the Convention will in fact be realized. To some degree the Lomé Convention acts as a precedent as well, showing that the developing countries, acting collectively, are able to change the conventional international division of labour of the capitalist world, formally, and structurally, working towards a truly new world economic order. One must stress that, from this point of view, increasing international detente as well is favourable, and could help the developing countries to obtain more concessions from the developed capitalist countries in the future. The latter also creates favourable conditions which help east-west cooperation in overcoming some of the major problems of the developing world, such as the shortage of food, and cultural backwardness. The socialist countries can be good partners in diversifying their economic relations.

Third: Regional integration schemes within zones must also be mentioned in any discussion of the economic growth of developing countries. There are a number of cases already. Integration there is largely meant to help overcome economic backwardness at greater speed, and this largely determines its direction, character, and most rational mechanisms. In the case of developing countries the collective mobilization of resources and the need for economic coordination are much more acute than in developed ones. What is required in respect of institutions and mechanisms therefore differs as well. A simple unification of markets can, in such circumstances, be of limited importance only. The coordination of development policies, and, in certain cases, joint industrialization plans, make political cooperation within the given zone increasingly important. Conditions are not always favourable for this. The internal socio-economic situation is also of decisive importance from the point of view of integration. Regional integration also creates more favourable conditions as regards obtaining and strengthening economic independence.

Part Three

THE CONVENTION AND A NEW INTERNATIONAL
ECONOMIC ORDER

Chapter 9

EUROPEAN COMMUNITY'S SECURITY OF SUPPLY WITH RAW MATERIALS AND THE INTERESTS OF DEVELOPING COUNTRIES: THE NEED FOR A COOPERATIVE STRATEGY.

by *Huub Coppens, Gerrit Faber and Ed Lof.* *

The negotiations for the Lomé Convention took place at a moment in history that, in retrospect, will perhaps be called a turning point in the relationships between the industrially developed nations and the poor developing ones. This turning point is marked by various events, of which the so-called oil crisis is probably the most notorious. Even though signs of change can be detected earlier, it was very much the successful operation of the OPEC that inspired the developing countries as a group to review their strategy of politely begging the developed ones for assistance and to recast it toward using concerted pressure to obtain a more favorable reaction to their demands. Such pressure can (and as a matter of fact did) take many forms, ranging from merely verbal acts at international conferences to combined producer action with regard to those raw materials[1] of which developing countries are among the major suppliers and on which developed countries depend in varying ways and degrees.

This changing atmosphere coincides with a growing awareness in many countries of the limits of earth's capacity to supply— amongst others aroused by the studies commissioned by the Club of Rome. These interrelated developments have resulted in some degree of concern in developed industrialised countries about their security of provision with raw materials. Therefore, one aspect of the present study is to investigate the actual state of security of

* The first draft of this chapter was written in consultation with a team operating under the auspices of the Working Group Peace Research of the Free University in Amsterdam. The authors owe much to P. Karsdorp, B. Oostenbrink, W.B.J. Smits and W. Uytenbogaardt for their cooperation in this team. Valuable comments were also given by Mrs. M.J. 't Hooft-Welvaars, H. Linneman and J. Vingerhoets.

1. In this text the terms raw materials, primary products and commodities will be used as synonyms.

161

raw material provision of one group of developed countries, the nine member states of the European Community (EC), and to see whether, and if so to what extent, the Lomé Convention can be expected to contribute to this security.

However, as a great number of the (actual and potential) security problems of the EC that will be touched upon in this study are in fact very much connected with the highly unequal distribution of resource use, wealth and power in the world at large, we deem it necessary to enlarge the scope of this investigation. The issue of a more assured access to supply of consumer countries is strongly interlinked with the issue of, what is since 1974 being called, a more equitable New International Economic Order. Therefore it is our strong conviction that real security in this field can only be obtained by policies of consuming countries that also take account, as much as possible, of the development needs of developing countries. For this reason we will also discuss what kind of policies would be required that strike a balance between the two issues mentioned and to what extent the Lomé Convention does meet these requirements. With regard to the latter a distinction is to be made between developing countries in Africa, the Caribbean and the Pacific area participating in the Convention (referred to as ACP countries) and the rest of the Third World.

Our approach in this study can be called a normative one. We will not discuss the likelihood of the full implementation by the relevant authorities of the policies we recommend. Disregarding eventual feelings of optimism or pessimism, we will simply confine ourselves to what, in our opinion, should be done in this respect.

In order to explain our views more clearly, we will start with a brief exposition of the so-called development needs of the Third World and its evolving strategy to put more pressure on the developed part of our interdependent world.

Development needs of the Third World

When we use the word development we mean the development of people in the first place. This is to say that we will only speak of development if it means improvement in the satisfaction of human needs, beginning with the basic needs for food, clothing, shelter, health and education of the poor who constitute the world's majority, and including the general human needs for freedom, equality and dignity. So, development refers to both welfare and well-being of individuals and social groups of both the present and future generations. With regard to the latter it should be stressed that development has to be pursued in harmony with the natural environment.

These elements can be taken as the fundamentals of the development process and they are in a sense universal. On the other hand, the very nature of this definition implies that the roads of development are many, since they have to answer to the specifics of a great variety of cultural and natural situations in the world.

In the words of the 1975 Dag Hammerskjöld Report:

> "Development is endogenous; it springs from the heart of each society, which relies first on its own strength and resources and defines in sovereignty the vision of its future, cooperating with societies sharing its problems and aspirations. At the same time, the international community as a whole has the responsibility of guaranteeing the conditions for the self-reliant development of each society, for making available to all the fruits of others' experience and for helping those of its members who are in need. This is the very essence of the new international order...".[2]

In this perspective *self-reliance* is a key-word—it being both a *means* for developing countries to escape from their historically grown dependency on the industrial centres, and a *goal* in itself. Self-reliance should neither be taken as a synonym for autarchy nor for isolation, though, for the majority of the developing countries it may imply, at least temporarily, a more selective approach to participation in interaction with the industrial centres. As an alternative to this interaction and as a means to strengthening the third world's bargaining power vis-à-vis the centre, self-reliance has been extended to *collective self-reliance*. Thus, developing countries having common interests and common goals join forces in mutual cooperation and collective action. The strategy of collective self-reliance is presently being executed at various levels (subregional and inter-regional) and with varying degrees of intensity and permanency.

One may wonder whether this new strategy of the developing countries will create an atmosphere of confrontation rather than one of cooperation along the lines of interdependence with the developed countries. In our opinion this will to a large extent depend on the reaction of the latter. In the words of the Dutch

2. *What Now.* The 1975 Dag Hammerskjöld Report, prepared on the occasion of the Seventh Special Session of the UN General Assembly, Uppsala, 1975, p. 7.

minister for development cooperation, Jan Pronk: "The demands of the developing countries are reasonable and are presented in a reasonable way. The refusal of the rich countries has often been both unreasonable and offensive. Such a refusal means real confrontation and polarisation".[3]

With regard to primary products, the specific demands of the Third World have been formulated and reformulated at various international conferences both of developing countries alone and of developed and developing ones together. Subject to negotiating tactics and changes in practical circumstances the exact wording of these demands has been shifting in the course of time. Since our analysis remains at a rather general level it is sufficient for the purpose of our study to base ourselves in a global manner on the various declarations and resolutions adopted in the recent period[4] and to summarise the Third World demands with respect to commodities in the following way.

Developing countries, still depending on their primary commodities export for 75 to 80 percent of their foreign exchange earnings, need and are willing to strive for:

1) obtaining and securing effective sovereign control over their natural resources and economic activities.

2) rapidly increasing production of food-stuffs by their own agricultural and fisheries sectors and receiving adequate financial, technical and material assistance (including fertilizers) to this end;

3) progressive promotion of raw material processing in their own national territories;

4) expanding shares in transport, marketing and distribution activities of goods they export;

5) appropriate international stocking and other forms of market arrangements for securing stable remunerative and equitable prices in the trade of primary commodities;

6) improved and non-discriminatory access to the developed economies' markets in such a way that they can expand and diversify their production and export packages, both with regard to commodity composition and geographical distribution; and

7) protection against export revenue fluctuations through im-

3. Pronk in his Final Address to the Symposium on a New International Economic Order, The Hague, May 1975 (Report, p. 79).

4. In particular those of the Sixth and Seventh Special Sessions of the UN General Assembly, the fourth conference of UNCTAD and the provisional positions taken in the Conference on International Economic Cooperation.

proved compensatory financing facilities and, eventually, through the introduction of some kind of indexation scheme to preserve the purchasing power of their exports.

We will take these demands as points of reference for both our outline of a cooperative strategy to be pursued by the EC (next paragraph) and our assessment of the Lomé Convention (see page 177).

EC's Security of Supply and Possible Remedying Action

It can be stated that a regular provision with raw materials is of vital importance to any economy. This provision depends, for each country, on two main sources: a) domestic production and b) foreign supply of these materials. The relative importance of both, different for each country, is determined primarily by the respective costs of procurement, which in turn largely depend on the quantity and quality of resources available.

We may distinguish between two kinds of potential threats to the security of provision of a particular country:
— inability of nature to supply (both temporary interruptions because of disasters, such as floods, droughts, earthquakes etc., and permanent interruption because of depletion);
— unwillingness of foreign suppliers to continue delivery at present conditions (e.g. price level).

A threat to the provision of raw materials may be translated into costs (e.g. by estimating the probability of future price increases). On the other hand, a threat could to a lesser or larger degree be warded off—for instance by substitution—but such protective action would certainly entail costs as well. In theory, the costs implied by the threat would have to be weighed against the costs of protection. In practice, this weighing process is virtually impossible because a host of subjective elements mingle with the facts. Even the question whether or not a security problem exists with regard to the provision with raw materials is a highly subjective matter. The perception of danger in this respect is directly linked with:
— the perception of one's own needs (both in terms of what one wants to receive from others and what one would be ready to yield in exchange);
— the perception of the supplying party's needs and demands and of the means he might use in order to attain his goals.

Therefore, in our opinion, the EC's security of provision with primary products does not lend itself to exact quantitative assessment; neither can minimum conditions for its guarantee be spelled out. The only realistic approach to this problem is to consider the various factors that seem to play a role, meanwhile stressing that the significance of each is largely a matter of judgement.

Factors Influencing the EC's Security of Provision

For a rough assessment of the EC's present position with regard to the provision with primary products, five interrelated factors may be distinguished as relevant:

Dependence on imports. The extent to which an economy is dependent on imports is a first indication of its vulnerability to external pressure. Unfortunately, readily available data do not permit a systematic and detailed picture for the nine countries of the EC of net imports of primary products and their share in domestic consumption. Further research to obtain these data—for the present as well as in the perspective of past and projected trends—is desirable.

The figures assembled in tables 6-9 allow the following general observations: Regarding *primary products from agriculture and forestry* (tables 6-7) distinction should be made between competing and non-competing products. The former are imported in competition with domestic products, with imports from other developed countries, and/or with synthetic substitutes. Non-competing products are those only produced by developing countries, such as coffee, tea, cocoa and bananas. For the latter group, the self-sufficiency ratio of the EC is, of course, nil (unless produced in dependent territories). For competing products the ratio is relatively high, 90% or more for several major products: potatoes, cereals, sugar, vegetables; the same is true of meat and dairy products. In this category self-sufficiency is low for tobacco, cotton, citrus fruits and oils and fats. Some products covered by the EC Common Agricultural Policy show rising self-sufficiency ratios due to the protectionist tendencies of that policy.

A much higher dependency on foreign sources exists for most *mineral primary products* (tables 8-9). The example of oil hardly needs elaborating; only 5% of EC-consumption is supplied from within. On the other hand, for the other two main fossil fuels—natural gas and coal—the ratio is very high, i.e. 98 and 90% respectively. For provision with metallic minerals the EC is again highly dependent: 75% of iron ore has to be imported, while for copper, bauxite, manganese, magnesium and tungsten the self-sufficiency ratio is negligible. Its effect is lessened only to the

166

degree that recycling is possible (as in the case of copper and aluminium). Other vital minerals for which the EC has a low self-sufficiency ratio are uranium (25%) and phosphates (1%).

Number and variety of foreign sources. It may be argued that provision is less secure when a certain commodity is supplied by only a few countries than when a great number of suppliers is available. Although even a large group of exporters may be able to join forces, one would expect this to be more difficult as the number increases and the interests diverge.

As illustrated in table 10, with regard to *products from agriculture and forestry* suppliers to the EC are dispersed geographically. In the cases where one country provides approximately one half or more of EC imports, these are other developed countries: for cereals and tobacco, the U.S.; for oranges Spain. In most cases the major supplier does not have a dominant share in EC imports, even in the case of highly climate-dependent products such as coffee and cocoa. It should be observed that the supply may be more concentrated than is apparent from the figures presented. EC cocoa imports, for instance, originate predominantly from five West African countries.

A higher concentration of suppliers is found with regard to *minerals,* but again the major supplier is often a developed country (e.g. Australia for copper ore and bauxite, Canada for nickel, South Africa for manganese ore). Developing countries are dominant in crude fertilizer (Morocco) and especially in copper, where three developing countries account for more than half of EC imports. The importance of the Third World, however, is understated by these figures as they do not show indirect dependencies. Some developed exporters of processed materials derive all or part of the ores from developing countries (e.g. Norway, whose predominance in aluminium exports is due to the availability of low-cost energy). The main reason for the concentration of mineral suppliers lies in the uneven spread of mineral deposits in the world. A striking example is oil: 59% of proven world reserves are located in the Middle East and 10% in Eastern Europe (incl. the U.S.S.R.).[5] Table 11 shows the geographical concentration of those metallic mineral reserves of which half or more is concentrated in one or two countries.

5. Computed from figures in "World Trends", in *World Oil,* Feb. 15, 1975, p. 44.

Role and position of EC companies in the Third World. Whether the exploration, exploitation, transport, marketing and distribution of its imports are controlled by European or by foreign firms, may be of considerable importance to the EC's security of provision with raw materials. This argument is based on the assumption that in general the interests of private companies tend to converge with the interests of their country or region of origin, rather than with those of the host country, and that the governments of the former have more means to influence such a company than host country governments do. This is self-evident in the case where public EC-companies operate in the Third World. The importance of this factor is recognized in the European Commission's recent statement that with regard to iron, bauxite and alumina, tungsten, and phosphates, the EC has only a small share in the exploitation outside its own area and therefore needs an investment policy.[6]

Comprehensive, up to date and sufficiently reliable data on the role of European companies in the exploitation of primary products in the Third World are hard to come by. An indication is given by the fact that in 1966/7, nearly half of the total stock of DAC investments in the Third World were in the sectors petroleum, mining and smelting. Of DAC investment stock in the African developing countries' oil sector, 20% was British, 27% French and 11% Dutch; for the sector mining and smelting these shares were 36%, 22% and nil respectively.[7] The same source observes that the pattern of European foreign investment reflects the former colonial ties. Supporting examples are French investments in the CFA-franc zone (uranium interests in Niger, Gabon and the Central African Republic that together fully cover French import needs); British investments in Nigeria (Shell and BP; Unilever) and Belgian investments in Zaïre (Société Générale). Gradually, however, the pattern is shifting as the old colonial powers are diversifying their interests (partly as a result of the EC association policy), while other developed countries, EC as well as non-EC, are increasing their involvement in the exploitation of the Third World's resources, often through international consortia. Thus, before its nationalization in 1974 iron was produced in Mauretania by MIFERMA, a consortium in which French, British, German and Italian interests participated, the majority share being French and 5% Mauretanian; and in Liberia by a consortium of

6. *Bulletin of the European Communities,* Supplement 1/75, p. 14.
7. *Multinational Corporations in World Development,* UNO, New York, 1973, p. 180.

168

American, Swedish and German companies with only a small Liberian share.[8]

In many cases, property titles have been transferred to national governments; the meaning of such transactions may be only symbolic, however, to the extent that foreign control is maintained through a "de facto" monopoly of management, know-how and/or research. Zambia's copper mines are 51% state owned, but the foreign partners obtained the right to veto important decisions such as those regarding expansion, research and exploration. In Zaïre, the Union Minière was awarded a management contract for its former expropriated mines, as part of a compensation agreement.[9]

At the same time, foreign firms are hedging against the loss of direct control by diversification of their activities; thus, British-Dutch Unilever has branched out into a variety of commercial and industrial activities in Africa and elsewhere. And regardless of property structures and access to skills and technology, foreign interests are often deeply embedded in elements of the cultural and political structure of the host country.

Although these data are incomplete, they indicate that European firms are considerably involved in the exploration and production in primary sectors in the Third World.

Political factors. Political factors do play a role in international trade and investment activities, although one is easily tempted to overstate their significance. Sudden political changes in supplying countries may cause interruptions in the flow of their exports, but economic necessity will usually force these countries to soon resume delivery. In general the concentration of trade and capital flows in the world economy seems to a large extent a function of diverging levels of economic development and growth rates, rather than of differences in economic and political systems.

There is no doubt, however, that the present uneven spread of known mineral resources in the world reflects to some extent the tendency of private mining companies to concentrate exploration and exploitation investments in countries whose government policies vis-à-vis foreign enterprise are considered favorable. Also, some developed market economy countries apparently consider their economic and political status and power so much connected

8. R.H. Green & A. Seidman, *Unity or Poverty?* (Penguin, 1968, p. 116).
9. D.N. Smith and L.T. Wells, "Mineral Agreements in Developing Countries," in: *American Journal of International Law*, 1975, p. 560.

with the present international economic order, that they approach the Third World's desire for a New International Economic Order rather negatively. In particular those countries that seem prepared to use their position as suppliers of vital commodities as an instrument for changing the rules of the game, are being watched suspiciously.

It seems worthwhile, in this context, to examine the conditions on which the success of producer action along the lines of OPEC seems to depend. [10]

a) The commodity has to be essential to the importers. This implies that it has to be imported in significant quantities, that the absolute price elasticity of demand is small and that the possibilities of substitution are limited.

b) The share of participants in the total supply of the commodity has to be substantial. It does not, however, seem necessary that this share comes close to 100%.

c) The number of participants should not be too large and their interests should not be conflicting.

d) The exporting countries should be able to bear the consequences of a temporary interruption of exports. This condition is not a purely economic one but has social and political aspects as well. It implies, for example, that the commodity concerned should not have too large a share in export earnings; that financial and technical means should be available to reduce production and to stock the commodity; that the foreign exchange position should be sufficiently sound to cushion temporary deficits and enable continuation of essential imports; and that the political stability and the level of welfare should be such as to enable the country to resist eventual foreign economic and political pressure (e.g. an embargo) and to cope with resulting domestic disturbances.

e) The structure of marketing and distribution of the commodity concerned should be such that an increase in prices imposed by the government of the exporting country is effective. It seems that this is more easy in cases where only a small number of firms control vital parts of the economic circuit than in cases where many competing firms operate, though in the case of governments faced with only a few giant multinational companies, their relative bargaining strength may be assumed to be weaker. Crucial is, how-

---

10. Partly based on: *Europe, Raw Materials and the Third World*, Commission of the European Communities, Brussels, 1974, pp. 19-20.

ever, whether their respective interests really diverge or not. With oil, for instance, there did not seem to be too much of a divergence of interests between the oil companies and the OPEC governments.

Simultaneous fulfilment of all these conditions is clearly not an absolute prerequisite for successful producer action. However, the conditions include several elements that could in a concrete situation be decisive.

Besides OPEC a considerable number of producer associations of varying character have been established or are in preparation, namely concerning mercury, phosphates, bauxite, copper, iron ore, natural rubber, silver, cane sugar, coffee, wood, groundnuts, tea, bananas, coconuts, pepper, fibres and cocoa. Too many imponderables remain, however, to allow for realistic forecasts of the number and scope of producer actions which could be expected.

In conclusion, we can say that political factors that give rise to threats to EC's raw material provision are easily overstated, while the chances for effective action by producer associations do seem rather limited.

Depletion of Natural Resources. Depletion of resources within the EC increases the dependence on imports. The threat of global depletion could provoke fierce competition for the materials concerned which might place some countries with more ample resources in a powerful position.

Agricultural production, forestry and fishing are in principle reproduceable, but that does not mean that they can be exploited at any rate or intensity. Bad maintenance or over-use (overdose of chemicals, overgrazing, deforestation, etc.) can for instance cause serious reduction of nature's capacity to produce.

Maximum food production in the world is, in theory, many times higher than present production. [11] Yet, food shortages occur in many regions of the world because income, and therefore production is spread unevenly. Significantly, in cases of temporary shortages in world supply of food stuffs it is the poorest groups in the Third World that are forced to accommodate by reducing their consumption. FAO forecasts a growth in world food production sufficient for a growing global demand, but production in the

11. See, for instance: P. Buringh, H.D.J. v. Heemst and G.J. Staring, *Computation of the Absolute Maximum Food Production of the World,* Agricultural University, Wageningen, Jan. 1975.

Third World will lag behind if no national and international measures are taken. [12]

For minerals the situation is quite different, as the quantities available are fixed even though these cannot be determined with precision. Distinction should be made here between reserves and resources. Reserves are defined, then, as known, identified deposits from which minerals can be extracted with existing technology and under present economic conditions. Resources additionally include deposits that may eventually become available. [13] Further exploration, changed market conditions and improved technology may enable resources to become reserves.

Considering hydrocarbons: oil reserves are 556 billion barrels, enough for 27 years' production of crude oil at the 1971 level. [14] Allowing for annual growth this reserve-index is much lower; Mesarović and Pestel arrive at 21 years on the basis of a 5% growth rate. For gas the static index is 41 years and the dynamic one 23 years. For coal these figures are 1,725 and 180 years respectively. Of late, large sums are being spent on exploration for new oil reserves in areas where the costs involved are much higher than in the traditional oil producing regions. The African shelves and the North Sea show promising results. Optimistic estimates of potentially recoverable resources arrive at 3,735 billion barrels. However, even these would be depleted in some 50 years if consumption grows by 5% per annum. [15]

For some metallic minerals, reserves are insufficient to sustain even a constant consumption level for the next 35 years. This is the case with gold (disregarding the large quantity of inactive monetary gold), silver, platinum, mercury, tin, lead and zinc (table 12).

Several attempts have been made at estimating available metallic mineral resources, notably by McKelvey, Erickson and Tooker. [16]

12. "Prognoses up to 1985" in: *Assessment of the World Food Situation, Present and Future,* FAO, E/Conf/65/63, Rome, Aug. 1974.

13. D.A. Probst and W.P. Pratt, "Introduction to U.S. Mineral Resources," in: *US Geological Survey,* Prof. paper 820, Washington, 1973.

14. See note (5).

15. M. Mesarović and E. Pestel, *Mankind at the turningpoint,* E.P. Dutton & Comp. Inc., 1974, Annex III, B.

16. E. McKelvey, "Mineral Resource Estimates and Public Policy," and R.L. Erickson, "Crustal Abundance of Elements and Mineral Reserves and Resources," both in: *US Geological Survey,* Prof. paper 820, Washington, 1973, pp. 9 and 21 resp. E.W. Tooker, *Challenges to Geological Exploration in the Next Three Decades,* Society of Mining Engineers of AIME, Reprint No. 74-H-20, New York, 1974.

Their conclusion should be regarded with caution as some of the underlying assumptions are rather heroic. Most experts agree, however, that for most metallic minerals fear of depletion in the foreseeable future is unfounded. Continental resources are estimated to be sufficient for another 200 or 300 years at the present level of consumption; in addition, metallic minerals might eventually be extracted from seawater and the ocean floors. [17] It should be stressed, however, that it is highly uncertain whether these resources can ever be exploited as the costs in energy required will rise steeply when less accessible sources are broached, while for ecological reasons rooting up the whole surface of the earth is hardly realistic.

In the EC, not much is left of its mineral reserves, while surprising discoveries of large resources are not to be expected. It has been proposed to make an inventory of what actually exists. [18] Although the known hydrocarbon deposits in the North Sea are small compared to those in the Middle East, some experts contend that these could provide for a substantial share in EC consumption if exploited at a rapid rate. Of course, this could only be the case for a correspondingly shorter period. [19]

So we can conclude that although EC's endowment with mineral reserves is very poor, depletion of world resources may not be expected in the near future (except for oil and gas).

A Cooperative Approach to the Problems of Provision

Whether or not the EC's security of supply is in fact endangered by the various factors discussed in the above section also depends on the question to what extent these factors may be changed by the EC itself. Some of the possible remedying action can be undertaken by the EC countries on their own, individually or as a group, since it only involves internal policies. Other approaches refer to relationships with outsiders and therefore necessarily also depend on their willingness to cooperate with the EC. But even with re-

17. *De toekomstige beschikbaarheid van metallische mineralen.* Advies no. 53, Nationale Advies Raad voor Ontwikkelingssamenwerking, Staatsuitgeverij, Den Haag, 1975, pp. 24/25.

18. Bureau de la Recherche Géologique et Minières—*Propositions en vue de la réalisation communautaire d'un ouvrage sur les ressources minérales de l'Europe.* SNG/MET/GIT no. 281, 10 févr. 1975.

19. E.g., P. Odell, "Het energievraagstuk—een overzicht," in: *Gas,* Orgaan van de koninklijke Vereniging van Gasfabrikanten in Nederland, Rijswijk, Juli 1975.

spect to the latter situation it may be argued that the EC, important as it is in the international community, to a considerable extent has it in its own hands whether its strivings will be successful or not. [20] Let us, however, start with some approaches in which the EC can act on a relatively independent basis. [21]

In the first place possibilities of *substitution* should be examined. "Unsecure" imports could be replaced by domestic products or imports that are considered safer (e.g. from other developed market economies). Also, other products could be substituted for them. It has been suggested, for instance, that for some uses aluminium could be replaced by timber. This has the added advantage that the latter is a reproduceable commodity (even though its rate of reproduction is rather low), the former being exhaustible. More frequently, however, the opposite happens when a synthetic product is substituted for a natural one, as in the case of rubber and fibres. Generally, substitution entails higher costs (apart from the case where it is induced by technical innovation), in particular where the new source is technically less accessible. For example, the extraction of oil from shales or tar sands was only seriously considered after the oil crisis and the resulting price rises. Costly research will often be required to develop feasible substitutes. Oil itself will not be fully replaceable by other sources of energy (nuclear, solar, geothermal, or energy from the wind, water power, or the tidal movement of the seas) within the next decade. For some mineral commodities substitution does not at present appear possible at all because of very specific applications in vital industrial processes, e.g. for uranium, cobalt, silver, lead, tungsten, platinum and tin.

A second approach to the problem is to devise ways to *recycle* used materials and waste. For some products this is already being done; according to estimates by the European Commission recaptured copper and aluminium account for 35 and 25% of EC con-

20. This is not meant to suggest the use of violent action, such as military intervention. Such rejectable action will not be discussed in this study, although it should not be neglected that it is being advocated in some quarters in times of rising tensions. In that respect the mere existence of NATO's power in general and the continuing foreign military presence in the Third World region may too easily create a temptation to use such means also for protecting developed countries' raw material interests.

21. For the views of the European Commission on the possible measures to be taken by the EC see: *Bulletin of the European Communities,* Suppl. 1/75.

sumption respectively. [22] Used paper is also being recycled.

In general, it may be possible to *economize* substantially with regard to the use of imported and/or exhaustible commodities. Such an approach would largely coincide with the ecological aims of restoring natural balances and preserving the environment. Advocates of these ideas have coined the slogan "toward a new way of life", implying that "the new style will make less demands on the material resources of the globe, but more on our moral resources". [23] It would take us too far to elaborate these ideas but they deserve very serious consideration.

Though the measures just mentioned largely belong to the field in which the EC is relatively autonomous, it would be wrong to think that in their consideration only internal factors have to be weighed. For instance, with respect to those mineral reserves facing depletion, it is important that steps are taken to expand exploration and exploitation of new deposits and/or of alternative resources. The cost of this should, however, be weighed against the price at which supplies are available from other sources. Artificially high floor prices to stimulate exploration and production in the EC region in order to lessen its dependence on imports from other regions may be called both inefficient from a world point of view and detrimental to those suppliers that depend on the EC market. The same objection can be raised against artificial promotion of high cost synthetic substitutes and against increasing agricultural production in the EC of those products for which capacity in the Third World is presently under-exploited because of lack of market outlets.

One could think of other examples of unscrupulous action aiming at provision security for the EC while fully disregarding vital interests of other countries. Some of them might even work to a certain extent and for a certain period. But pursuing such policies in those areas where it is thought to be possible for the EC will inevitably affect other areas in which the EC is not able to manage full security of provision relying on internal resources alone. Our previous section has shown that the latter is the case in

22. Source: See note (10). It is noteworthy that comparable figures for the U.S. are much lower, i.e. 20% for copper and 5% for aluminium. (*Mining and Minerals Policy, 1973,* Second Annual Report of the Secretary of the Interior under the Mining and Minerals Policy Act of 1970, p. 20).

23. G. Adler–Karlsson, "New Way of Life in Developed Countries," in: *Report of the Symposium on a New International Economic Order,* The Hague, May 1975, p. 69.

the fields of tropical products and minerals. [24] Because of this dependence it simply does not make sense for the EC to contemplate policies (in other fields) that neglect interests of outsiders. It would be an illusion to think that a partial dependency problem can be tackled by partial approaches. He who demands cooperation from others in one field must be prepared to offer cooperation in other fields or, as has been said: "...as ye would that men should do to you, do ye also to them likewise" (St. Luke 6 : 31).

The cooperative strategy we advocate for the EC is, therefore, based on the conviction that a proper balance is needed between the interests of the EC and those of its suppliers of raw materials. Let us illustrate this by mentioning a few approaches that reflect this attitude:

— One could think of a series of international negotiations in which the interests of both importing and exporting countries are represented, e.g. through the conclusion of world wide trading arrangements, establishment of international buffer stock schemes covered by common financing arrangements, and the other elements of the comprehensive and integrated commodity programme, as proposed in UNCTAD, including safeguards and gradual increases of the purchasing power of developing countries' exports, and recognition of producer associations' right to take action.

— Promoting greater participation of developing countries in the processing of their raw materials and expanding their industrial capacity, supported by measures to improve the access of these exports to the EC markets, would contribute to a new international division of labour which would gradually decrease the EC's dependence on raw material imports.

— Stimulating exploration and exploitation of resources in developing countries by European companies in cooperation with local entrepreneurs and governments (including compliance with development needs and programmes and gradual transfers of ownership of assets) would both enlarge the world's available reserves and reduce potential sources of conflict.

— Increasing EC's security of provision through deconcentration

24. In passing it may be noted that EC's dependence on external mineral resources differs quite considerably from that of the USA, which does not make it very recommendable to follow the rather hard line that has been advocated in the USA in these matters.

of supply can in some cases be obtained by curbing or preventing oligopolistic business practices, which may also be in the interest of exporting developing countries.

— Geographical diversification of sources of supply, as well as of market outlets, is an objective which is relevant for both rich and poor countries; its implementation requires negotiations among parties concerned in order to prevent abrupt changes and to open up alternative supplies and outlets where needed.

— Earth's limited supply capacity demands measures to economize energy and raw material use and to expand recycling of used materials and waste in all countries, especially in the industrially developed ones; when these measures are part of a wider strategy that actively strives for a global redistribution of economic activity traditional exporters may gradually find alternative market outlets in areas that are presently underdeveloped.

These were only a few examples. But they support our belief that it is both feasible and politically sensible for the EC to secure its imports through policies that aim at cooperation with the Third World rather than at confrontation.

Of course, there is always the temptation to apply the principle of cooperation only to a restricted area, by concluding agreements with certain supplying developing countries to the detriment of others. Such a policy of "divide et impera" may seem promising in the short run, but it entails the risk that the premiums needed for special allies eventually become costly as well, while never giving absolute certainty about the ally's loyalty. Such policies may even provoke the same action by other importers and then result in separate regional trading blocs or fragmented international markets, which surely are bad from a world point of view and tend to put the burden of market adaptation on outsiders. Real cooperation requires inclusion of all parties concerned, developed and developing ones; only then the chance is minimized that agreements will be disturbed from within or without. Most likely that is the best security one can get.

The Lomé Convention

In this paragraph we will discuss the Lomé Convention from the point of view of the EC and the Third World respectively, in particular with regard to trade in primary products. In the first two sections special attention will be given to the question to what degree the ACP countries might be able to provide the primary products the EC needs, and whether this would be possible in harmony with the development interests of these ACP countries.

A third section will concentrate on the likely effects of the Lomé Convention on the rest of the Third World.

Fulfilling the EC needs

In this section the importance of ACP exports of primary products to the EC will be analysed in two ways. First, we will present the percentage shares the ACP countries had in the EC imports in 1973 (see table 13). Next, we will give an indication of the potential supply capacity of the ACP countries comparing their total primary exports to all destinations (tables 14 and 15, 1st column) with the net import needs of these products of the EC (tables 6 and 8, 1st column). This latter exercise, undertaken with 1972 data, gives an approximation of the degree in which EC's import needs would theoretically have been covered by ACP countries if all their exports of primary products would have gone to the EC. Of course, this exercise can in no way be taken as a serious forecast of future trade flows. In addition, it must be noted that some product categories are so heterogeneous that a simple comparison of net imports and exports is not very meaningful. With regard to other products, however, this exercise gives an indication of the highest possible share of ACP countries in EC imports based on the former's export capacity in 1972.

Let us first look at the EC imports of *primary products from agriculture and forestry* from ACP countries. In 1973, a large part of some agricultural products came from the ACP countries. The most important cases are tropical fruit—excluding bananas—(33.4 per cent of EC imports coming from ACP countries), sugar (78.3), coffee (30.9), cocoa beans (90.1) and products (cocoa paste 98.6 and cocoa butter 51.1), groundnuts and peanuts (65.0), palmnuts and kernels (92.2), peanut and groundnut oil (62.0), and wood—rough or squared—(46.6). According to our computation of the highest possible shares in 1972, a higher share was possible for sugar (100), for coffee (50), for tea (50 instead of the actual 26.4 in 1973), and for crude rubber (25 instead of the actual 12.4 in 1973).

In relation to some products for which the EC had an important net import need (pulp and paper, fruit and vegetables, cereals and meat) the 1972 exports of the ACP were only minor.

As to *mineral products*, a large part of EC imports in 1973 (see table 13) came from the ACP countries in the case of ores of uranium and thorium (99.3 per cent), and in the case of copper (41.1). The ACP countries had a smaller share in the EC imports of phosphates (21.7) and iron ore (21.5). The highest possible shares in

178

1972 were higher for copper (100 per cent), zinc (75 instead of the actual 8.8 in 1973), tin (33 instead of the actual 16.8 in 1973), crude oil (12 instead of the actual 7.0 in 1973) and aluminium (20 instead of the actual 5.7 in 1973).

From these figures the conclusion may be drawn that the ACP countries are important suppliers of some primary products to the EC, and may be more so in the future. As to this latter aspect of potential future supplies not only the actual 1972 ACP exports to all destinations are of relevance but also the future production capacity of the ACP countries concerned. With regard to minerals figures relating to reserves give an indication in this respect. As table 16 shows, ACP countries do have important reserves of some metallic minerals (notably bauxite, cobalt, copper, and manganese) and of uranium. These reserves could still be substantially increased by further exploration.

This brings us to the important question whether the Lomé Convention offers an instrument through which both a continuation of present ACP exports of primary products to the EC and an increase of these exports in future may be stimulated.

The first thing that calls attention in this respect is the Stabex mechanism (Title II of the Convention) which provides the ACP countries concerned with fairly stable revenues for those commodities exported to the EC market in primary and/or limited processed forms (although the funds reserved for this purpose are rather limited). Several of the products from agriculture and forestry just mentioned are covered by this mechanism. [25] So these exports may be expected to continue and most probably to increase gradually. On the other hand it is noteworthy that with regard to mineral products, in which field the EC is highly dependent on external sources, Stabex contains only one product: iron ore. So the idea that Stabex has been introduced specifically as a means to enhance the EC's security of provision can hardly be substantiated in this respect.

Other specific elements in the Lomé Convention that could be called instrumental in maintaining or even stimulating raw material exports from the ACP to the EC are lacking or are only operative in a limited and indirect way. One could think of the paragraphs

25. At present, the full list includes groundnut products, cocoa products, coffee products, cotton products, coconut products, palm, palmnut and kernel products, raw hides, skins and leather, wood products, fresh bananas, tea, raw sisal and iron ore (art. 17.1). Article 17.3 specifies the conditions in which this list may be expanded.

on financial and technical cooperation (art. 46 mentions amongst others capital projects in the field of rural development, energy, and mining and schemes to improve the structure of agricultural production) and on trade promotion (chapter 2 of Title I on commercial cooperation), which may in effect increase ACP countries' production capacity and perhaps also their exports to the EC. However, since various of these measures are not specifically limited to raw material production and export, they may also have the opposite effect of stimulating local processing in and exports of processed and manufactured goods by ACP countries.

To conclude this assessment: through the Lomé Convention the EC seems to have established firm relationships with a considerable number of developing countries supplying all or a significant part of its import needs of some primary products. The ACP group's contribution to the EC's security of raw material provision, both actually and, through the Convention also potentially, is important. On the other hand, our analysis shows in an indirect way that other suppliers, among which non-ACP developing countries, remain indispensable for the EC as well.

The interests of the ACP countries

The ACP countries have of course divergent interests. But, as developing countries, they do have various interests in common which are related to their development needs. In addition most ACP members have had colonial ties with countries of the EC.

We want to focus attention on the needs of the ACP-countries by taking the demands of the developing countries, as summarized above, as guide lines. We will compare these demands with the text of the Convention of Lomé.

Sovereignty over economic activities and natural resources. The right to exercise sovereignty over one's own economic activities and natural resources is not explicitly recognized in the Convention.

Instead, the principle of non-discrimination is followed with regard to the arrangements that may be applied in matters of establishment and provision of services (art. 62) and to measures related to foreign exchange transactions linked with investments and current payments (art. 66). Concerning the latter, parties agreed that "they shall refrain from taking action (...) which would be incompatible with their obligations under this Convention resulting from the provisions relating to trade in goods, to services, establishment and industrial cooperation" (art. 65).

180

There are possibilities for both the EC and the ACP countries to escape from the strict application of these rules. With regard to capital movements and current payments both parties may take the necessary protective measures "should this be justified by reasons relating to serious economic difficulties or severe balance of payment problems" (art. 65).

Article 66 states that discriminatory measures shall be avoided "as far as possible" and that to the extent that they are unavoidable "they will be maintained or introduced in accordance with international monetary rules and every effort will be made to minimize any adverse effects on the Parties concerned".

With regard to matters of establishment and provision of services it appears that the non-discrimination principle may be evaded, since art. 62 continues that if a party "is unable to provide such treatment, the Member States or the ACP States, as the case may be, shall not be bound to accord such treatment for this activity to the nationals and companies or firms of the State concerned". The latter formulation also constitutes the only sanction to be found in Title V of the Convention.

So, as a rule, ACP governments should not refuse the establishment of a company from a particular EC country, and leave companies from other EC countries free. By these uniform arrangements the scope for a national development policy may be narrowed in certain fields (e.g. investments, social policy). Moreover, it is an explicit goal of the Convention to stimulate establishment of EC companies in the ACP countries "where those States so desire and in accordance with their economic and social objectives" (art. 26g).

In our opinion, agreements between parties with a very unequal level of economic development and power should distribute much more economic advantages to the weaker than to the stronger party, and should not be based on non-discrimination principles as is the case with the Convention of Lomé. Stressing these principles creates a restrictive atmosphere with regard to the exercise of sovereignty by the appropriate ACP authorities. Furthermore the latter agreed that "in their trade with the Community the ACP States shall not discriminate among the Member States, and shall grant to the Community treatment no less favourable than the most-favoured-nation treatment" (art. 7.2. (a)); so it will not be possible for them to participate in producer associations and the like, that interrupt supply to one or more of the EC member countries and not to the whole of the developed world. Of course, the arrangements for stabilisation of export earnings (Stabex) are another disincentive to such producer action with regard to products covered by it. Finally, the monetary ties between France and the countries of the CFA-zone will not be influenced by the Convention, as may be derived from art. 66.

Expanding food production. This objective is not explicitly mentioned in the Convention. Nevertheless, the conditions for increasing food production may be improved, because the financial cooperation includes capital projects in the field of rural development, schemes to improve the structure of agricultural production, and microprojects for grassroots development, in particular in rural areas (art. 46).

Diversification of production and export (with regard to commodities and geographical distribution) and processing of primary products. In the Convention the need for diversification of the ACP countries' economies is stressed, particularly in title III about industrial cooperation, the object of which is—among others—"to promote the development and diversification of industry in the ACP States and to help bring about a better distribution of industry both within those States and between them" (art. 26).

The European Community will try to stimulate this by financing programs for industrial infrastructures and ventures, training, technology and research, industrial information and promotion, and trade cooperation. The Community shall contribute to the setting up and extension of industries (processing raw materials and manufacturing finished and semi-finished products) (art. 29). So, the Community will play a stimulating and supporting role, trying to create the conditions for diversification.

To this end two institutions are established: a Committee on Industrial Cooperation supervising a Centre for Industrial Development. Both institutions have the task to give advice and information, and to bring about contacts between Community and ACP States' industrial policy-makers, promoters and firms, and financial institutions (see further chapter 5).

Diversification is further supported by trade cooperation (in the sense that all ACP exports may enter the EC freely, except those products coming under the Common Agricultural Policy; these only receive preferential treatment), and by trade promotion activities (art. 13). The same may be said of the scheme for the stabilization of export earnings, which not only applies to raw materials, but also to (in some degree) processed primary products.

On the other hand, Stabex is a disincentive to further forms of

182

processing (which could of course be said of any action to improve export revenues of primary products of developing countries). The free access of exports of the ACP countries to the EC market gives these countries a lead in competition with other countries. No doubt they will export more to the EC than they would have done without the Convention, while their exports to other markets need not necessarily diminish.

Expanding shares in transport, marketing and distribution. The Convention says nothing about stimulating ACP countries to transport larger parts of their exports by their merchant marines. Art. 13 sums up measures for trade promotion: improvement of organizations, departments or firms contributing to the development of the foreign trade of ACP States, or setting up of these; training; participation by ACP States in fairs and the like; market-research, etc. It remains uncertain whether the ACP countries will get a greater share in marketing and distribution of their exports.

Stable, remunerative and equitable prices for primary products. The Convention contains no direct interventions in the markets of primary products, except for the special arrangement for sugar (Protocol 3). The EC undertakes to purchase 1.4 million tons of sugar annually at a guaranteed price (in line with prices paid to Community farmers), if the supplying countries concerned are not able to sell this quantity in the EC at a price equal to or higher than this guaranteed price (see further chapters 2 and 7).

Protection against export revenue fluctuations. For a limited number of products (more products may be added, art. 17.3) the export revenues from sales to the EC (or to all destinations in some cases) are stabilized out of the Stabex fund; for cases where the lowering of revenues exceeds 7.5 (in some cases 2.5) per cent of the reference level the ACP country receives the difference in the form of an interest-free loan or a grant (arts. 17-25). When their earnings from exporting a Stabex-product exceed the reference level, they have to pay back former loans received in the stabilization scheme (see further chapter 4).

Considering the above points, it is not clear what will really happen in the future. Much depends on the practical implementation of the articles and on the degree to which the ACP countries feel themselves restricted by the Convention in taking autonomous decisions.

In our opinion the ACP States are offered considerable advantages. In comparison with the previous association agreements, this Convention is certainly an improvement. But this is not sufficient reason to call the Convention of Lomé a perfect agreement, because there is a chance that part of the ACP countries' political and economic decision making is actually shared with or lost to EC countries and/or companies. The latter would be a hindrance to their striving for self-reliance.

Effects on other developing countries

The Lomé Convention has been heralded by some of its EC sponsors as a breakthrough in the relations between rich and poor countries, and a first concrete step toward a new economic world order. Critics have pointed out, however, that this association, by-passing as it does the emerging international frameworks through which the developing countries have made their greatest effort to forward their cause (such as UNCTAD), will on the contrary frustrate the advance. [26] The latter argument may be stretched to the suggestion that the EC has done so deliberately in order to break, or to prevent unity among the developing countries, thus safeguarding its provision with raw materials at conditions more favorable than might otherwise be the case.

The text of the Convention hardly gives ground for such suspicions. In the preamble to the agreement the signatories resolve "to establish a new model for relations between developed and developing states, compatible with the aspirations of the international community toward a more just and more balanced economic order". Regarding the danger of alienating ACP countries from the rest of the Third World, art. 7.2 (b) stipulates that the most-favoured-nation treatment to be granted to the EC "shall not apply in respect of trade or economic relations between ACP States or between one or more ACP States and other developing countries". Also, 10% of the community aid is reserved for the financing of contributions by ACP countries to regional projects, while financial and technical assistance may also go directly to regional or interstate bodies to which ACP States belong (arts. 47 and 49).

Nevertheless, the critique is not unfounded. Even though 17 of the ACP countries are among the 25 "least developed developing countries" and another 10 of them belong to the group of countries "most seriously affected by economic crises", the present

26. Most notably by the Dutch member of the European Parliament A. v.d. Hek; see for instance his: "De Associatie-politiek van de Europese Gemeenschap," in: *Internationale Spectator*, Sept. 1975.

46 account for but a small fraction of the world's poor in terms of population. The most deprived areas in that respect—i.e. in South Asia—are not represented. Moreover, the channeling of funds for financial and technical assistance through the Lomé Convention may have a negative effect on an efficient and equitable aid allocation in so far as from a given volume of aid less would be available for regions outside the ACP area where it might be more urgently needed. Thus the reduction of the EC aid budget for 1976 fell entirely on non-ACP countries as the amount allocated for the ACP countries had already been agreed upon in the Convention. As a consequence Community aid to other developing countries almost exclusively consisted of food aid. [27] The same tendency of shifting funds from non-ACP to ACP countries could well be followed when EC States reduce their bilateral aid to the former because of the obligation to contribute to the Community programme.

Regarding trade, little can be said with certainty about the effects of the Lomé Convention on relations between rich and poor countries in general. The claim that the agreement is a step toward similar approaches on a world scale is not very convincing. For instance, with regard to global action to stabilize developing countries' export revenues the European Commission seems to prefer schemes that exclude as much as possible the products that are already covered by the Lomé Convention's Stabex. The Commission stated that Stabex "...must keep its specific character and (that) the Community will obviously have to continue to be responsible for and to pay for the system". [28]

The Convention actually affects the unity of the Third World, because it discriminates among developing countries. As an illustration of this, one can think of three kinds of negative effects for non-ACP countries:

— Non-associated countries may lose markets in the EC to ACP countries. This is relevant in particular for those Commonwealth developing countries that used to have preferential access to the British market but were not allowed to participate in the Lomé negotiations.

— The relative security of part of the ACP exports to the EC and the likely resulting changes in trade flows might increase fluctuations of commodity prices on world markets (in particular those that are already residual in character—such as sugar).

27. *Europa van Morgen,* Vol. V, no. 35, Okt. 8, 1975, p. 468.
28. *Bulletin of the European Communities,* Supplement 6/75, p. 50.

— The Convention may weaken the motivation of ACP countries to join other developing countries in the strategy to press for international commodity agreements, general preferences, adequate development assistance, etc.—or, for that matter, in the bearing of pressure on developed countries to these ends—as they could thereby lose their special advantages. (For instance, at the Manilla Conference of the Group of 77 "the African bloc ... refused to give up its position which gives its members preferential access" to the EC under the Lomé Convention. [29]

In conclusion, from a global point of view the Lomé Convention has to be regarded with reservation. It is hard to see how it could greatly contribute to the emergence of radically different relations between rich and poor countries, while as a model it does in several respects run counter to the means by which the Third World as a group is presently trying to change these relations.

Conclusions

On the basis of the foregoing analysis we arrive at the conclusion that the actual security of provision with raw materials of the EC does in some cases (in particular minerals) require careful attention, but that it does certainly not warrant alarm. There seems to be ample scope both for autonomous internal action and for cooperative approaches with regard to the Third World supplying part of the EC's import needs. The Lomé Convention, though it contains various elements of such a cooperative approach, nevertheless suffers from some serious shortcomings, due mainly to its restricted geographical coverage. From the point of view of the EC's security of supply, the Convention may offer an important contribution with regard to some primary products, but not to all of its import needs. From the point of view of the development interests of the Third World, it must be concluded that, though most of the ACP countries may be expected to gain in several respects, other developing countries may well be harmed by the Convention, both directly and indirectly. As such the Convention is still an extension of the EC's traditionally regionalistic orientation towards the Third World, in spite of the fact that the number of developing countries involved has grown considerably. Indeed, one may wonder whether the mere existence of the Lomé Convention will continue to hamper a more world-wide orientation of the Community towards the problem of development.

29. *Financial Times*, Febr. 2, 1976, p. 17.

Our analysis has underlined the need for a more global approach. The kind of particularistic policies that still seem to dominate the Community's attitude in these matters (besides the Lomé Convention, the Community's Mediterranean policy and the Euro-Arab dialogue) will not solve the problems dealt with in this chapter. It may be added, moreover, that these problems are not specific to the EC or to any other region or group of countries; they are the problems of mankind as such. Security is indivisible and requires global cooperation.

Chapter 10

LOMÉ AND BEYOND

by *Frans A.M. Alting von Geusau*

The negotiation and conclusion of the Lomé Convention—from July 1973 to February 1975—broadly coincided with efforts in the United Nations to lay down principles and rules for a new international economic order—from the Lima conference of non-aligned countries in September 1973 to the Special Session of the UN General Assembly in September 1975.

According to EC Commissioner Cheysson: "It is at a time when too many countries and too many people, in the industrial countries and in the Third World, are talking in terms of confrontation, that we have firmly committed ourselves to the dynamics of cooperation" in the Lomé Convention.[1]

Compared to the outcome of deliberations in the UN framework, the Lomé Convention could indeed be seen as a "new model for relations between developed and developing States", at least in formal terms. As was written in Chapter 1 (supra, p. 8) "its integrated approach, its binding character, the elements of automaticity and long term commitments, its concentration on the poorest countries and the poorest population strata, the participatory structure of decision making, and some of the policy instruments are likely to constitute useful precedents".

In a world in which relations between developed and developing states are in fact based on inequality, cooperation can be dynamic only, if and whenever it contributes to equality.

As has been explained in chapter 2, the Lomé Convention replaced a set of arrangements—the Yaoundé and Arusha conventions and Commonwealth arrangements—which were considered to express relationships between unequal partners. A mere continuation of such old links would not therefore contribute to the elimination of injustice and inequality. Hence, the Lomé Convention

1. *The Courrier*. "European Community-Africa-Caribbean-Pacific." No. 31.—Special Issue—March 1975, p. 13.

can be termed a new model for dynamic cooperation only to the extent it constitutes a new departure from—if not a break with— the previous links between the European Communities and the developing states concerned.

For this reason the analysis of the Lomé Convention in the preceding chapters has focused attention on those provisions, which are said to be innovations compared to previous agreements between the European Communities and developing countries. Each of the authors has addressed himself to two basic questions submitted to him:

(1) Do the innovations contained in the Lomé Convention constitute a new departure or are they no more than limited adaptations in the relations between the European Community and the ACP States; and

(2) Can the innovations stand model for—and be precursors to— new relations between developed and developing countries, or are they—by the fact of being part of a "regional" arrangement—likely to hamper agreement on world-wide rules for a new international economic order.

What seems to emerge from the analyses in the preceding chapters, is that the Lomé Convention contains several significant improvements over the previous Yaoundé Convention.

According to Stordel in chapter 3, "the Lomé Convention might therefore be considered as an example of what a generalized system of preferences could look like given the political will for an effective trade cooperation between developed and developing countries" (p. 74).

A similar conclusion is reached in chapter 4 by Persaud: "Stabex could be the basis of a (global scheme for compensatory financing) if it could be extended to cover more products, all developing countries, earnings in all markets and the improvements" discussed by him (p. 90).

Anyiwo in chapter 5 sees the Lomé Convention "as a modern example in international cooperation between developed and developing countries" (p. 93), opening possibilities for a new international division of labor more favorable to developing countries and providing a realistic basis for transfer of technology to them.

Voorhoeve in chapter 6 underlines the substantial improvement with respect to aid in the Lomé Convention as compared to the Yaoundé Conventions (p. 113). The terms of EC aid, moreover, compare favorably to other official development aid; the same could be said of its concentration on the poorest countries and its emphasis on regional integration projects among developing countries.

Even with respect to agricultural cooperation—the area of the much criticised CAP of the European Communities—have several modern aspects of development policy been realized, according to Dams in chapter 7. The protocol on sugar is mentioned by him—as by the authors of chapter 2—as the first example of an indexing of the returns received by developing countries for their primary products (p. 124). The new orientation of aid on agricultural projects for the least developed countries and the poorest strata of their populations is of particular importance in this respect.

All authors of the preceding chapters have attached great importance to the unity and solidarity of the ACP countries shown during the negotiations of the new convention. The authors of chapter 2 explain why this unity has largely contributed to the innovations in the rules governing relations between the EC and the ACP countries.

In the context of world-wide efforts towards a new international economic order, the unity of the ACP countries is important for at least three reasons. *First,* their unity has been a major factor in bringing about an improved relationship between a group of developed and developing countries. It shows that unity between economically weak countries should not be brandished as a strategy of confrontation, but accepted as a necessary step towards the creation of new relations based on equality and justice. *Second,* ACP unity has not been an isolated phenomenon. It is both part and example of the growing negotiating unity of developing countries in their dealings with developed countries on a global level. *Third,* ACP unity has also produced a number of provisions towards developing relations between ACP and non-ACP developing countries. The provisions of art. 7 of the Lomé Convention, the more flexible rules of origin and the promotion of regional integration may be cited as examples.

Some of the provisions of the new Convention have of course also been criticized, especially in the context of discussions on a new international economic order. The preferences accorded to ACP countries, do in fact discriminate in favor of a limited group of developing countries; by their very existence they may well render a global preferential system more difficult (Stordel, chapter 2). Stabex, as explains Persaud in chapter 3, still contains many shortcomings. Among them he mentions in particular, the absence of an up-to-date reference period; the fact that the scheme is based on nominal instead of real earnings; the use of a sharp cut-off point of 7.5% instead of a graduated system for the determination of eligibility for transfers; and the inadequacy of the Fund (p. 86). More serious a shortcoming may reside in the fact that at least one EC member is unwilling to see compensatory financing as no more than a supplementary measure in a comprehensive attack on the commodity-problem.[2]

The amount of EDF aid according to Voorhoeve in chapter 6 is not sufficient for the desired impact and both Voorhoeve and Dams (chapter 7) note that EC aid is not sufficiently—if at all—related to member states' national aid programs. According to Dams, moreover, the food aid policies of the EC may well demonstrate the unresolved long-range conflict between the agricultural policies of the industrialized countries and the interests of the developing countries (p. 130).

More severe criticisms against the Lomé Convention have been voiced by Palánkai in chapter 8c. His criticisms no doubt reflect the approach of the CMEA countries, which have sofar hardly played a meaningful role in establishing a new international economic order.

Does the Lomé Convention, in final analysis, contribute to more just and more equal relations between developed and developing countries, in short, to a new international economic order? The answer to this question can be given only by the way in which the Convention will be implemented, and especially by the willingness of the EC countries—as written in chapter 9—to meet the demands of the developing countries in a cooperative development strategy.

Such a development strategy would require the developed nations to revise their conceptions on the principles to govern the new international law. As Röling wrote already years ago,[3] mutual interdependence instead of national independence should be the all-embracing concept of a world of nations. The international law of liberty, created by the prosperous nations for themselves, should be replaced by a law of nations, which prime function is to

---

2. Compare: *Commodities*, "Action on Commodities, including decisions on an integrated programme in the light of the need for change in the world commodity economy." Report by the UNCTAD Secretariat. UNCTAD. Fourth Session. Nairobi, 5 May 1976. Item 8 of the Agenda. TD/184.

3. International Law in an Expanded World. Amsterdam 1960.

protect the weaker nations against the strong. Only a cooperative development strategy of the EC countries and a further strengthening of the unity of the developing countries can contribute to transforming these principles into binding rules for a new international economic order.

ANNEX I

ACP Countries			Per Capita Income (1973) in US Dollars	Exports[1] in % of GNP (1973)	Population (000) (1973)	Status Prior to Lomé Convention[2]	Totals		
A. Low Exportable Surplus	B. Dependent on Export Primary Products	C. Large Population and internal Market (industrialization)					A	B	C
Group I: Per Capita Income Less Than $ 200.							Group I States		
West Africa									
Upper Volta×			70	4	5,714	A			
Chad×			80	10	3,873	A			
Mali×			70	6	5,370	A			
	Guinea×		110	—	5,243	D			
Niger×			100	10	4,357	A			
	Zaire		140	30	23,438	A			
	Dahomey×		110	18	2,947	A			
Gabia×			130	—	493	C			
CAR×			160	14	1,710	A			
	Togo×		180	28	2,119	A			
	Sierra Leone		160	30	2,787	C			
East Africa									
Rwanda×			70	10	3,980	A			
Burundi×			80	10	3,580	A			
Ethiopia×			90	11	26,550	D			
	Somalia×		80	20	3,042	A			
Lesotho×			100	—	1,165	C			
	Malawi×		110	22	4,833	D			
	Sudan×		130	20	17,051	D			
	Tanzania×		130	25	13,974	B			
Madagascar×			150	14	8,301	A	11	11	0
	Uganda×		150	21	10,829	B			
	Kenya		170	27	12,480	B			
						Population	65,093	98,743	0

ANNEX I (continued)

| ACP Countries | | | Per Capita Income (1973) in US Dollars | Exports[1] in % of GNP (1973) | Population (000) (1973) | Status Prior to Lomé Convention[2] | Totals | | |
A. Low Exportable Surplus	B. Dependent on Export Primary Products	C. Large Population and internal Market (industrialization)					A	B	C
Group II. Per Capita Income $ 200 – $ 499									
West Africa									
		Nigeria	210	—	71,262	C			71,262
Mauretania×)			200	52	1,257	A			
Cameroon			250	20	6,206	A	5	13	1
Guinee-Bissau×)			330	—	510	D			
Eg. Guinea×)			260	—	313	D			
	Liberia		310	50	1,452	D			
	Senegal		280	20	4,070	A			
	Congo		340	15	1,199	A			
	Ivory Coast		380	34	5,887	A	*Group II States*		
	Ghana		300	23	9,313	C			
East Africa									
Botswana×)			230	10	641	C			
Swaziland			330	69	463	C	*Population*		
Mauritius×)			410	56	860	A	1,57	36,373	
Zambia×)			430	60	4,646	C			
Latin America									
Guyana			410	63	772	C			
Grenada×)			330	—	106	C			
Pacific									
Western Samoa×)			250	40	153	C			
Tonga×)			210	40	95	C			

Group III. Per Capita Income $ 500— $ 1.999

					Group III States
West Africa:					0 5
Gabon (oil)	1.310	—	520	A	0 _Population_ 0 4,336
Latin America:					0
Barbados^x	1.000	38	239	C	
Jamaica^x	990	38	1,967	C	
Trinidad/Tobago^x	1.310	71	1,059	C	
Pacific:					
Fiji^x	650	40	551	C	

Group IV. Per Capita Income $ 2.000— $ 4.999

D. Developed Economies				
Latin America: Bahamas^x	2.320		190	C
Western Europe: Belgium	4.560		9,760	E
Denmark	5.210		5,020	E
France	4.540		52,160	E
Ireland	2.150		3,030	E
Italy	2.450		54,890	E
Luxembourg	4.560		350	E
Netherlands	4.330		13,430	E
United Kingdom	3.060		56,000	E

Group V. Per Capita Income More Than $ 5.000

German Federal Republic	5.320		61,970	E

Population EC: 256,610

Source: World Bank Atlas 1975
1) European Communities.
Key: 2) A: party to Yaoundé Conventions
B: party to Arusha Convention
C: associable state following enlargement EC.
D: other states
E: Member EC.

x) Countries to which STABEX applies if export earnings of product or products listed in article 17 of the Convention represented at least 2.5% of its total earnings from merchandise exports. For the other countries it is 7.5%.

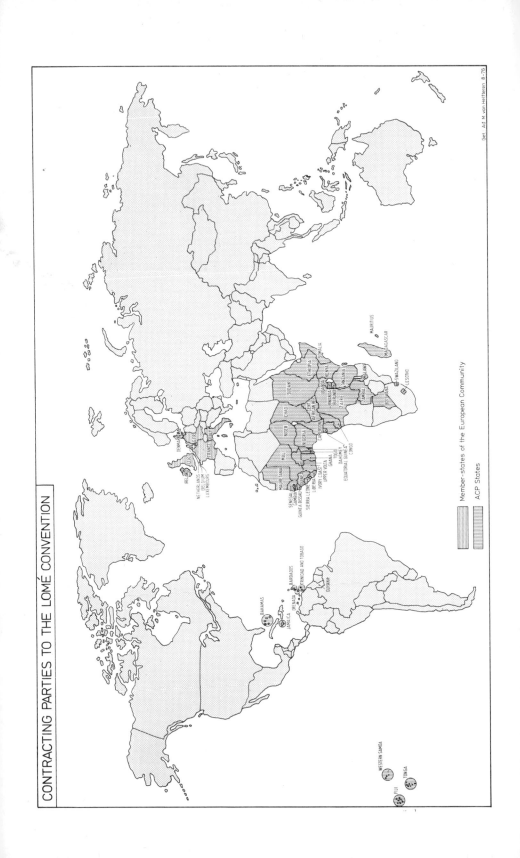

CONTRACTING PARTIES TO THE LOMÉ CONVENTION

Member-states of the European Community

ACP States

Get. Ad. M. van Heffteren 8-75

ANNEX II

ACP—EEC CONVENTION OF LOME*

His Majesty the King of the Belgians,
Her Majesty the Queen of Denmark,
The President of the Federal Republic of Germany,
The President of the French Republic,
The President of Ireland,
The President of the Italian Republic,
His Royal Highness the Grand Duke of Luxemburg,
Her Majesty the Queen of the Netherlands,
Her Majesty the Queen of the United Kingdom of Great Britain and Northern Ireland,

Contracting parties to the Treaty establishing the European Economic Community signed at Rome on 25 March 1975 (hereinafter called the 'Treaty'), whose States are hereinafter called 'Member States';
and the Council of the European Communities, of the one part, and

The Head of State of the Bahamas,
The Head of State of Barbados,
The President of the Republic of Botswana,
The President of the Republic of Burundi,
The President of the United Republic of Cameroon,
The President of the Central African Republic,
The President of the People's Republic of the Congo,
The President of the Republic of the Ivory Coast,
The President of the Republic of Dahomey,
The President of the Provisional Administrative Military Council, President of the Government of Ethiopia,
Her Majesty the Queen of Fiji,
The President of the Gabonese Republic,
The President of the Republic of the Gambia,
The President of the National Redemption Council of the Republic of Ghana,
The Head of State of Grenada,
The President of the Republic of Guinea,
The President of the Council of State of Guinea Bissau,
The President of the Republic of Equatorial Guinea,
The President of the Cooperative Republic of Guyana,
The President of the Republic of Upper Volta,
The Head of State of Jamaica,
The President of the Republic of Kenya,
The King of the Kingdom of Lesotho,
The President of the Republic of Liberia,
The President of the Republic of Malawi,
The Head of State and of Government of the Malagasy Republic,
The President of the Military Council of National Liberation of Mali, Head of State,

* Protocols, Agreement and Declarations omitted; see for a list of these documents the Final Act, p. 489.

President of the Government,
Her Majesty the Queen of Mauritius,
The President of the Islamic Republic of Mauritania,
The President of the Republic of Niger,
The Head of the Federal Military Government of Nigeria,
The President of the Republic of Rwanda,
The President of the Republic of Senegal,
The President of the Republic of Sierra Leone,
The President of the Somali Democratic Republic, President of the Supreme Revolutionary Council,
The President of the Democratic Republic of the Sudan,
The King of the Kingdom of Swaziland,
The President of the United Republic of Tanzania,
The President of the Republic of Chad,
The President of the Republic of Togo,
The Head of State of Tonga,
The Head of State of Trinidad and Tobago,
The President of the Republic of Uganda,
The Head of State of Western Samoa,
The President of the Republic of Zaïre,
The President of the Republic of Zambia,
whose States are hereinafter called the 'ACP States', of the other part,

HAVING REGARD to the Treaty establishing the European Economic Community;
ANXIOUS to establish, on the basis of complete equality between partners, close and continuing co-operation, in a spirit of international solidarity;
RESOLVED to intensify their efforts together for the economic development and social progress of the ACP States;
WISHING to demonstrate their common desire to maintain and develop the friendly relations existing between their countries, according to the principles of the United Nations Charter;
RESOLVED to promote, having regard to their respective levels of development, trade co-operation between the ACP States and the Community and to provide a sound basis therefor in conformity with their international obligations;
CONSCIOUS of the importance of developing co-operation and trade among the ACP States;
RESOLVED to establish a new model for relations between developed and developing States, compatible with the aspirations of the international community towards a more just and more balanced economic order;
DESIROUS of safeguarding the interests of the ACP States whose economies depend to a considerable extent on the exportation of commodities;
ANXIOUS to promote the industrial development of the ACP States by wider co-operation between these States and the Member States of the Community;
HAVE DECIDED TO CONCLUDE THIS CONVENTION, and to this end have designated as their Plenipotentiaries:

HIS MAJESTY THE KING OF THE BELGIANS:
   Renaat VAN ELSLANDE,
   Minister of Foreign Affairs;
etc., etc.
....

198

WHO, having exchanged their full powers, found in good and due form,
HAVE AGREED AS FOLLOWS:

Title I. Trade co-operation

Article 1

In the field of trade co-operation, the object of this Convention is to promote trade between the Contracting Parties, taking account of their respective levels of development, and, in particular, of the need to secure additional benefits for the trade of ACP States, in order to accelerate the rate of growth of their trade and improve the conditions of access of their products to the market of the European Economic Community, (hereinafter called the "Community") so as to ensure a better balance in the trade of the Contracting Parties.

To this end the Contracting Parties shall apply Chapters 1 and 2 of this Title.

Chapter 1. Trade arrangements

Article 2

1. Products originating in the ACP States shall be imported into the Community free of customs duties and charges having equivalent effect, but the treatment applied to these products may not be more favourable than that applied by the Member States among themselves.

For the purpose of the first subparagraph the transitional provisions in force relating to the residual customs duties and charges having equivalent effect resulting from the application of Articles 32 and 36 of the Act concerning the Conditions of Acession and the Adjustments to the Treaties shall have no application.

2. (a) Products originating in the ACP States:
- listed in Annex II to the Treaty when they come under a common organization of the market within the meaning of Article 40 of the Treaty, or
- subject, on importation into the Community, to specific rules introduced as a result of the implementation of the common agricultural policy; shall be imported into the Community notwithstanding the general arrangements applied in respect of third countries, in accordance with the following provisions:
(i) those products shall be imported free of customs duties for which Community provisions in force at the time of importation do not provide, apart from customs duties, for the application of any other measure relating to their importation;
(ii) for products other than those referred to under (i), the Community shall take the necessary measures to ensure, as a general rule, more favourable treatment than the general treatment applicable to the same products originating in third countries to which the most-favoured-nation clause applies.
(b) These arrangements shall enter into force at the same time as this Convention and shall remain applicable for its duration.

If, however, during the application of this Convention, the Community,
- subjects one or more products to common organization of the market or to specific rules introduced as a result of the implementation of the common agricultural policy, it reserves the right to adapt the import treatment for these products originating in the ACP States, following consultations within the Council of Ministers. In such cases, paragraph 2 (a) shall be applicable;
- modifies the common organization of the market in a particular product or the specific rules introduced as a result of the implementation of the common agricultural policy, it reserves the right to modify the arrangements laid down for products originating in the ACP States, following consultations within the Council of Ministers. In such cases, the

Community undertakes to ensure that products originating in the ACP States continue to enjoy an advantage comparable to that previously enjoyed in relation to products originating in third countries benefiting from the most-favoured-nation clause.

Article 3

1. The Community shall not apply to imports of products originating in the ACP States any quantitative restrictions or measures having equivalent effect other than those which the Member States apply among themselves.

2. Paragraph 1, however, shall not prejudice the import treatment applied to the products referred to in the first indent of Article 2 (2) (a).

The Community shall inform the ACP States when residual quantitative restrictions are eliminated in respect of any of these products.

3. This Article shall not prejudice the treatment that the Community applies to certain products in implementation of world commodity agreements to which the Community and the ACP States concerned are signatory.

Article 4

Nothing in this Convention shall preclude prohibitions or restrictions on imports, exports or goods in transit justified on grounds of public morality, public policy or public security; the protection of health and life of humans, animals and plants; the protection of national treasures possessing artistic, historic or archaeological value or the protection of industrial and commercial property.

Such prohibitions or restrictions shall not, however, constitute a means of arbitrary discrimination or a disguised restriction on trade.

Article 5

Where new measures or measures stipulated in programmes adopted by the Community for the approximation of laws and regulations in order to facilitate the movement of goods are likely to affect the interests of one or more ACP States the Community shall, prior to adopting such measures, inform the ACP States thereof through the Council of Ministers.

In order to enable the Community to take into consideration the interests of the ACP States concerned, consultations shall be held upon the request of the latter with a view to reaching a satisfactory solution.

Article 6

Where existing rules or regulations of the Community adopted in order to facilitate the movement of goods or where the interpretation, application or administration thereof affect the interests of one or more ACP States, consultations shall be held at the request of the latter with a view to reaching a satisfactory solution.

With a view to finding a satisfactory solution, the ACP States may also bring up within the Council of Ministers any other problems relating to the movement of goods which might result from measures taken or to be taken by the Member States.

The competent institutions of the Community shall to the greatest possible extent inform the Council of Ministers of such measures.

Article 7

1. In view of their present development needs, the ACP States shall not be required, for the duration of this Convention, to assume, in respect of imports of products originating in the Community, obligations corresponding to the commitments entered into by the Community in respect of imports of the products originating in the ACP States, under this Chapter.

2. (a) In their trade with the Community, the ACP States shall not discriminate among the Member States, and shall grant to the Community treatment no less favourable than the most-favoured-nation treatment.

(b) The most-favoured-nation treatment referred to in subparagraph (a) shall not apply in respect of trade or economic relations between ACP States or between one or more ACP States and other developing countries.

Article 8

Each Contracting Party shall communicate its customs tariff to the Council of Ministers within a period of three months following the entry into force of this Convention. It shall also communicate any subsequent amendments to that tariff as and when they occur.

Article 9

1. The concept of "originating products" for the purposes of implementing this Chapter, and the methods of administrative co-operation relating thereto, are laid down in protocol No. 1.

2. The Council of Ministers may adopt any amendment to Protocol No. 1.

3. Where the concept of 'originating products' has not yet been defined for a given product in implementation of paragraphs 1 or 2, each Contracting Party shall continue to apply its own rules.

Article 10

1. If, as a result of applying the provisions of this Chapter, serious disturbances occur in a sector of the economy of the Community or of one or more of its Member States, or jeopardize their external financial stability, or if difficulties arise which may result in a deterioration in a sector of the economy of a region of the Community, the latter may take, or may authorize the Member State concerned to take, the necessary safeguard measures. These measures and the methods of applying them shall be notified immediately to the Council of Ministers.

2. For the purpose of implementing paragraph 1, priority shall be given to such measures as would least disturb the trade relations between the Contracting Parties and the attainment of the objectives of the Convention. These measures shall not exceed the limits of what is strictly necessary to remedy the difficulties that have arisen.

Article 11

In order to ensure effective implementation of the provisions of this Convention in the field of trade co-operation, the Contracting Parties agree to inform and consult each other.

Consultations shall take place, at the request of the Community or of the ACP States, in accordance with the conditions provided for in the rules of procedure in Article 74, particularly in the following cases:

1. Where Contracting Parties envisage taking any trade measures affecting the interest of one or more Contracting Parties under this Convention, they shall inform the Council of Ministers thereof. Consultations shall take place, where the Contracting Parties concerned so request, in order to take into account their respective interests.

2. Where the Community envisages concluding a preferential trade agreement it shall inform the ACP States thereof. Consultations shall take place, where the ACP States so request, in order to safeguard their interests.

3. Where the Community or the Member States take safeguard measures in accordance with Article 10, consultations on these measures may take place within the Council of Ministers, where the Contracting Parties concerned so request, notably with a view to ensuring compliance with Article 10 (2).

4. If, during the application of this Convention, the ACP States consider that agricultural products covered by Article 2 (2) (a), other than those subject to special treatment, call for special treatment, consultations may take place within the Council of Ministers.

Chapter 2. *Trade promotion*

Article 12
With a view to attaining the objectives they have set themselves as regards trade and industrial co-operation the Contracting Parties shall carry out trade promotion activities which will be aimed at helping the ACP States to derive maximum benefit from Title I, Chapter 1 and Title III and to participate under the most favourable conditions in the Community, regional and international markets.

Article 13
The trade promotion activities provided for in article 12 shall include:
(a) improving the structure and working methods of organizations, departments or firms contributing to the development of the foreign trade of ACP States, or setting up such organizations, departments or firms;
(b) basic training or advanced vocational training of staff in trade promotion;
(c) participation by the ACP States in fairs, exhibitions, specialized international shows and the organization of trade events;
(d) improving co-operation between economic operators in the Member States and the ACP States and establishing links to promote such co-operation;
(e) carrying out and making use of market research and marketing studies;
(f) producing and distributing trade information in various forms within the Community and the ACP States with a view to developing trade.

Article 14
Applications for financing of trade promotion activities shall be presented to the Community by the ACP State or ACP States concerned under the conditions laid down in Title IV.

Article 15
The Community shall participate, under the conditions laid down in Title IV and in Protocol No. 2, in financing trade promotion activities for promoting the development of exports of ACP States.

Title II. Export earnings from commodities

Chapter 1. *Stabilization of export earnings*

Article 16
With the aim of remedying the harmful effects of the instability of export earnings and of thereby enabling the ACP States to achieve the stability, profitability and sustained growth of their economies, the Community shall implement a system for guaranteeing the stabilization of earnings from exports by the ACP States to the Community of certain products on which their economies are dependent and which are affected by fluctuations in price and/or quantity.

Article 17
1. Exports earnings to which the stabilization system applies shall be those accruing from

the exportation by the ACP States to the Community of the products on the following list, drawn up taking account of factors such as employment, deterioration of the terms of trade between the Community and the ACP State concerned, the level of development of the State concerned and the particular difficulties of the least developed, landlocked or island ACP States listed in Article 24:

a. *Groundnut products*
(aa) groundnuts, shelled or not
(ab) groundnut oil
(ac) groundnut oilcake

b. *Cocoa products*
(ba) cocoa beans
(bb) cocoa paste
(bc) cocoa butter

c. *Coffee products*
(ca) raw or roasted coffee
(cb) extracts, essences or concentrates of coffee

d. *cotton products*
(da) cotton, not carded or combed
(db) cotton linters

e. *coconut products*
(ea) coconuts
(eb) copra
(ec) coconut oil
(ed) coconut oilcake

f. *Palm, palm nut and kernel products*
(fa) palm oil
(fb) palm nut and kernel oil
(fc) palm nut and kernel oilcake
(fd) palm nuts and kernels

g. *Raw hides, skins and leather*
(ga) raw hides and skins
(gb) bovine cattle leather
(gc) sheep and lamb skin leather
(gd) goat and kid skin leather

h. *Wood products*
(ha) wood in the rough
(hb) wood roughly squared or half-squared, but not further manufactured
(hc) wood sawn lengthwise, but not further prepared

i. *Fresh bananas*

k. *Tea*

l. *Raw sisal*

m. *Iron ore*
 Iron ores and concentrates and roasted iron pyrites.

The statistics used for implementation of the system shall be those obtained by cross-checking the statistics of the ACP States and of the Community, account being taken of the fob values.

The system shall be implemented in respect of the products listed above where they are:
(a) released for home use in the Community;
(b) brought under the inward processing arrangements there in order to be processed.
2. The system shall apply to an ACP State's export earnings from the products listed above if, during the year preceding the year of application, earnings from the export of the product or products to all destinations represented at least 7.5% of its total earnings from merchandise exports: for sisal, however, the percentage shall be 5%. For the least developed, landlocked or island ACP States listed in Article 24 the percentage shall be 2.5%.
3. Nonetheless if, not sooner than 12 months following the entry into force of this Convention, one or more products not contained in this list, but upon which the economies of one or more ACP States depend to a considerable extent, are affected by sharp fluctuations, the Council of Ministers may decide whether the product or products should be included in the list, without prejudice to Article 18 (1).
4. For certain special cases the system shall apply to exports of the products in question irrespective of destination.
5. The ACP States concerned shall certify that the products to which the stabilization system applies have originated in their territory.

Article 18
1. For the purposes specified in Article 16 and for the duration of this Convention, the Community shall allocate to the stabilization system a total amount of 375 million units of account to cover all its commitments under the said system. This amount shall be managed by the Commission of the European Communities (hereinafter called the 'Commission').
2. This total amount shall be divided into five equal annual instalments. Every year except the last, the Council of Ministers may authorize, where required, the use in advance of a maximum of 20% of the following year's instalment.
3. Whatever balance remains at the end of each year of the first four years of the application of this Convention shall be carried forward automatically to the following year.
4. On the basis of a report submitted to it by the Commission, the Council of Ministers may reduce the amount of the transfers to be made under the stabilization system.
5. Before the expiry of this Convention, the Council of Ministers shall decide on the use to which any balance remaining from the total amount referred to in paragraph 1 is to be put and also on the terms to be laid down for the further use of amounts still to be paid by the ACP States, under Article 21, after the expiry of this Convention.

Article 19
1. In order to implement the stabilization system a reference level shall be calculated for each ACP State and for each product.
This reference level shall correspond to the component of export earnings during the four years preceding each year of application.
2. An ACP State shall be entitled to request a financial transfer if, on the basis of the results of a calendar year, its actual earnings, as defined in Article 17, from each of the products considered individually, are at least 7.5% below the reference level. For the least developed, landlocked or island ACP States listed in article 24 the percentage shall be 2.5%.
3. The request from the ACP State concerned shall be addressed to the Commission, which shall examine it in the light of the volume of resources available.
The difference between the reference level and actual earnings shall constitute the basis of the transfer.
4. However,

204

(a) should examination of the request, to be undertaken by the Commission in conjunction with the ACP State concerned, show that the fall in earnings from exports to the Community of the products in question is the result of a trade policy measure of the ACP State concerned adversely affecting exports to the Community in particular, the request shall not be admissible;

(b) should examination of the total exports of the requesting ACP State show a significant change, consultations shall be held between the Commission and the requesting State to determine whether such changes are likely to have an effect on the amount of the transfer, and if so to what extent.

5. Except in the case referred to in paragraph 4 (a) the Commission shall, in conjunction with the requesting ACP State, draw up a draft decision to make a transfer.

6. All necessary steps shall be taken to ensure that transfers are made rapidly, for example by means of advances, normally sixmonthly.

Article 20

The recipient ACP State shall decide how the resources will be used. It shall inform the Commission annually of the use to which it has put the resources transferred.

Article 21

1. The amounts transferred shall not bear interest.

2. The ACP States which have received transfers shall contribute, in the five years following the allocation of each transfer, towards the reconstitution of the resources made available for the system by the Community.

3. Each ACP State shall help reconstitute the resources when it is found that the trend of its export earnings will so permit.

To this effect, the Commission shall determine, for each year and for each product, and on the conditions specified in Article 17 (1), whether

– the unit value of the exports is higher than the reference unit value;

– the quantity actually exported to the Community is at least equal to the reference quantity.

If the two conditions are met at the same time, the recipient ACP State shall pay back into the system, within the limit of the transfers it has received, an amount equal to the reference quantity multiplied by the difference between the reference unit value and the actual unit value.

4. If, on expiry of the five-year period referred to in paragraph 2, the resources have not been fully reconstituted, the Council of Ministers, taking into consideration in particular, the situation of and prospects for the balance of payments, exchange reserves and foreign indebtedness of the ACP States concerned, may decide that:

– the sums outstanding are to be reconstituted wholly or partially, in one or more instalments;

– rights to repayment are to be waived.

5. Paragraphs 2, 3 and 4 shall not apply to the ACP States listed in Article 48.

Article 22

For each transfer a 'transfer agreement' shall be drawn up and concluded between the Commission and the ACP State concerned.

Article 23

1. In order to ensure that the stabilization system functions efficiently and rapidly, statistical and customs co-operation shall be instituted between the Community and the ACP States. The detailed arrangements for such co-operation shall be established by the Council of Ministers.

2. The ACP States and the Commission shall adopt by mutual agreement any practical measures facilitating the exchange of necessary information and the submission of requests for transfers, for example by producing a form for requesting transfers.

Article 24

The least developed, landlocked or island ACP States referred to in Article 17 (1) and (2) and Article 19 (2) are as follows:

- the Bahamas
- Barbados
- Botswana
- Burundi
- Central African Republic
- Chad
- Dahomey
- Equatorial Guinea
- Ethiopia
- Fiji
- the Gambia
- Grenada
- Guinea
- Guinea-Bissau
- Jamaica
- Lesotho
- Madagascar
- Malawi
- Mali
- Mauritania
- Mauritius
- Niger
- Rwanda
- Somalia
- Sudan
- Swaziland
- Tanzania
- Togo
- Tonga
- Trinidad and Tobago
- Uganda
- Upper Volta
- Western Samoa
- Zambia

Chapter 2. *Specific provisions concerning sugar*

Article 25

1. Notwithstanding any other provisions of this Convention the Community undertakes for an indefinite period to purchase and import, at guaranteed prices, specific quantities of cane sugar, raw or white, which originate in the ACP States producing and exporting cane sugar and which those States undertake to deliver to it.
2. Protocol No. 3 annexed to this Convention determines the conditions of implementation of this Article.

Title III. Industrial co-operation

Article 26

The Community and the ACP States, acknowledging the pressing need for the industrial development of the latter, agree to take all measures necessary to bring about effective industrial co-operation.

Industrial co-operation between the Community and the ACP States shall have the following objectives:

(a) to promote the development and diversification of industry in the ACP States and to help bring about a better distribution of industry both within those States and between them;

(b) to promote new relations in the industrial field between the Community, its Member States and the ACP States, in particular the establishment of new industrial and trade links between the industries of the Member States and those of the ACP States;

(c) to increase the links between industry and the other sectors of the economy, in particular agriculture;

(d) to facilitate the transfer of technology to the ACP States and to promote the adaptation of such technology to their specific conditions and needs, for example by expanding the capacity of the ACP States for research, for adaptation of technology and for training in industrial skills at all levels in these States;

(e) to promote the marketing of industrial products of the ACP States in foreign markets in order to increase their share of international trade in those products;

(f) to encourage the participation of nationals of ACP States, in particular that of small and medium-sized industrial firms, in the industrial development of those States;

(g) to encourage Community firms to participate in the industrial development of the ACP States, where those States so desire and in accordance with their economic and social objectives.

Article 27

In order to attain the objectives set out in Article 26, the Community shall help to carry out, by all the means provided for in the Convention, programmes, projects and schemes submitted to it on the initiative or with the agreement of the ACP States in the fields of industrial infrastructures and ventures, training, technology and research, small and medium-sized firms, industrial information and promotion, and trade co-operation.

Article 28

The Community shall contribute to the setting up and the extension of the infrastructure necessary for industrial development, particularly in the fields of transport and communications, energy and industrial research and training.

Article 29

The Community shall contribute to the setting up and the extension in the ACP States of industries processing raw materials and industries manufacturing finished and semi-finished products.

Article 30

At the request of the ACP States and on the basis of the programmes submitted by the latter, the Community shall contribute to the organization and financing of the training, at all levels, of personnel of the ACP States in industries and institutions within the Community.

In addition, the Community shall contribute to the establishment and expansion of industrial training facilities in the ACP States.

Article 31

With a view to helping the ACP States to overcome obstacles encountered by them in matters of access to and adaptation of technology, the Community is prepared in particular to:

(a) keep the ACP States better informed on technological matters and assist them in selecting the technology best adapted to their needs;

(b) facilitate their contacts and relations with firms and institutions in possession of the appropriate technological know-how;

(c) facilitate the acquisition, on favourable terms and conditions, of patents and other industrial property, in particular through financing and/or through other suitable arrangements with firms and institutions within the Community;

(d) contribute to the establishment and expansion of industrial research facilities in the ACP States with particular reference to the adaptation of available technology to the conditions and needs of those States.

Article 32

The Community shall contribute to the establishment and development of small and medium-sized industrial firms in the ACP States through financial and technical co-operation schemes adapted to the specific needs of such firms and covering inter alia:

(a) the financing of firms,

(b) the creation of appropriate infrastructure and industrial estates,

(c) vocational and advanced training,

(d) the setting up of specialized advisory services and credit facilities.

The development of these firms shall, as far as possible, be conductive to the strengthening of the complementary relationship between small and medium-sized industrial firms and of their links with large industrial firms.

Article 33

Industrial information and promotion schemes shall be carried out in order to secure and intensify regular information exchanges and the necessary contacts in the industrial field between the Community and the ACP States.

These schemes could have the following aims:

(a) to gather and disseminate all relevant information on the trends of industry and trade in the Community and on the conditions and possibilities for industrial development in the ACP States;

(b) to organize and facilitate contacts and meetings of all kinds between Community and ACP States' industrial policy-makers, promoters and firms;

(c) to carry out studies and appraisals aimed at pinpointing the practical opportunities for industrial co-operation with the Community in order to promote the industrial development of the ACP States;

(d) to contribute, through appropriate technical co-operation schemes, to the setting up, launching and running of the ACP States' industrial promotion bodies.

Article 34

In order to enable the ACP States to obtain full benefit from trade and other arrangements provided for in this Convention, trade promotion schemes shall be carried out to encourage the marketing of industrial products of ACP States both in the Community as well as in other external markets. Furthermore, programmes shall be drawn up jointly between the Community and the ACP States in order to stimulate and develop the trade of industrial products among the said States.

Article 35

1. A Committee on Industrial Co-operation shall be established. It shall be supervised by the Committee of Ambassadors.

2. The Committee on Industrial Co-operation shall:

(a) see to the implementation of this Title;

(b) examine the problems in the field of industrial co-operation submitted to it by the ACP States and/or by the Community, and suggest appropriate solutions;

(c) guide, supervise and control the activities of the Centre for Industrial Development referred to in Article 36 and report to the Committee of Ambassadors and, through it, to the Council of Ministers;

(d) submit from time to time reports and recommendations which it considers appropriate to the Committee of Ambassadors;

(e) perform such other functions as may be assigned to it by the Committee of Ambassadors.

3. The composition of the Committee on Industrial Co-operation and the details for its operation shall be determined by the Council of Ministers.

Article 36

A Centre for Industrial Development shall be set up. It shall have the following functions:

(a) to gather and disseminate in the Community and the ACP States all relevant information on the conditions of and opportunities for industrial co-operation;

(b) to have, at the request of the Community and the ACP States, studies carried out on the possibilities and potential for industrial development of the ACP States, bearing in mind the necessity for adaptation of technology to their needs and requirements, and to ensure their follow-up;

(c) to organize and facilitate contacts and meetings of all kinds between Community and ACP States' industrial policy-makers, promoters, and firms and financial institutions;

(d) to provide specific industrial information and support services;

(e) help to identify, on the basis of needs indicated by ACP States, the opportunities for industrial training and applied research in the Community and in the ACP States, and to provide relevant information and recommendations.

The Centre's Statutes and rules of operation shall be adopted by the Council of Ministers on a proposal from the Committee of Ambassadors upon the entry into force of this Convention.

Article 37

Programmes, projects or schemes undertaken in the field of industrial co-operation and involving Community financing shall be implemented in accordance with Title IV, taking into account the particular characteristics of interventions in the industrial sector.

Article 38

1. Each ACP State shall endeavour to give as clear an indication as possible of its priority areas for industrial co-operation and the form it would like such co-operation to take. It will also take such steps as are necessary to promote effective co-operation within the framework of this Title with the Community and the Member States or with firms or nationals of member States who comply with the development programmes and priorities of the host ACP State.

2. The Community and its member States, for their part, shall endeavour to set up measures to attract the participation of their firms and nationals in the industrial development efforts of the ACP States concerned, and shall encourage such firms and nationals to adhere to the aspirations and development objectives of those ACP States.

Article 39

This Title shall not prevent any ACP State or groups of ACP States from entering into specific arrangements for the development in ACP States of agricultural, mineral, energy and other specific resources with a Member State or States of the Community, provided that these arrangements are compatible with this Convention. Such arrangements must be complementary to the efforts on industrialization and must not operate to the detriment of this Title.

Title IV. Financial and technical co-operation

Article 40

1. The purpose of economic, financial and technical co-operation is to correct the structural imbalances in the various sectors of the ACP States' economies. The co-operation shall relate to the execution of projects and programmes which contribute essentially to the economic and social development of the said States.

2. Such development shall consist in particular in the greater well-being of the population, improvement of the economic situation of the State, local authorities and firms, and the introduction of structures and factors whereby such improvement can be continued and extended by their own means.

3. This co-operation shall complement the efforts of the ACP States and shall be adapted to the characteristics of each of the said States.

Article 41

1. The Council of Ministers shall examine at least once a year whether the objectives referred to in Article 40 are being attained and shall also examine the general problems resulting from the implementation of financial and technical co-operation. It shall take stock, on the basis of information gathered both by the Community and the ACP States, of action undertaken in this context by the Community and by the ACP States. This stocktaking shall also cover regional co-operation and measures in favour of the least developed ACP States.

As regards the Community, the Commission shall submit to the Council of Ministers an annual report on the management of Community financial and technical aid. This report shall be drawn up in collaboration with the European Investment Bank (hereinafter called the 'Bank') for the parts of the report which concern it. It shall in particular show the position as to the commitment, implementation and utilization of the aid, broken down by type of financing and by recipient State.

The ACP States for their part shall submit to the Council of Ministers any observations, information or proposals on the problems concerning the implementation, in their respective countries, of the economic, financial and technical co-operation, and also on the general problems of this co-operation.

The work on the annual stocktaking of financial and technical co-operation shall be prepared by the experts of the Community and of the ACP States who are responsible for the implementation of that co-operation.

2. On the basis of the information submitted by the Community and the ACP States and of the examination referred to in paragraph 1, the Council of Ministers shall define the policy and guidelines of financial and technical co-operation and shall formulate resolutions on the measures to be taken by the Community and the ACP States in order to ensure that the objectives of such co-operation are attained.

Article 42

For the duration of this Convention, the overall amount of the Community's aid shall be 3,390 million units of account.

This amount comprises:

1. 3,000 million units of account from the European Development Fund (hereinafter called the 'Fund'), allocated as follows:

(a) for the purposes set out in Article 40: 2,625 million units of account, consisting of:

– 2,100 million units of account in the form of grants,

– 430 million units of account in the form of special loans,

– 95 million units of account in the form of risk capital;

(b) for the purposes set out in Title II, up to 375 million units of account, likewise from the Fund, in the form of transfer for the stabilization of export earnings.

2. For the purposes set out in Article 40, up to 390 million units of account in the form of loans from the Bank, made from its own resources on the terms and conditions provided for in its Statute, and supplemented, as a general rule, by a 3% interest rate subsidy, under the conditions laid down in Article 5 of Protocol No. 2.

The total cost of the interest rate subsidies shall be charged against the amounts of aid provided for in 1 (a) above.

210

Article 43

1. The method or methods of financing which may be contemplated for each project or programme shall be selected jointly by the Community and the ACP State or States concerned with a view to the best possible use being made of the resources available and by reference to the level of development and the economic and financial situation of the ACP State or ACP States concerned. Moreover, account shall be taken of the factors which ensure the servicing of repayable aid.

The definitive choice of methods of financing for projects and programmes shall be made only at an appropriate stage in the appraisal of such projects and programmes.

2. Account shall also be taken of the nature of the project or programme, of its prospects of economic and financial profitability and of its economic and social impact.

In particular, productive capital projects in the industrial, tourism and mining sectors shall be given priority financing by means of loans from the Bank and risk capital.

Article 44

1. Where appropriate, a number of methods may be combined for financing a project or programme.

2. With the agreement of the ACP State or ACP States concerned, financial aid from the Community may take the form of co-financing with participation by, in particular, credit and development agencies and institutions, firms, Member States, third countries or international finance organizations.

Article 45

1. Grants and special loans may be made available to or through the ACP State concerned.

2. Where these funds are on-lent through the ACP State concerned, the terms and procedure for the onlending by the intermediate recipient to the final borrower shall be laid down between the Community and the State concerned in an intermediate financing agreement.

3. Any benefits accruing to the intermediate recipient, either because that recipient receives a grant or a loan for which the interest rate or the repayment period is more favourable than that of the final loan, shall be employed by the intermediate recipient for the purposes and on the terms set out in the intermediate financing agreement.

Article 46

1. The financing of projects and programmes comprises the means required for their execution, such as:

- capital projects in the fields of rural development, industrialization, energy, mining, tourism, and economic and social infrastructure;
- schemes to improve the structure of agricultural production;
- technical co-operation schemes, in particular in the fields of training and technological adaptation or innovation;
- industrial information and promotion schemes;
- marketing and sales promotion schemes;
- specific schemes to help small and medium-sized national firms;
- microprojects for grassroots development, in particular in rural areas.

2. Financial and technical co-operation shall not cover current administrative, maintenance and operating expenses.

3. Financial aid may cover import costs and local expenditure required for the execution of projects and programmes.

Article 47

1. In the implementation of financial and technical co-operation, the Community shall provide effective assistance for attaining the objectives which the ACP States set themselves in the context of regional and interregional co-operation. This assistance shall aim to:

(a) accelerate economic co-operation and development both within and between the regions of the ACP States;

(b) accelerate diversifivation of the economies of the ACP States;

(c) reduce the economic dependence of the ACP States on imports by maximizing output of those products for which the ACP States in question have real potential;

(d) create sufficiently wide markets within the ACP States and neighbouring States by removing the obstacles which hinder the development and integration of those markets in order to promote trade between the ACP States;

(e) maximize the use of resources and services in the ACP States.

2. To this end approximately 10% of the total financial resources provided for in Article 42 for the economic and social development of the ACP States shall be reserved for financing their regional projects.

Article 48

1. In the implementation of financial and technical co-operation, special attention shall be paid to the needs of the least developed ACP States so as to reduce the specific obstacles which impede their development and prevent them from taking full advantage of the opportunities offered by financial and technical co-operation.

2. The following ACP States shall be eligible, according to their particular needs, for the special measures established under this Article:

Botswana	Mauritania
Burundi	Niger
Central African Republic	Rwanda
Chad	Somalia
Dahomey	Sudan
Ethiopia	Swaziland
the Gambia	Tanzania
Guinea	Togo
Guinea-Bissau	Tonga
Lesotho	Uganda
Malawi	Upper Volta
Mali	Western Samoa.

3. The list of ACP States in paragraph 2 may be amended by decision of the Council of Ministers:

– where a third State in a comparable economic situation accedes to this Convention;

– where the economic situation of an ACP State undergoes a radical and lasting change either so as to necessitate the application of special measures or so that this treatment is no longer warranted.

Article 49

1. The following shall be eligible for financial and technical co-operation:

(a) the ACP States;

(b) the regional or interstate bodies to which the ACP States belong and which are authorized by the said States;

(c) the joint bodies set up by the Community and the ACP States and authorized by the latter to attain certain specific objectives, notably in the field of industrial and trade co-operation.

2. Subject to the agreement of the ACP State or ACP States concerned, the following shall be eligible for such co-operation in respect of projects or programmes approved by the latter:

(a) local authorities and public or semi-public development agencies of the ACP States, in particular their development banks;

(b) private bodies working in the countries concerned for the economic and social development of the population of those ACP States;

(c) firms carrying out their activities, in accordance with industrial and business management methods, which are set up as companies or firms of an ACP State within the meaning of Article 63;

(d) groups of producers that are nationals of the ACP States or like bodies, and, where no such groups or bodies exist, the producers themselves;

(e) for training purposes, scholarship holders and trainees.

Article 50

1. There shall be close co-operation between the Community and the ACP States in implementing aid measures financed by the former. This co-operation shall be achieved through active participation by the ACP State or group of ACP States concerned in each of the various stages of a project: the aid programming, the submission and appraisal of projects, the preparation of financing decisions, execution of projects and final evaluation of the results, in accordance with the various procedures laid down in Articles 51 to 57.

2. As regards project financing for which the Bank is responsible, application of the principles defined in Articles 51 to 58 may be adapted, in concert with the ACP State or ACP States concerned, to take account of the nature of the operations financed and of the Bank's procedures under its Statute.

Article 51

1. Community aid, which is complementary to the ACP States' own efforts, shall be integrated in the economic and social development plans and programmes of the said States so that projects undertaken with the financial support of the Community dovetail with the objectives and priorities set up by those States.

2. At the beginning of the period covered by this Convention, Community aid shall be programmed, in conjunction with each recipient State in such a way that the latter can obtain as clear an idea as possible of the aid, in particular as regards the amount and terms, it can expect during that period and especially of specific objectives which this aid may meet. This programme shall be drawn up on the basis of proposals made by each ACP State, in which it has fixed its objectives and priorities. Projects or programmes already identified on an indicative basis may be the subject of a provisional timetable as regards preparation.

3. The Community indicative aid programme for each ACP State shall be drawn up by mutual agreement by the competent bodies of he Community and those of the ACP State concerned. It shall then be the subject of an exchange of views, at the beginning of the period covered by this Convention, between the representatives of the Community and those of the ACP State concerned.

This exchange of views shall enable the ACP State to set out its development policy and priorities.

4. The aid programmes shall be sufficiently flexible to enable account to be taken of changes occuring in the economic situation of the various ACP States, and any modifications of their initial priorities. Therefore, each programme may be reviewed whenever necessary during the period covered by this Convention.

5. These programmes shall not cover the exceptional aid referred to in Article 59 or the measures for stabilizing export earnings referred to in Title II.

Article 52

1. Preparation of the projects and programmes which come within the framework of the Community aid programme drawn up by mutual agreement shall be the responsibility of the ACP States concerned or of other beneficiaries approved by them. The Community may, where those States so request, provide technical assistance for drawing up the dossiers of projects or programmes.

2. Such dossiers shall be submitted to the Community as and when they are ready by the beneficiaries specified in Article 49 (1), or, with the express agreement of the ACP State or ACP States concerned, by those specified in Article 49 (2).

Article 53

1. The Community shall appraise projects and programmes in close collaboration with the ACP States and any other beneficiaries. The technical, social, economic, trade, financial, organizational and management aspects of such projects or programmes shall be reviewed systematically.

2. The aim of appraisal is:

(a) to ensure that the projects and programmes stem from economic or social development plans or programmes of the ACP States;

(b) to assess, as far as possible by means of an economic evaluation, the effectiveness of each project or programme by setting the effects it is expected to produce against the resources to be invested in it. In each project the expected effects shall be the practical expression of a number of specific development objectives of the ACP State or ACP States concerned.

On this basis, appraisal shall ensure that, as far as possible, the measures selected constitute the most effective and profitable method of attaining these objectives, taking into account the various constraints on each ACP State;

(c) to verify that the conditions guaranteeing the successful conclusion and the variability of the projects or programmes are met, which involves:

– verifying that the projects as conceived are suitable for bringing about the effects sought and that the means to be used commensurate with the circumstances and resouces of the ACP State or region concerned;

– and furthermore guaranteeing that the staff and other means, particularly financial, necessary for operating and maintaining the investments and for covering incidental project costs are actually available. Particular attention shall be paid here to the possibility of the project being managed by national personnel.

Article 54

1. Financing proposals, which summarize the conclusions of the appraisal and are submitted to the Community's decision-making body, shall be drawn up in close collaboration between the competent departments of the Community and those of the ACP State or ACP States concerned.

The final version of each financing proposal shall be transmitted by the competent departments of the Community simultaneously to the Community and to the ACP States concerned.

2. All projects or programmes put foward officially in accordance with Article 52 by an ACP State or ACP States, whether or not selected by the competent departments of the Community, shall be brought to the attention of the Community body responsible for taking financing decisions.

3. Where the Community body responsible for delivering an opinion on projects fails to deliver a favourable opinion, the competent departments of the Community shall consult the representatives of the ACP State or ACP States concerned on further action to be taken,

in particular on the advisability of submitting the dossier afresh, possibly in a modified form, to the relevant Community body.

Before that body gives its final opinion, the representatives of the ACP State or ACP States concerned may request a hearing by the representatives of the Community in order to be able to state their grounds for the project.

Should the final opinion delivered by that body not be favourable, the competent departments of the Community shall consult afresh with the representatives of the ACP State or APC States concerned before deciding whether the project should be submitted as it stands to the Community's decision-making bodies or whether it should be withdrawn or modified.

Article 55

The ACP States, or the other beneficiaries authorized by them, shall be responsible for the execution of projects financed by the Community.

Accordingly, they shall be responsible for negotiating and concluding works and supply contracts and technical co-operation contracts.

Article 56

1. As regards operations financed by the Community, participation in tendering procedures and other procedures for the award of contracts shall be open on equal terms to all natural and legal persons of the Member States and ACP States.
2. Paragraph 1 shall be without prejudice to measures intended to assist construction firms or manufacturing firms of the ACP States concerned, or of another ACP State, to take part in the execution of works contracts or supply contracts.
3. Paragraph 1 does not mean that the funds paid over by the Community must be used exclusively for the purchase of goods or for the remuneration of services in the Member States and in the ACP States.

Any participation by certain third countries in contracts financed by the Community must, however, be of an exceptional nature and be authorized case-by-case by the competent body of the Community, account being taken in particular of a desire to avoid excessive increases in the cost of projects attributable either to the distances involved and transport difficulties or to the delivery dates.

Participation by third countries may also be authorized where the Community participates in the financing of regional or interregional co-operation schemes involving third countries and in the joint financing of projects with other providers of funds.

Article 57

1. The effects and results of completed projects, and the physical state of the work carried out, shall be evaluated regularly and jointly by the competent departments of the Community and of the ACP State or ACP States concerned in order to ensure that the objectives set are attained under the best conditions.

Evaluations may also be made of projects in progress where this is warranted by their nature, importance or difficulty of execution.
2. The competent institutions of the Community and of the ACP States concerned shall, each for their respective parts, take the measures which evaluation shows to be necessary. The Council of Ministers shall be kept informed of such measures by the Commission and each ACP State for the purposes of Article 41.

Article 58

1. The management and maintenance of work carried out within the context of financial and technical co-operation shall be the responsibility of the ACP States or other beneficiaries.

2. Exceptionally, and by way of derogation from Article 46 (2), in particular under the circumstances specified in Article 10 of Protocol No. 2, supplementary aid may be provided temporarily and on a diminishing scale in order to ensure that full use is made of investments which are of special importance for the economic and social development of the ACP State concerned and the running of which temporarily constitutes a truly excessive burden for the ACP State or other beneficiaries.

Article 59

1. Exceptional aid may be accorded to ACP States faced with serious difficulties resulting from natural disasters or comparable extraordinary circumstances.
2. For the purposes of financing the exceptional aid referred to in paragraph 1, a special appropriation shall be constituted within the Fund.
3. The special appropriation shall initially be fixed at 50 million units of account. At the end of each year of application of this Convention this appropriation shall be restored to its initial level.

The total amount of monies transferred from the Fund to the special appropriation during the period of application of the Convention may not exceed 150 million units of account.

Upon expiry of the Convention any monies transferred to the special appropriation which have not been committed for exceptional aid shall be returned to the Fund proper for financing other schemes falling within the field of application of financial and technical co-operation, unless the Council of Ministers decides otherwise.

In the event of the special appropriation being exhausted before the expiry of this Convention, the Community and the ACP States shall adopt, within the relevant joint bodies, appropriate measures to deal with the situations described in paragraph 1.
4. Exceptional aid shall be non-reimbursable. It shall be allocated on a case-by-case basis.
5. Exceptional aid shall help finance the most suitable means of remedying the serious difficulties referred to in paragraph 1.

These means may take the form of works, supplies or provision of services, or cash payments.
6. Exceptional aid shall not be used for dealing with the harmful effects of the instability of export earnings, which are the subject of Title II.
7. The arrangements for allocating exceptional aid, for payments and for implementing the programmes shall be worked out under an emergency procedure, with account being taken of the provisions of Article 54.

Article 60

The fiscal and customs arrangements applicable in the ACP States to contracts financed by the Community shall be adopted by a decision of the Council of Ministers at its first meeting following the date of entry into force of this Convention.

Article 61

In the event of failure of an ACP State to ratify this Convention pursuant to Title VII, or denunciation of this Convention in accordance with that Title, the Contracting Parties shall be obliged to adjust the amounts of the financial aid provided for in this Convention.

Title V. Provisions relating to establishment, services, payments and capital movements

Chapter 1. *Provisions relating to establishment and services*

216

Article 62

As regards the arrangements that may be applied in matters of establishment and provision of services, the ACP States on the one hand and the Member States on the other shall treat nationals and companies or firms of Member States and nationals and companies or firms of the ACP States respectively on a non-discriminatory basis. However, if, for a given activity, an ACP State or a Member State is unable to provide such treatment, the Member States or the ACP States, as the case may be, shall not be bound to accord such treatment for this activity to the nationals and companies or firms of the State concerned.

Article 63

For the purpose of this Convention 'companies or firms' means companies or firms constituted under civil or commercial law, including co-operative societies and other legal persons governed by public or private law, save for those which are non-profit-making.

"Companies or firms of a Member State or of an ACP State" means companies or firms formed in accordance with the law of a Member State or ACP State and whose registered office, central administration or principal place of business is in a Member State or ACP State; however, a company or firm having only its registered office in a Member State or ACP State must be engaged in an activity which has an effective and continuous link with the economy of that Member State or ACP State.

Article 64

At the request of the Community or of the ACP States, the Council of Ministers shall examine any problems raised by the application of Articles 62 and 63. It shall also formulate any relevant recommendations.

Chapter 2. *Provisions relating to current payments and capital movements*

Article 65

With regard to capital movements linked with investments and to current payments, the Contracting Parties shall refrain from taking action in the field of foreign exchange transactions which would be incompatible with their obligations under this Convention resulting from the provisions relating to trade in goods, to services, establishment and industrial co-operation. These obligations shall not, however, prevent the Contracting Parties from adopting the necessary protective measures, should this be justified by reasons relating to serious economic difficulties or severe balance of payments problems.

Article 66

In respect of foreign exchange transactions linked with investments and current payments, the ACP States on the one hand and the Member States on the other shall avoid, as far a possible, taking discriminatory measures vis-à-vis each other or according more favourable treatment to third States, taking full account of the evolving nature of the international monetary system, the existence of specific monetary arrangements and balance of payments problems.

To the extent that such measures or treatment are unavoidable they will be maintained or introduced in accordance with international monetary rules and every effort will be made to minimize any adverse effects on the Parties concerned.

Article 67

Throughout the duration of the loans and risk capital operations provided for in Article 42, each of the ACP States undertakes:
- to place at the disposal of the beneficiaries referred to in Article 49 the currency

necessary for the payment of interest and commission on and amortization of loans and quasi-capital aid granted for the implementation of aid measures on their territory;
– to make available to the Bank the foreign exchange necessary for the transfer of all sums received by it in national currency which represent the net revenue and proceeds from transactions involving the acquisition by the Community of holdings in the capital of firms.

Article 68

At the request of the Community or of the ACP States, the Council of Ministers shall examine any problems raised by the application of Articles 65 to 67. It shall also formulate any relevant recommendations.

Title VI.   Institutions

Article 69

The Institutions of this Convention are the Council of Ministers, assisted by the Committee of Ambassadors, and the Consultative Assembly.

Article 70

1. The Council of Ministers shall be composed, on the one hand, of the members of the Council of the European Communities and of members of the Commission of the European Communities and, on the other hand, of a member of the Government of each of the ACP States.
2. Any member of the Council of Ministers unable to attend may be represented. The representative shall exercise all the rights of the accredited member.
3. The proceedings of the Council of Ministers shall be valid only if half the members of the Council of the European Communities, one member of the Commission and two thirds of the accredited members representing the Governments of the ACP States are present.
4. The Council of Ministers shall lay down its rules of procedure.

Article 71

The office of President of the Council of Ministers shall be held alternately by a member of the Council of the European Communities and a member of the Government of an ACP State, the latter to be designated by the ACP States.

Article 72

1. Meetings of the Council of Ministers shall be called once a year by its President.
2. The Council of Ministers shall, in addition, meet whenever necessary, in accordance with the conditions laid down in its rules of procedure.

Article 73

1. The Council of Ministers shall act by mutual agreement between the Community on the one hand and the ACP States on the other.
2. The Community on the one hand and the ACP States on the other shall each, by means of an internal protocol, determine the procedure for arriving at their respective positions.

Article 74

1. The Council of Ministers shall define the broad outlines of the work to be undertaken in the context of the application of this Convention.
2. The Council of Ministers shall periodically review the results of the arrangements under this Convention and shall take such measures as may be necessary for the attainment of the objectives of this Convention.

3. Where provided for in this Convention, the Council of Ministers shall have the power to take decisions; such desicions shall be binding on the Contracting Parties, which must take such measures as are required to implement these decisions.

4. The Council of Ministers may likewise formulate such resolutions, recommendations or opinions as it may deem necessary to attain the common objectives and to ensure the smooth functioning of the arrangements of this Convention.

5. The Council of Ministers shall publish an annual report and such other information as it considers appropriate.

6. The Council of Ministers may make all the arrangements that are appropriate for ensuring the maintenance of effective contacts, consultations and co-operation between the economic and social sectors of the Member States and of the ACP States.

7. The Community or the ACP States may raise in the Council of Ministers any problems arising from the application of this Convention.

8. Where provided in this Convention, consultations shall take place, at the request of the Community or of the ACP States, within the Council of Ministers, in accordance with the conditions laid down in the rules of procedure.

9. The Council of Ministers may set up committees or groups and ad hoc working groups, to undertake such activities as it may determine.

10. At the request of one of the Contracting Parties, exchanges of view may take place on questions having direct repercussions on the matters covered by this Convention.

11. By agreement among the parties, exchanges of views may take place on other economic or technical questions which are of mutual interest.

Article 75

The Council of Ministers may, where necessary, delegate to the Committee of Ambassadors any of its powers. In this event, the Committee of Ambassadors shall give its decisions in accordance with the conditions laid down in Article 73.

Article 76

The Committee of Ambassadors shall be composed, on the one hand, of one representative of each Member State and one representative of the Commission and, on the other, of one representative of each ACP State.

Article 77

1. The Committee of Ambassadors shall assist in the performance of its functions the Council of Ministers and shall carry out any mandate entrusted to it by the Council of Ministers.

2. The Committee of Ambassadors shall exercise such other powers and perform such other duties as are assigned to it by the Council of Ministers.

3. The Committee of Ambassadors shall keep under review the functioning of this Convention and the development of the objectives as defined by the Council of Ministers.

4. The Committee of Ambassadors shall account for its actions to the Council of Ministers particularly in matters which have been the subject of delegation of powers. It shall also submit to the Council of Ministers any pertinent proposal and such resolutions, recommendations or opinions as it may deem necessary or consider appropriate.

5. The Committee of Ambassadors shall supervise the work of all the committees and all other bodies or working groups, whether standing or ad hoc, established or provided for by or under this Convention and submit periodical reports to the Council of Ministers.

Article 78

The office Chairman of the Committee of Ambassadors shall be held alternately by a representative of a Member State designated by the Community and a representative of an ACP State designated by the ACP States.

The Committee of Ambassadors shall lay down its rules of procedure which shall be submitted to the Council of Ministers for approval.

Article 79

The secretariat duties and other work necessary for the functioning of the Council of Ministers and the Committee of Ambassadors or other joint bodies shall be carried out on a basis of parity and in accordance with the conditions laid down in the rules of procedure of the Council of Ministers.

Article 80

1. The Consultative Assembly shall be composed on a basis of parity of members of the Assembly on the side of the Community and of the representatives designated by the ACP States on the other.
2. The Consultative Assembly shall appoint its Bureau and shall adopt its own rules of procedure.
3. The Consultative Assembly shall meet at least once a year.
4. Each year, the Council of Ministers shall submit a report on its activities to the Consultative Assembly.
5. The Consultative Assembly may set up ad hoc consultative committees to undertake such specific activities as it may determine.
6. The Consultative Assembly may adopt resolutions on matters concerning or covered by this Convention.

Article 81

1. Any dispute which arises between one or more Member States or the Community on the one hand, and one or more ACP States on the other, concerning the interpretation or the application of this Convention may be placed before the Council of Ministers.
2. Where circumstances permit, and subject to the Council of Ministers being informed, so that any parties concerned may assert their rights, the Contracting Parties may have recourse to a good offices procedure.
3. If the Council of Ministers fails to settle the dispute at its next meeting, either Party may notify the other of the appointment of an arbitrator, the other Party must then appoint a second arbitrator within two months. For the application of this procedure, the Community and the Member States shall be deemed to be one party to the dispute.

The Council of Ministers shall appoint a third arbitrator.

The decisions of the arbitrators shall be taken by majority vote.

Each Party to the dispute must take the measures required for the implementation of the arbitrators' decision.

Article 82

The operating expenses of the Institutions under this Convention shall be defrayed in accordance with the terms set out in Protocol No. 4 to this Convention.

Article 83

The privileges and immunities for the purpose of this Convention shall be as laid down in Protocol No. 5 to this Convention.

Title VII.   General and final provisions

Article 84

No treaty, convention, agreement or arrangement of any kind between one or more Member States and one or more ACP States may impede the implementation of this Convention.

Article 85

1. This Convention shall apply to the European territories to which the Treaty establishing the European Economic Community applies, in accordance with the conditions set out in that Treaty, on the one hand, and to the territories of the ACP States on the other.
2. Title I of this Convention shall also apply to the relations between the French Overseas Departments and the ACP States.

Article 86

1. As regards the Community, this Convention shall be validly concluded by a decision of the Council of the European Communities taken in accordance with the provisions of the Treaty and notified to the Parties.

It will be ratified by the Signatory States in conformity with their respective constitutional requirements.

2. The instruments of ratification and the act of notification of the conclusion of the Convention shall be deposited, as concerns the ACP States, with the Secretariat of the Council of the European Communities and, as concerns the Community and its Member States, with the Secretariat of the ACP States. The Secretariats shall forthwith give notice thereof to the Signatory States and the Community.

Article 87

1. This Convention shall enter into force on the first day of the second month following the date of deposit of the instruments of ratification of the Member States and of at least two thirds of the ACP States, and of the act of notification of the conclusion of the Convention by the Community.
2. Any ACP State which has not completed the procedures set out in Article 86 by the date of the entry into force of this Convention as specified in paragraph 1 may do so only within the twelve months following such entry into force and shall be able to proceed with these procedures only during the twelve months following such entry into force, unless before the expiry of this period it gives notice to the Council of Ministers of its intention to complete these procedures not later than six months after this period and on condition that it undertakes the deposit of its instrument of ratification within the same time-limit.
3. As regards those ACP States which have not completed the procedures set out in Article 86 by the date of entry into force of this Convention as specified in paragraph 1, this Convention shall become applicable on the first day of the second month following the completion of the said procedures.
4. Signatory ACP States which ratify this Convention in accordance with the conditions laid down in paragraph 2 shall recognize the validity of all measures taken in implementation of this Convention between the date of its entry into force and the date when its provisions become applicable to them. Subject to any extension which may be granted to them by the Council of Ministers they shall, not later than six months following the completion of the procedures referred to in Article 86, carry out all the obligations which devolve upon them under the terms of this Convention or of implementing decisions adopted by the Council of Ministers.
5. The rules of procedure of the Institutions set up under this Convention shall lay down

whether and under what conditions the representatives of Signatory States which, on the date of entry into force of this Convention have not yet completed the procedures referred to in Article 86, shall sit in those Institutions as observers. The arrangements thus adopted shall be effective only until the date on which this Convention becomes applicable to these States; such arrangements shall in any case cease to apply on the date on which, pursuant to paragraph 2, the State concerned may no longer ratify the Convention.

Article 88
1. The Council of Ministers shall be informed of any request by any State for membership of, or association with, the Community.
2. The Council of Ministers shall be informed of any request made by any State wishing to become a member of an economic grouping composed of ACP States.

Article 89
1. Any request for accession to this Convention by a country or territory to which Part Four of the Treaty applies, and which becomes independent, shall be referred to the Council of Ministers.

With the approval of the Council of Ministers, the country in question shall accede to this Convention by depositing an instrument of accession with the Secretariat of the Council of the European Communities which shall transmit a certified copy to the Secretariat of the ACP States and shall give notice thereof to the Signatory States.
2. That State shall then enjoy the same rights and be subject to the same obligations as the ACP States. Such accession shall not adversely affect the advantages accruing to the ACP States signatory to this Convention from the provisions on financial and technical co-operation and on the stabilization of export earnings.

Article 90
Any request for accession to this Convention submitted by a State whose economic structure and production are comparable with those of the ACP States shall require approval by the Council of Ministers. The State concerned may accede to this Convention by concluding an agreement with the Community.

That State shall then enjoy the same rights and be subject to the same obligations as the ACP States.

The Agreement may however stipulate the date on which certain of these rights and obligations shall become applicable to that State.

Such accession shall not, however, adversely affect the advantages accruing to the ACP States signatory to this Convention from the provisions on financial and technical co-operation, the stabilization of export earnings and industrial co-operation.

Article 91
This Convention shall expire after a period of five years from the date of its signature, namely 1 March 1980.

Eighteen months before the end of this period the Contracting Parties shall enter into negotiations in order to examine what provisions shall subsequently govern relations between the Community and its Members States and the ACP States.

The Council of Ministers shall adopt any transitional measures that may be required until the new Convention comes into force.

Article 92
This Convention may be denounced by the Community in respect of eacht ACP State and by each ACP State in respect of the Community, upon six months' notice.

Article 93

The Protocols annexed to this Convention shall form an integral part thereof.

Article 94

This Convention, drawn up in two copies in the Danish, Dutch, English, French, German and Italian languages, all texts being equally authentic, shall be deposited in the archives of the General Secretariat of the Council of the European Communities and the Secretariat of the ACP States which shall both transmit a certified copy to the Government of each of the Signatory States.

FINAL ACT

The Plenipotentiaries of
His Majesty the King of the Belgians,
etc., etc.
. . . . .

meeting at Lomé this twenty-eighth day of February in the year one thousand nine hundred and seventy-five for the purpose of signing the ACP-EEC Convention of Lomé, have adopted the following texts:

The ACP-EEC Convention of Lomé.

and the following Protocols and Declaration:

Protocol No. 1 concerning the definition of the concept of "originating products" and methods of administrative co-operation

Protocol No. 2 on the application of financial and technical co-operation

Protocol No. 3 on ACP sugar

Protocol No. 4 on the operating expenditure of the Institutions

Protocol No. 5 on privileges and immunities

Protocol No. 6 on bananas

Protocol No. 7 on rum

Joint declaration on fishing activities.

The Plenipotentiaries of the Member States and the Plenipotentiaries of the ACP States have also adopted the text of the Agreement on products within the province of the European Coal and Steel Community.

The Plenipotentiaries of the Member States and of the Community and the Plenipotentiaries of the ACP States have also adopted the texts of the Declarations listed below and annexed to this Final Act:

1. Joint declaration on the presentation of the Convention to GATT (Annex I)
2. Joint declaration on Article 11 (4) of the Convention (Annex II)
3. Joint declaration on Article 59 (6) of the Convention (Annex III)
4. Joint declaration on Article 60 of the Convention (Annex IV)
5. Joint declaration on representation of regional economic groupings (Annex V)
6. Joint declaration on Article 89 of the Convention (Annex VI)
7. Joint declaration on Article 4 (1) of Protocol No. 2 (Annex VII)
8. Joint declaration on Article 20 (c) of Protocol No. 2 (Annex VIII)
9. Joint declaration on Article 22 of Protocol No. 2 (Annex IX)
10. Joint declaration on Article 23 of Protocol No. 2 (Annex X)
11. Joint declaration on Article 26 of Protocol No. 2 (Annex XI)
12. Joint declaration on trade between the European Economic Community and Botswana, Lesotho and Swaziland (Annex XII)

13. Joint declaration concerning possible requests for participation in Protocol No. 3 (Annex XIII)

The Plenipotentiaries of the ACP States have also taken note of the Declarations listed below and annexed to this Final Act:

1. Declaration by the Community on Article 2 of the Convention (Annex XIV)

2. Declaration by the Community on Article 3 of the Convention (Annex XV)

3. Declaration by the Community on Article 10 (2) of the Convention (Annex XVI)

4. Declaration by the Community on the unit of account referred to in Article 42 of the Convention (Annex XVII)

5. Declaration by the Community on Article 3 of Protocol No. 2 (Annex XVIII)

6. Declaration by the Community on Article 4 (3) of Protocol No. 2 (Annex XIX)

7. Declaration by the Community on any additional financing by the European Investment Bank during the implementation of the Convention (Annex XX)

8. Declaration by the Community concerning sugar originating in Belize, St. Kitts-Nevis-Anguilla and Surinam (Annex XXI)

9. Declaration by the Community on Article 10 of Protocol No. 3 (Annex XXII)

10. Declaration by the Representative of the Government of the Federal Republic of Germany concerning the definition of German nationals (Annex XXIII)

11. Declaration by the Representative of the Government of the Federal Republic of Germany concerning the application to Berlin of the ACP-EEC Convention of Lomé (Annex XXIV).

Table 1. *Official Development Assistance From the European Communities,*
1970–1974
(disbursements)

	1970	1971	1972	1973	1974
Official Development Assistance (ODA)					
a) in million currents units of account	211.6	258.2	226.5	314.4	490.5
b) relative to 1970, in 1970 prices	100.0%	113.2%	96.6%	112.0%	148.0%

Source: OECD, *Development Cooperation; 1975 Review* (Paris: OECD, 1975),
hereinafter referred to as DAC Statistics.

Table 2. *Official Development Assistance from the European Community*[1]
in million current dollars
(disbursements)

	1970	1971	1972	1973	1974
1. ODA of the Community	212	258	246	375	598
2. ODA of EC Members[2]					
Belgium	120	146	193	235	263
Denmark	59	74	96	132	168
France	971	1075	1320	1488	1638
Germany (FRG)	599	734	808	1102	1435
Italy	147	183	102	192	204
Netherlands	196	216	307	322	429
United Kingdom	447	562	609	603	722
	2539	2990	3435	4074	4859
3. Total ODA (all donors)	6811	7690	8538	9378	11304
4. Community ODA relative to Member States' ODA	8.3%	8.6%	7.2%	9.2%	12.3%
5. Community ODA relative to Total ODA	3.1%	3.4%	2.9%	4.0%	5.3%
6. EC Members' ODA relative to Total ODA	37.3%	38.9%	40.2%	43.4%	43.0%

[1] Including Denmark and Great Britain before their accession to the Rome
Treaty.
[2] Luxembourg and Ireland are not DAC donor states.
Source: DAC Statistics.

225

Table 3. *Resources of The European Development Fund*[1]
(in millions)

Fund No.	I	II	III	IV
Period:	1959-63	1964-69	1970-74	1975-80
Convention:	Rome	Yaoundé I	Yaoundé II	Lomé
Units of Account	581	800	1000	3550
Current Dollars	581	800	1000	4419
In 1974 Dollars	1157	1493	1645	4419

[1] Including financial resources from the European Investment Bank for projects in countries associated under the Yaoundé and Lomé Conventions.
Source: DAC Statistics.

Table 4. *Financial Resources under the Lomé Convention 1975–1980*

	Million u/a	Million 1974 Dollars	Per Cent
1. EDF	3,000	3,734	88.5
— Non-repayable grants	2,100	2,614	61.9
— Loans on special terms	430	535	12.7
— Risk capital participations	95	118	2.8
— Stabex (commodity export stabilization)	375	467	11.1
2. EIB loans on normal terms	390	485	11.5
TOTAL (1 + 2)[1]	3,390	4,220	100.0

[1] Not including 160 million u/a for overseas countries, territories, and departments.

Table 5. *Population, Food Supply and Demand for Food in ACP-Countries (least developed, landlocked or islands)*

Country	Percentage rate of growth/year[3]			Dietary energy supply[2,4]	Protein supply[5] gr/caput per day
	Population	Food Prod.	Domestic demand[1]		
Barbados	0,6	−0,1	−	−	−
Botswana	2,0	2,3	−	87	65
Burundi	2,0	2,4	2,4	88	62
Central African R.	1,8	2,8	1,1	98	49
Chad	2,1	0,9	1,2	109	77
Dahomey	2,3	1,5	0,1	98	56
Ethiopia	1,8	2,3	3,0	93	72
Gambia	1,8	4,4	−	104	64
Guinea	2,0	2,0	3,4	88	45
Jamaica	1,9	1,9	3,3	105	63
Lesotho	1,6	0,5	−	−	−
Madagascar	2,4	2,8	2,1	111	58
Malawi	2,5	4,7	3,7	95	63
Mali	2,1	1,6	4,3	88	64
Mauritania	2,0	2,4	3,0	85	68
Mauritius	2,6	1,3	3,0	104	48
Niger	2,8	4,1	2,2	89	74
Rwanda	2,6	1,8	1,9	84	58
Somalia	2,2	1,1	1,5	79	56
Sudan	2,9	4,3	3,9	92	63
Tanzania	2,4	3,1	3,0	98	63
Togo	2,3	5,4	2,4	101	56
Trinidad/Tobago	2,5	1,9	4,8	98	64
Uganda	2,4	1,8	3,2	91	61
Upper Volta	1,8	4,7	1,2	72	59
Zambia	2,9	4,3	4,8	112	68

[1] Total food, including fish. − Calculated on basis of growth of population and per caput income, and estimates of income elasticity of farm value of demand in FAO Commodity Projections 1970−1980. Rome, 1971

[2] 1969−71 average

[3] Exponential trend 1952−72

[4] Revised standards of average requirements (physiological requirements plus 10% for waste at household level)

[5] Minimum requirement: 60 gr/day

Source: World Food Conference, Rome 1974.

227

Table 6. *Net imports and exports (marked with−) of the EC (nine members) in 1972 in mln. U.S. $ of primary products from agriculture and forestry (excl. internal trade)*

SITC	Product	1 Total net imports[1]	2 Net imports from develop- ing countries[4] as a % of 1
25	Pulp and paper	3,009.6	0.5
24	Wood, lumber, cork	2,199.1	31.6
05	Fruit and vegetables	2,197.5	54.6
04	Cereals and preparations	1,689.3	5.9
01	Meat and meat preparations	1,682.6	41.8
07	Coffee, tea, cocoa, spices and man	1,612.6	111.3[3]
	071 Coffee	1,153.7	102.8[3]
	072 Cocoa	280.1	128.6[3]
	073 Chocolate	−72.0	24.9[2]
	074 Tea and maté	191.9	120.0[3]
	075 Spices	53.0	93.0
26	Textile fibres not manufactured	1,433.7	38.7
22	Oil seeds, nuts and kernels	1,237.6	28.6
42	Fixed vegetable oils and fats	1,021.8	37.6
08	Feeding stuff for animals	988.1	57.5
00	Live animals	695.2	8.3
12	Tobacco and manufactures	567.7	22.0
21	Hides, skins and furskins	468.8	39.1
231.1	Crude natural rubber, gums	268.8	97.0
41	Animal oils and fats	147.6	26.3
29	Crude animal and veg. material, n.e.s.	134.7	124.7[1]
06	Sugar, sugar preparations, honey	54.5	216.8[3]
43	Processed an. and veg. oils and fats	−31.4	60.7[2]
09	Miscellaneous food preparations	−144.2	58.6[2]
02	Dairy products and eggs	−340.8	131.5[2] [3]
11	Beverages	1,111.2	20.2[2]

[1]   External import − external exports
   Sources: 1. for EC (6): OECD − Trade by commodities, country sum-
            maries, serie B nr. 6
            Figures for EC (6) were corrected for trade between old and
            new members of the Community
          2. for Denmark: UN Statistical Papers Series D Vol. XXII
            no. 1-1; for Ireland: id. no. 1-5; for United Kingdom: id.
            no. 1-8. Trade between Ireland, Denmark and United King-
            dom has also been excluded.

Table 7. *Selfsufficiency rates of the EC for some agricultural products*

Product	1956/60 EG-6	1972 EG-6	1972 EG-9	1973 EG-6	1973 EG-9
Total cereals	85	98	91	97	90
Rice	83	112	92	85	67
Potatoes	101	101	100	102	101
Sugar	104	122	100	116	92
Vegetables	104	100	—	97	94
Fresh fruit	90	87	—	82	76
Citrus fruit	47	52	—	41	34
Wine	89	95	93	91	89
Milk, basis product	100	100	99	—	—
Eggs	90	99	99	100	99
Total meat	95	91	92	91	—
Total fats and oils	36	44	44	—	—

Eurostat — 1974 Yearbook of Agricultural Statistics p. 192

2   Percentage of net exports

3   Part of the net imports from developing countries was re-exported to countries outside the EC (9).

4   Including dependent overseas territories.

Table 8. Net imports and exports (marked with —) of the EC (nine members) in 1972 in mln. U.S. $ of mineral primary products (excl. internal trade)

SITC	Product	1 Total net imports[1]	2 Net imports from developing countries as a % of 1	3 Net imports from North America as a % of 1	4 Net imports from New Zealand and South Africa as a % of 1	5 Net import from centrally planned countries[16] as a % of 1
3	Mineral fuels	11,138	110.4[3]	2.2	0.1	12.9
32	Coal, coke, briquettes	464.0	[13]	62.8[4]	3.7[11]	106.6[3]
33	Petroleum and products	10,649.0	115.2[3]	[5]	n.i.[14]	8.9
33.1	Crude petroleum	12,398.2	99.0			3.4
34	Gas, natural and manufactured	28.1	165.3[3]	[6]	n.i.[14]	22.7
28	Metalliferous ores and scrap	2,699.4	38.4	21.0	2.1	7.5
28.1	Iron ore and concentrates	1,216.8	51.2	8.8	0.2	3.1
28.2	Iron and steel scrap	55.2	2.8	50.8	n.i.[14]	109.5[3]
28.3	Ores and conc. of non fer. base metals[2]	976.0	35.7	36.7	4.1	4.3
28.4	Non fer. metal scrap	151.0	25.3	36.1	5.3	26.7
28.5	Silver and platinum ores	105.9	6.1	11.2	6.1	6.9
28.6	Ores and conc. of uranium, thorium	13.9	0.9	0	n.i.[14]	0
27	Crude fertilizer and minerals (no fuel)	848.9	19.1	28.4	5.4	16.7
27.1	Fertilizer crude	244.9	68.1	17.7	0	18.5

Code	Commodity					
27.3	Stone, sand, gravel	49.3				8.6
27.4	Sulphur, iron pyrites	67.9	5.4[8]	53.6[7]	19.8[12]	77.4[10]
27.5	Natural abrasives	18.2	0.1[9]	53.5	1.5	16.9
27.6	Other crude minerals[15]	304.9		47.6	12.3	
67	Iron ore and steel	−2,523				
68	Non ferrous metals	2,053				
68.1	Silver, platinum etc.	15				
68.2	Copper	1,450				
68.3	Nickel	99				
68.4	Aluminium	209				
68.5	Lead	101				
68.6	Zinc	45				
68.7	Tin	108				
68.8		—				
68.9	Miscellanious non ferrous base metals	71				

1 External imports — external exports see note 1 table 1
2 Incl. copper, nickel, bauxite, lead, zinc, tin, manganese, chromium, tungsten, titanium, vanadium, molybdeen. Part of the net imports from developing countries were re-exported to countries outside EC (9).
4 net export: $ 42.7 mln.
5 id. $ 1.8 mln.
6 id. $ 1.9 mln.
7 id. $ 1.6 mln.
8 id. $ 5.3 mln.
9 id. $ 0.7 mln.
10 id. $ 17.9 mln.
11 id. $ 4.1 mln.
12 id. $ 1.8 mln.
13 id. $ 13.6 mln.
14 not indicated, in most cases very small
15 clay, salt, asbestos etc.
16 Eastern Europe, USSR, Mongolia, China (mainland), North Korea and North Vietnam.

Table 9. *EC Dependency rates*[1] *for selected minerals in 1972*[2]

Product	Dep. rate
Uranium	89%
Oil	95%
Natural gas	2%
Coal	10%[3]
Iron ore	75%
Copper	65% (35% recapture[4])
Bauxite	74% (25% recapture[4])
Phosphates	99%
Tin ore	86%
Magnesium	100%
Manganese	100%
Tungsten	95%

[1] Imports as a percentage of consumption.
[2] *Sources*:   a. Commission of the European Communities: Europe, raw materials and The Third World, (May 1974).

b. OECD — Energy Statistics 1959—1973.

[3] hard coal.
[4] See our observation in text note 22.

Table 10. *Selected EC Imports by Major Supplying Countries, 1973*

SITC	Product[1]	Net imports x $ 1.000.000	of which from: % country	% country	% country	% country[2]
01	Meat & prep.	2.561	25 Argentina	14 New. Zeal.	10 Austral.	
04	Cereals & prep.	2.774	60 U.S.A.	19 Argentina	15 Canada	
0511	Oranges etc.	575	53 Spain	18 Morocco	15 Israel	
0711	Coffee	1.517	32 Brasil	12 Colombia	7 Ivory C.	
072	Cocoa	530	23 Ivory Coast	20 Ghana	16 Nigeria	14 Cameron
08	Feeding stuff for an.	2.045	35 U.S.A.	12 Brasil	9 Argentina	
121	Tobacco unmanufactured	876	45 U.S.A.	6 Canada	5 Brasil	
22	Oil seeds, nuts, kernels	2.093	53 U.S.A.	17 Brasil	7 Canada	
42	Vegetable oil & fats	902	11 Malaysia	9 Spain	9 Argentina	
242	Wood, rough	907	30 Ivory Coast	11 Gabon	7 Ghana	
263	Cotton	1.040	13 U.S.A.	11 Turkey	10 U.S.S.R.	
271	Fertilizer, crude	310	44 Morocco	15 U.S.A.	12 Tugo	10 U.S.S.R.
281	Iron ore & conc.	1.668	24 Sweden	18 Brasil	15 Liberia	11 Canada
671	Pig iron etc.	494	19 Fr. Ocean	18 Norway	7 South Afr.	
2831	Ores & conc. copper	226	47 Australia	10 Canada	9 South Afr.	
682	Copper	2.938	21 Zaïre	17 Zambia	14 Chile	
2832	Ores & conc. nickel	161	71 Canada	21 Fr. Ocean	8 South Afr.	
683	Nickel	263	28 Canada	16 Norway	13 Austral.	10 U.S.A.
2833	Bauxite & al. conc.	77	43 Austral.	11 Guyana	11 Yugoslav.	
684	Aluminium	753	38 Norway	11 U.S.A.	9 Greece	
2837	Ores & conc. manganese	106	43 South Afr.	24 Gabon	8 Brasil	
331	Crude petroleum	17.323	30 Saudi Ar.	16 Iran	15 Lybia	12 Kuwait

Source: Trade by Commodities – Market Summaries: Imports, Jan.-Dec. 1973, OECD, Paris.

Notes: [1] The spread may vary considerably as a broader or narrower category is taken.

[2] A fourth country is listed only if its share is 10% or more. Of course, the number and spread of further suppliers may change the significance of the share of the 3 or 4 biggest suppliers.

Table 11. *Concentration of metallic mineral reserves in the world. Two countries posses half or more than half of the known recoverable reserves of the following metallic minerals[1]:*

Bauxite:	Australia 34%, Guinea 21%
Antimony:	China 68%, Bolivia 8%
Chromium:	South Africa 74%, Rhodesia 23%
Cobalt:	Zaïre 27%, New Caledonia — incl. Australia — 27%
Industrial diamond:	Zaïre 80%, South Africa 8%
Gold:	South Africa 60%, USSR 20%
Manganese:	USSR 41%, South Africa 10%[2]
Mercury:	Spain 49%, Yugoslavia 9%
Lead:	USA 37%, Canada 13%
Molybdenum:	USA 58%, USSR 18%
Platinum metals:	South Africa 64%, USSR 32%
Uranium:	USA 30%, South Africa 23%
Vanadium:	USSR 59%, South Africa 20%
Tungsten:	China 74%, USA 7%

[1] *Source*: W. Uytenbogaardt "De rol van grondstoffen in de wereldpolitiek; zegen of conflictstof" (in AR-Staatkunde, juni 1975) p. 185.

[2] Figure computed from: Commodity Data Summaries 1974 (Appendix I to: Mining and Minerals Policy, Bureaux of Mines, US dept. of interior) p. 97.

Table 12. *World-wide reserves, production, lifetime of reserves, average yearly rate of increase of production*

Raw Material	Reserves on 1.1.1972 (×10³ tons)	Production 1971 (×10³ tons)	Static life-time (years)	Increase in production	Dynamic life-time (years)
Copper	348,000	6,336	54.9	4.1	28.7
Lead	94,000	3,419	27.3	3.2	19.1
Zinc	118,000	5,500	21	4.5	14
Bauxite (50% Al_2O_3)	12,451,000	59,994	207.5	7.1	38.3
Tin	4,200	236	17.8	2.1	14.7
Tungsten	1,146	32	39.3	4.5	17.6
Nickel	68,000	686	99.1	5.8	32.2
Cobalt	2,500	16	124	5.8	35
Chrome ore	2,400,000	6,996	408	2.3	101.1
Molybdenum	4,200	74	58	6.5	23.2
Iron ore	254,334,000	765,000	333	3.3	75
Manganese ore	4,000,000	19,000	205	2.1	80.3
Fluorite (CaF_2 cont.)	130,000	4,654	27.9	ca. 7.0	14.7
Mercury	183	9.6	19.0	1.1	17
Platinum metals	15.5	0.12	125.6	7.0	31.9
Silver	170	9.5	18.0	2.1	15.6
Gold	31.1	1.5	20.8	0.2	20.4

Source: communicated by E. Pestel at a conference in Bad Homberg "Geoscience in a finite world" of the IUGS-Comittee Geoscience and Man, July 22-24, 1974.

Table 13. *Shares of EC imports of primary products coming from ACP countries (main products exported by ACP) in 1973*

Product	Total import	Share of ACP in %
Meat of bovine animals, fresh	1,110	3.6
Other prepared or preserved meat	197	6.8
Fish, fresh chilled or frozen	265	4.2
Crustacea and molluscs	655	28.0
Idem, prepared or preserved	289	5.9
Rice, glazed or polished	50	5.0
Fresh bananas	353	15.4
Tropical fruit (excl. bananas)	47	33.4
Fruit juice and vegetable	91	6.1
Fruit and nuts, prepared or preserved	375	6.6
Beans, peas, lentils, dried	178	11.1
Vegetables, prepared or preserved, n.e.s.	161	7.6
Raw and refined sugar	264	78.3
Coffee	1,270	30.9
Cocoa paste	17	98.6
Cocoa beans	352	90.1
Cocoa butter	85	51.1
Tea	236	26.4
Pepper and pimento	40	12.1
Oil seed cake	1,190	11.1
Tobacco, unmanufactured	769	7.3
Groundnuts, peanuts	173	65.0
Copra	94	2.0
Palm nuts and kernels	39	92.2
Oil seeds, oil nuts and oil kernels, n.e.s.	173	13.0
Natural rubber	388	12.4
Wood, rough or simply squared	1,213	46.6
Raw cotton	843	18.2
Sisal	76	41.7
Natural phosphates	253	21.7
Natural graphite	29	6.5
Iron ore	1,411	21.5
Copper ore	179	2.5
Zinc ore	205	1.3
Tin ore	73	18.7
Manganese ore	89	30.9
Ores of uranium and thorium	25	99.3
Natural gums, resins, lacs	39	42.6
Vegetable material for plaiting	16	7.5
Plants, seeds, flowers used in perfume/pharm.	39	15.0
Crude petroleum	14,830	7.0
Groundnut, peanut oil	147	62.0
Palm oil	151	19.7
Essential oils	97	5.0
Diamond, not industrial	1,975	1.0
Copper and other unrefined copper	2,389	41.1
Aluminium and alloys	493	5.7
Zinc and alloys	161	8.8
Tin and alloys	171	16.8

Source: Eurostat-ACP: Yearbook of foreign trade statistics (statistical abstract 1968–1973), Brussels 1975; figures were taken and computed from pp 75. Total imports are in million UA.

Table 14. *Exports of primary products from agriculture and forestry by the ACP-countries in 1972, in 1,000 US $ and the main exporters among them in percentages[1]*

Sitc	Product	Exported value	Main exporting countries in % of total ACP exports			
0	Food	2,097,049	Ivory Coast 14	Nigeria 11	Uganda 9	Kenya 7
01	Meat and meat prep.	54,418	Kenya 25	Madagasc. 22	Ethiopia 12	Tanzania 11
02	Dairy prod. and eggs.	9,597	Ghana 59	Kenya 39	Madagasc. 17	Sudan 11
04	Cereals and preparations	45,321	Guyana 28	Ghana 26	Jamaica 17	Ethiopia 11
05	Fruit and vegetables	140,792	Ivory Coast 20	Tanzania 20	Guyana 17	Fiji 12
06	Sugar and sugar preparations	303,067	Mauritius 32	Jamaica 15	Nigeria 14	Uganda 11
07	Coffee, tea, cocoa and spices	1,537,622	Ghana 16			
071	Coffee	695,125	Ivory C. 23	Uganda 23	Ethiopia 12	Kenya 10
072	Cocoa	662,866	Ghana 38	Nigeria 32	Ivory C. 14	Cameroon 9
073	Chocolate	2,724	Cameroon 100			
074	Tea and maté	101,680	Kenya 45	Tanzania 45	Malawi 15	Tanzania 7
075	Spices	72,364	Madagasc. 49	Madagasc. 49	Ethiopia 2	Zaïre 13
08	Feeding stuff for animals	82,078	Sudan 20	Nigeria 19	Senegal 16	
09	Miscellanious food prep.	5,378	Trinidad 56	Barbados 25	Ghana 16	
11	Beverages	30,661	Bahamas 40	Jamaica 26	Barbados 10	Guyana 9
12	Tobacco	60,607	Malawi 59	Zambia 11	Zambia 7	Jamaica 6
21	Hides, skins and furskins	65,470	Kenya 16	Sudan 14	Nigeria 10	Uganda 9
22	Oil seeds, nuts and kernels	233,281	Nigeria 35	Sudan 24	Malawi 4	Niger 5
231.1	Crude natural rubber	68,317	Liberia[2] 43	Nigeria 25	Zaïre 19	
24	Wood, lumber and cork	216,104	Ivory C. 49	Gabon 20	Cameroon 9	Congo 8
26	Textile fibres not manufactured	438,323	Sudan 49	Tanzania 15	Uganda 12	Cameroon 8
29	Crude animal and vegetable mat.	64,501	Sudan 43	Kenya 26	Tanzania 10	Chad 12
41	Animal oils and fats	5,272	Ghana 100			
43	Processed animal and vegetable oils and fats	713	Ethiopia 73	Madagasc. 19	CAR 8	
42	Fixed vegetable oils and fats	150,144	Zaïre 27	Nigeria 21	Senegal 18	Sudan 8

1 *Source:* U.N. Yearbook of International Trade Statistics 1972/1973. For the next countries only figures for 1971 were available: Ivory Coast, Dahomey, Upper Volta, Mauritania, Niger, Nigeria, Senegal, Togo, CAR, Chad, Congo, Gabon, Madagascar; for Zaïre and Zambia only figures for 1970 were available.

2 incl. synthetic rubber

237

Table 15. Exports of mineral primary products by the ACP-countries in 1972 in 1,000 US $ and the main exporters among them in percentages[1]

SITC	Product	Exported value	Main exporting countries as a % of total ACP exports							
27	Crude fertilizer, minerals	55,898	Togo	31	Senegal	27	Bahamas	10	Madagasc.	5
	27.1 Fertilizer crude	30,862	Togo	56	Senegal	44				
	27.3 Stone, sand, gravel	1,774	Jamaïca	100						
	27.5 Natural abrasives	8,379	Liberia	75	Ivory C.	25				
	27.6 Other crude minerals	14,208	Bahamas	38	Madagasc.	21	Trinidad	12	Senegal	10
28	Metalliferous ores, scrap	602,832	Jamaica	40	Liberia	30	Mali	13	Guyana	11
	28.1 Iron ore and concentrates	273,588	Liberia	68	Mali	27	Sierra Leone	5		
	28.3 Ores and conc. of non ferrous base metals	371,061	Jamaïca	64	Guyana	17	Gabon	9	Zaïre	6
	28.31 Ores and conc. copper	4,666	Mali	80	Congo	20				
	28.33 Bauxite	241,552	Jamaïca	98	Sierra Leone	2				
	28.35 Ores and conc. zinc	1,087	Zaïre	100						
	28.36 Ores and conc. tin	20,496	Zaïre	74	Rwanda	26				
	28.37 Ores and conc. manganese	35,906	Gabon	94	Zaïre	6				
	28.39 Idem 28.3 n.e.s.	8,446	Madagasc.	36	Niger	25	Nigeria	20	Rwanda	18
	28.4 Non ferrous metal scrap	5,923	Zambia	67	Kenya	20	Sierra L	7		
	28.6 Uranium	5,495	Gabon	100						
3	Mineral fuels	2,244,991	Nigeria	60	Trinidad	19	Bahamas	11	Gabon	4
	33 Petroleum and products	2,244,380	Nigeria	60	Trinidad	19	Bahamas	11	Gabon	4
	33.1 Crude petroleum	1,499,536	Nigeria	89	Gabon	5	Trinidad	4	Ghana	2
	34 Gas	300	Senegal	100						
67	Iron and steel	2,046	Togo	51	Senegal	22	Zaïre	11	Ivory C.	7
68	Non ferrous metals	1,576,473	Zambia	62	Zaïre	31	Niger	2	Cameroon	1
	68.2 Copper	1,462,210	Zambia	65	Zaïre	34				
	68.4 Aluminium	20,772	Cameroon	90	Ghana	10				
	68.5 Lead	6,824	Zambia	100						
	68.6 Zinc	32,077	Zaïre	52	Zambia	48				
	68.7 Tin	38,691	Nigeria	90	Zaïre	10				
	68.9 Miscellanious non ferrous base metals	45,687	Zaïre	81	Zambia	19				

Table 16. *Mineral Reserves in the ACP-countries as a percentage of World Reserves*

Mineral	World Reserve		ACP-share	Main countries
Bauxite	15.5	billion long dry tons	30%	Guinea, Guyana, Jamaïca
Cobalt	2.7	million short tons	42%	Zaïre, Zambia
Copper	370	million ,, ,,	13%	Zaïre, Zambia
Iron Ore	96.7	billion tons	1%	Liberia
Manganese	1.4	billion short tons	16%	Gabon
Phosphate	5	million ,, ,,	2%	Senegal, Togo
Tin	4.2	,, long ,,	5%	Nigeria, Zaïre
Uranium	1.1	,, short ,,	7%	Gabon, Niger
Crude Oil	74.5	million tons	4%	Nigeria
Coal	6,641	billion tons	9%	Nigeria, Zambia

Sources: for Metals: Commodity Data Summaries 1974 (Appendix I to Mining and Minerals Policy), US Dept. of the Interior.
for Oil: World Oil, February 15, 1975, p. 44.
for Coal: Courrier de l'Association, Jan/Febr. 1975, p. 16.

INDEX OF AUTHORS AND SUBJECTS

n-note = footnote

242

246

247

Venice, 17
Vessels, their –, 43, 44
Vingerhoets, J., 161n
Voorhoeve, Dr. I.J.J.C., 111, 189, 191

Weil, Gordon L., 16n, 20n
Welfare, 162
Wellbeing, 162
Wells, L.T., 169n
Western European sphere, 156
Westhoff, Dr. J., 15
Willingness of EC-countries, 191
Wilson, Prime Minister, 145
World:
    Bank Group, 111n, 114-116, 118, 126
    Food Conference, 126, 129

Yaoundé conventions: 7, 12, 15, 16, 20, 21, 22n, 28-31, 33, 34, 38-42, 52, 53, 57, 58n, 64, 68, 69ff, 78, 113, 115, 125, 133, 135-137, 140-144, 188, 189
    First: 146, 152
    Second: 146, 152

Zaire, 39, 168, 169
Zambia, 169
Zartman, I. William, 134, 138n, 141n
Zinc, 172, 179
"Zône franc", 16

249